THE
SOUTHERN
ENIGMA

From the Old South to the New: Essays on
the Transitional South
Walter J. Fraser, Jr., and Winfred B. Moore, Jr., editors

American Political Trials
Michal R. Belknap

The Evolution of American Electoral Systems
*Paul Kleppner, Walter Dean Burnham, Ronald P. Formisano,
Samuel P. Hays, Richard Jensen, and William G. Shade*

Class, Conflict, and Consensus: Antebellum Southern
Community Studies
Orville Vernon Burton and Robert C. McMath, Jr., editors

Toward A New South? Studies in Post-Civil War
Southern Communities
Orville Vernon Burton and Robert C. McMath, Jr., editors

To Free A People: American Jewish Leaders and The Jewish
Problem in Eastern Europe, 1890-1914
Gary Dean Best

Voting in Revolutionary America: A Study of Elections
in the Original Thirteen States, 1776-1789
Robert J. Dinkin

Good and Faithful Labor: From Slavery to Sharecropping
in the Natchez District, 1860-1890
Ronald L. F. Davis

Reform and Reformers in the Progressive Era
David R. Colburn and George E. Pozzetta, editors

History of Black Americans: From the Emergence of the
Cotton Kingdom to the Eve of the Compromise of 1850
Philip S. Foner

History of Black Americans: From the Compromise of 1850
to the End of the Civil War
Philip S. Foner

THE SOUTHERN ENIGMA

Essays on Race, Class, and Folk Culture

Edited by Walter J. Fraser, Jr.,
and Winfred B. Moore, Jr.

Contributions in American History, Number 105

GREENWOOD PRESS
WESTPORT, CONNECTICUT • LONDON, ENGLAND

Library of Congress Cataloging in Publication Data
Main entry under title:

The Southern enigma.

(Contributions in American history, ISSN 0084-9219 ;
no. 105)
Papers presented at the Citadel Conference on the
South, April, 1981.
Bibliography: p.
Includes index.
1. Southern States—Race relations—Congresses.
2. Afro-Americans—Southern States—History—Congresses.
3. Social classes—Southern States—History—Congresses.
4. Southern States—Social conditions—Congresses.
5. Southern States—Historiography—Congresses.
I. Fraser, Walter J. II. Moore, Winfred B.,
1949- . III. Citadel Conference on the South (1981)
IV. Series.
E185.92.S685 1983   305.8'0975   82-20966
ISBN 0-313-23640-2 (lib. bdg.)

Library of Congress Catalog Card Number: 82-20966
ISBN: 0-313-23640-2
ISSN: 0084-9219

First published in 1983

Greenwood Press
A division of Congressional Information Service, Inc.
88 Post Road West
Westport, Connecticut 06881

Printed in the United States of America

10 9 8 7 6 5 4 3 2 1

CONTENTS

TABLES

PREFACE

Throughout the years, many volumes of essays on southern history have been published. This volume is an anthology of fifteen essays selected from more than eighty papers presented in April 1981 at The Citadel Conference on the South. As such, it is the product of one of those regional symposia that George B. Tindall once characterized as "one of the flourishing minor industries of the region." While we plead guilty to being a part of this industry, we believe that periodic volumes of essays are a vital part of the constant reevaluation of southern history. The essays in this volume examine aspects of three of the most powerful forces in southern life: race, class, and folk culture. Whether attacking, defending, or modifying existing interpretations, each article offers suggestive insights on the southern experience, an experience that continues to be something of an enigma for many Americans. We believe that these articles shed new light on their respective topics. Therefore, it is our hope that this volume will help to unravel the southern enigma and advance the continuing dialogue, reexaminations, and reevaluations of southern history.

In producing this volume we are indebted to the president of The Citadel, Lieutenant General James A. Grimsley, for his encouragement and support in undertaking such projects in the humanities. We are similarly indebted to our other colleagues and our chairman, John S. Coussons, of The Citadel History Department. We also wish to thank Delene Hiott for patiently and efficiently handling the tedious secretarial chores without complaint. Those individuals who participated in the conference and offered suggestions on the papers have contributed greatly to whatever merit this volume may have. Among those persons are: James Tice Moore, Paul D. Escott, David Chalmers, Randall Miller, Ernest M. Lander, Jr., Leslie Rowland, Lee Drago, Paolo E. Coletta, James O. Breeden, Vernon Burton, Steven Hahn, Augustus M. Burns III, and Drew Gilpin Faust. Special thanks are due to Jon L. Wakelyn, the general editor of the Greenwood Press series, Contributions in American History. Finally and most important, a huge debt of gratitude is owed to The Citadel Development Foundation whose generous financial support made possible both The Citadel Conference on the South and this volume.

THE
SOUTHERN
ENIGMA

RACE

The study of racial issues has been a focal point of southern historiography ever since U. B. Phillips' famous essay labeled white supremacy as the central theme of southern history. Over the last twenty-five years a flood of monographs and journal articles has explored different aspects of this topic. Even so, the richness, complexity, and tragic legacy of persistent racial discrimination continues to make it a fruitful area for historical investigation. It is especially interesting in the years between the collapse of slavery and the turn of the present century, for it was during these years that much of the framework for modern racial patterns was established.

Beginning with Leon F. Litwack's "The Ordeal of Black Freedom," the first five articles in this anthology examine what freedom meant for Afro-Americans in the thirty years after emancipation. Litwack demonstrates that former slaves used every available strategy in their attempt to translate legal freedom into equal opportunity and upward mobility. Labor negotiations, politics, militance, self-help, and accommodation all foundered in turn on the seemingly immovable rock of white supremacy. This state of affairs, Litwack argues eloquently, revealed the existence of a "Catch-22," a central paradox in the southern black experience. White society told blacks to prove themselves worthy of acceptance by attaining white standards of moral rectitude and economic progress. Those blacks who were unable to overcome the formidable, white-imposed obstacles to these ends were condemned as unworthy of respect. Yet, those blacks who somehow made significant progress were considered even more dangerous because of the symbolic threat they posed to white domination. White repression usually increased in proportion to black gains. For black Americans, therefore, to succeed was only to risk greater failure. Litwack concludes unhappily that this "frustrating and debilitating" paradox of an "unbeatable" white America continues to be the central problem of Afro-Americans.

Illustrating the economic aspect of this paradox in greater detail is "Labor and Ideology in the South Carolina Up-Country: The Transition to Free-Labor Agriculture" by Lacy Ford. In the three years after Appomatox the Carolina up-country underwent severe dislocations that forced major changes in its pre-war economic structure. With Freedmen's Bureau agents refereeing the conflict, it was only the lack of capital that prevented landowners from reimposing plantation methods. The lack of northern support for confiscation denied independent farm status to blacks. At the same time, white merchants emerged as the dominant factor in the economy. The white need for black labor in a drought-stricken, war-torn land, enabled black laborers to win some concessions in the form of share-tenancy contracts. Although the contracts enabled them to negotiate loans with white merchants and thus become more independent of the old planter class from whom they rented, before long, Ford concludes, blacks realized that their apparent minor victory was illusory. The economic strings were still in the hands of men committed to white supremacy, whether they were old landowners or new merchants. To quote one South Carolinian of the time, "Can not freedmen be organized and disciplined as well as slaves? Is not the dollar as potent as the lash? The belly as tender as the back?"

White dominance also was reestablished in the South Carolina low country in the years after Lee's surrender. The events leading to this, however, were significantly different from those in the up-country, according to John Scott Strickland's essay, " 'No More Mud Work': The Struggle for the Control of Labor and Production in Low Country South Carolina, 1863-1880." Strickland argues that a variety of circumstances unique to coastal Carolina made the economic struggle there "more intense and of longer duration than that of . . . other regions of the state and the South." Under slavery, the widespread pattern of absentee ownership and the use of the task system had given the low country's black majority an unusually high degree of autonomy over their daily labor. This autonomy was increased as former slaves occupied lands abandoned during the war. After the war, a coalition of northern and southern whites tried to reimpose prewar labor patterns, but the former slaves, drawing on their autonomous tradition and the knowledge that they were crucial to white economic recovery, resisted the attempt with a degree of solidarity that approached quasi-union status. Whether refusing to work, setting contract standards for entire areas, or resorting to armed resistance, blacks extracted liberal contract concessions that for a time raised the tantalizing possibility of economic independence. Only the combined efforts of southern whites, the Union army, and white control of emergency rations during the drought of 1867-68 forestalled that possibility and forced blacks to abandon many of their demands. Even so, Strickland finds that the heroic effort of low country blacks left them with more economic self-determination than could be found elsewhere. It well demonstrates the variety and complexity of the black response to emancipation.

These themes of complexity and paradox also arise in education and politics as Richard B. Westin writes in "Blacks, Educational Reform, and Politics in North Carolina, 1897-1898." Perhaps the least orthodox of the southern states, North Carolina elected a Populist-Republican fusion ticket that controlled the state government from 1894 to 1898. Ostensibly more friendly to blacks, the fusion government inherited a public education system in which each school constituted a separate school district run by a three-man committee. In the name of efficiency and improved education for all, the fusionist government consolidated single school districts into township districts run by centralized five-man committees. The law rapidly backfired as both whites and blacks protested that it had become possible for members of one race to run the other's schools. This in part led to increased racial friction, the defeat of increased school taxes, and the return of the Democrats in the bloody, Red Shirt Campaign of 1898. In a classic example of shooting oneself in the foot, The Tarheel faction most sympathetic to blacks helped to unleash the forces of their own doom. Westin concludes that the crowning paradox of this episode was the Democratic manipulation of the fusionist school law to eliminate what little control blacks previously had held over their own schools, thus leading to a decline in the quality of black education in North Carolina.

A final reflection on the cruel paradoxes entrapping black Americans is given by Peter H. Wood in "Waiting in Limbo: A Reconsideration of Winslow Homer's *The Gulf Stream*." Painted in 1899, *The Gulf Stream* depicts a sailing accident off Key West. A quizzical black man is adrift on a crippled boat loaded with sugar cane. Sharks circle the stormy and blood-stained waters around it while a vessel on the horizon steams along oblivious to the black man's fate. Homer's famous work received a mixed critical reception, interpreted alternately as a literal representation of a shipwreck and a universal statement on the human condition. In an innovative mixture of art criticism and historical study, Wood traces artistic portrayals of blacks in general and in Homer's work in particular to suggest that *The Gulf Stream* may better be interpreted as "a rich portrayal of both the historical and the contemporary situation of blacks in America." Adrift in an uncertain world, surrounded by historical nemeses (sharks, sugar cane, and indifferent whites), Afro-Americans survived but only in a suspended world of limbo created by white America.

1

THE ORDEAL OF BLACK FREEDOM

Leon F. Litwack

With the passage of time, the black men and women who had endured enslavement came to articulate a disillusionment that encompassed both their bondage and the tortured freedom they had enjoyed since emancipation. Patsy Mitchner was "'bout 12 years old" when the Union soldiers passed through North Carolina. Taught by her master and mistress to fear the Yankees, she chose to hide, but when the other slaves left, she ran away and settled in a nearby town. "I have wurked for white folks, washin', cookin', an' wurkin' at a laundry ever since freedom come." Some seventy years after emancipation, when interviewed about her life, she had no reason to recall her bondage with nostalgia. Her master had treated blacks "mean"; she had seen her mother beaten; the food, clothing, and sleeping quarters had been "bad"; and her mother, brother, and sister had been sold to a slave speculator and shipped to Mississippi "in a box-car." Reflecting on her enslavement and freedom, she could talk only of different kinds of oppression:

Slavery wus a bad thing an' freedom, of de kin' we got wid nothin' to live on wus bad. Two snakes full of pisen. One lyin' wid his head pintin' north, de other wid his head pintin' south. Dere names wus slavery an' freedom. De snake called slavery lay wid his head pinted south an' de snake called freedom lay wid his head pinted north. Both bit de nigger, an' dey wus both bad.[1]

What Patsy Mitchner suggested, the experience of four-million black men and women after the Civil War confirmed: the theory and practice of white supremacy transcended regional boundaries. Emancipation introduced still other forms of white duplicity and coercion, and the attitudes and behavior that had justified and underscored enslavement persisted in different guises. The dominant society refused to rearrange its values and priorities to grant to black southerners the positive assistance that seemed mandated by the inequalities they had suffered and the magnitude of the problems they faced. More than a century of black freedom has not altered significantly Patsy Mitchner's assessment. It has only sharpened it, only deepened its tragic implications, only underscored the terrible paradox of black men and women seeking admission into a society that refuses to recognize their essential humanity.

The death of slavery in the South is an episode as dramatic as any in the history of the American people. Few, if any, experiences in American lives have been felt so deeply and so intensely by so many. And few experiences in our history have been so replete with paradox, ambiguity, and irony, with both tragedy and triumph. From the moment the Civil War broke out, the nearly four-million enslaved black men and women of the South were placed in an anomalous and precarious position. They constituted the muscle of a military and economic effort designed to perpetuate their bondage; they were the cause of the war and indispensable to the Confederacy. But could they be trusted? The answer came slowly in some cases, quickly in others: the more desperate the Confederate cause became, the more the white South depended on the labor and loyalty of its blacks. The more they were needed, the less they could be trusted.

Throughout the history of slavery, the attitudes blacks manifested toward their enslavers varied considerably. The most loyal and devoted would be enshrined forever in white southern mythology—in story, in legend, even in statues and song. The deeds of a Nat Turner were equally well known. One can only speculate on how many slaves resembled the cook in a North Carolina family who spit in the biscuits and pissed in the coffee to get back at her white folks.[2] Every slave had the capacity for outrage and resistance. No slaveholding family, even one that thought it commanded the affection and loyalty of its blacks, could know for certain when any one of them might choose to give expression to his or her outrage and what form that expression might take.

The Civil War and emancipation swept away the pretenses, dissolved the illusions, and laid bare the tensions and instability inherent in the master-slave relationship. Neither whites nor blacks were untouched by the physical and emotional demands of the war. Both races suffered, and each evinced some sympathy for the plight of the other. There was, however, a critical difference, and that difference grew in importance with each passing month. If the slaves evinced a compassion for beleaguered masters and mistresses, if they deplored the ravagement of the land and crops by Union soldiers who brutalized and looted whites and blacks alike, at some moment in the war many of these same slaves and still others came to the realization that in the very suffering and defeat of their white folks lay their only hope for freedom. That revelation was no less far-reaching in its implications than the white southerners' acknowledgment that they were facing danger on both sides—from the Yankees and from their own black folk. "We have already been twice betrayed by negroes," Joseph LeConte noted, as he made his way to the safety of the Confederate lines, "we avoid them as carefully as we do Yankees."[3]

With emancipation, each black family, each black man and woman, would need to determine the meaning, the dimensions, and the immediate implications of freedom. How would they now feed, house, and clothe themselves? Where could they go? To make certain of their freedom, would they need to separate themselves from those who had previously owned them? If they chose to remain, what relations would they sustain with their former owners? Whether they left or stayed, how could they safely manifest their freedom? And, perhaps most critically, what could they aspire to in a society in which whites commanded the land, the tools, the crops, and the law, and in which the prospect of four-million newly freed black men and women made it all the more imperative for whites to maintain their domination? George King, a former South Carolina slave, remembered having been raised on "two-hundred acres of Hell" ("the white folks called it Samuel Roll's plantation"). It was there that he had watched "the old she-devil Mistress . . . whip his mammy 'till she was just a piece of living raw meat." And he remembered as well how his master chose to tell the slaves they were free: "The Master he says we are all free, but it don't mean we is white. And it don't mean we is equal. Just equal for to work and earn our own living and not depend on him for no more meats and clothes."[4]

Within such perceptions of reality, newly freed black men and women determined the content of their freedom. To experience "de feel of bein' free," they adopted different priorities and found themselves driven in many directions at the same time. Most often the difference between slavery and freedom could be perceived in the choices that became available to them, in the opportunities to expand their personal and psychological autonomy, to secure families, to locate loved ones, to formalize marital ties, to take new surnames or to reveal old ones, to educate themselves, to withdraw the women from the white folks' kitchens and fields, to worship in their own churches, to assemble for political and community purposes, and to work at a pace and under terms commensurate with their new status.[5] For some, freedom took on meaning only when they left the places they had worked as slaves; still others found sufficient satisfaction in abandoning only their slave domiciles. Even if they chose to work on the same place, many freedmen acted quickly to break up the slave quarter by removing their cabins from the residence of the former master or by erecting new ones on plots they now rented.

To suggest, as some contemporary observers did, that emancipation made no difference in the lives of black men and women is to judge emancipation solely by its economic content and to ignore how blacks themselves perceived their freedom. To those who had endured enslavement, even as they acknowledged the burdens of freedom, even as they conceded new insecurities in their day-to-day lives, even as they recognized the white man's superiority in rights, power, and resources, freedom made a difference. "Dere is sumpin' 'bout bein' free," a former Alabama slave recalled, "and dat makes up for all de hardships. I'se been both slave and free and I knows. Course, while I was a slave I didn' have no 'sponsibility, didn' have to worry 'bout where sumpin to eat and wear and a place to sleep was comin' from, but dat don't make up for bein' free." Nor was there any ambiguity in the response of a former Florida slave, when he observed that "even the best masters in slavery couldn't be as good as the worst person in freedom." Still another former slave placed even his circumscribed freedom above the security allegedly enjoyed in slavery:

Every time I think of slavery and if it done the race any good, I think of the story of the coon and dog who met. The coon said to the dog "Why is it you're so fat and I am so poor, and we is both animals?" The dog said: "I lay round Master's house and let him kick me and he gives me a piece of bread right on." Said the coon to the dog: "Better then that I stay poor." Them's my sentiment. I'm lak the coon, I don't believe in 'buse.[6]

Whatever the frustrations, failures, and hardships black men and women experienced during and after the Civil War, they acted on the assumption that freedom made a difference. In doing so, they demonstrated unmistakably that the slavery they had endured, no matter how brutal and oppressive, had not succeeded in reducing them to docile, irresponsible, childish Sambos, as the well-meaning missionaries and teachers from the North soon learned. The former slaveowning class also came to realize this, as it endured changes in the demeanor and behavior of former slaves who became transformed from faithful servants and workers—or so they had seemed—into unrecognizable men and women. The distance black men and women chose to place between themselves and their old status could not always be measured by how far they traveled from their place of bondage. As many former masters and mistresses came to discover, black men and women found ways to manifest their freedom even as they labored in the same fields and kitchens they had labored in as slaves. "Henney is still with me," a South Carolina white woman informed her niece, "but not the same person that she was."[7]

The transition from slavery to freedom took some ironic twists. The same class that had loved to boast of how it looked after old and decrepit slaves now beheld the spectacle of former slaves caring for and refusing to abandon old and decrepit whites who had recently been their masters and mistresses. The same class that had thought blacks to be tied to them by feelings of dependency found themselves painfully dependent on blacks, unable to look after themselves. The testimony of white mistresses forced to assume responsibility for the daily chores once undertaken by their black help is unanimous on this point; the cries of despair reflected both physical exhaustion and psychic humiliation. Yet, none of the many white women who testified to the agonies of performing such chores thought to ask how their black help had performed these tasks day after day, while at the same time in many instances caring for a husband and children. If few former slaveowning families ever paused to scrutinize their own lives and dependency, the blacks who worked for them knew only too well. "Dey was glad to have a heap of colored people bout dem," Josephine Bacchus recalled, "cause white folks couldn' work den no more den dey can work dese days like de colored people can."[8]

Nothing in the experience of the slaveowning class had prepared it to deal with blacks as free workers, and in many respects it was less equipped to make the transition to freedom than its former slaves. Few seemed capable of learning new ways and shaking off old attitudes. Whatever comfort and inspiration this class found in the aftermath of the Civil War seemed confined to an evocation, a celebration of the past, to an elaboration of myths about the "Old South" and the "lost cause." In acknowledging emancipation, former slaveowners had not surrendered the convictions with which they had held black men and women as slaves, and they fully expected those men and women to maintain the old slave demeanor. The kinds of questions they chose to ask about the future revealed only a grim determination to recover the past, to find new ways of exploiting black labor and commanding black lives. "Can not freedmen be organized and disciplined as well as slaves?" a white South Carolinian asked. "Is not the dollar as potent as the lash? The belly as tender as the back."[9] Nothing in the postwar behavior and attitudes of the former slaveholders suggests that the ownership of slaves had compromised their values or tortured their consciences or made them feel morally reprehensible or guilt ridden. The only problem, some conceded, had been with those few slaveholders who had abused the institution. Like any northern employer, the former slaveholder insisted that the excesses of the few should not be visited upon the system itself, which had been essentially benign. If some felt a measure of guilt, none questioned the absolute necessity of maintaining the domination of the superior race.

After emancipation nearly every field hand aspired to the chance to work for himself on his own plot of land, to become the independent proprietor of a small farm. That was the most American of aspirations, the stamp of respectability in an agricultural society, the way to enter the mainstream of American life. For many former slaves, the certain confirmation of freedom was to own the land on which they had worked and which they had made productive and valuable by their own labor. Such aspirations were not to be realized, at least not on any significant scale, as they conflicted with prevailing values involving confiscation, the rights of property, and how success ought to be achieved in a capitalist society. Such aspirations also conflicted with the perceived needs of the planter class, which wanted a black agricultural proletariat, not an independent black yeomanry and therefore after the war moved quickly to prevent blacks from acquiring land or from pursuing nonagricultural employment. For blacks to succeed in becoming proprietors of small farms posed dangers as great as those raised by the spectre of blacks succeeding as voters or legislators.

If emancipation created in the victorious North a rhetorical commitment to helping blacks help themselves, it was never translated into a significant measure of economic opportunity for the newly freed slaves. What evolved was a federal policy that placed former slaves at work for the same men who had previously commanded their labor. In South Carolina, a federal official took pains to explain to a group of freedmen the meaning of free labor, what he chose to call "the price you pay for your freedom."

There are different kinds of work. One man is a doctor, another is a minister, another a soldier. One black man may be a field hand, one a blacksmith, one a carpenter, and still another a house-servant. Every man has his own place, his own trade that he was brought up to, and he must stick to it. . . . If a man works, no matter in what business, he is doing well. The only shame is to be idle and lazy.

You do not understand why some of the white people who used to own you, do not have to work in the field. It is because they are rich. If every man were poor, and worked in his own field, there would be no big farms, and very little cotton or corn raised to sell; there would be no money, and nothing to buy. Some people must be rich, to pay the others, and they have the right to do no work except to look out for their property. It is so everywhere, and perhaps by hard work some of you may by-and-by become rich yourselves.[10]

The message seemed clear enough to the federal official and the government he represented, if not to the assembled freedmen. What the federal government and the nation said in effect was that special consideration did not need to be accorded the freed slaves to correct two centuries of special inequality and exploitation.

In the postwar South, the relationship of slave and master was transformed into that of worker and employer. Without land of his own, the question for the newly freed black and for the first generation born in freedom was the degree to which the white man's dependence on his labor could be transformed into a weapon with which to bargain and expand his autonomy, improve his day-to-day life, and enhance his prospects for the future. Few expressed the new relationship more eloquently or more cogently than Ned Cobb (Nate Shaw), the sharecropper born in Alabama in 1885 and made a part of our historical consciousness through Theodore Rosengarten's *All God's Dangers: The Life of Nate Shaw.*

If you don't make enough to have some left you aint done nothin, except givin the other fellow your labor. That crop out there goin to prosper enough for him to get his and get what I owe him; he's makin his profit but he aint goin to let me rise. . . .
    Now it's right for me to pay you for usin what's yours—your land, stock, plow tools . . . But how much . . . is a man due to pay out? . . . You got a right to your part—rent; and I got a right to mine. But who's the man ought to decide how much? The one that owns the property or the one that works it?[11]

Since both sides perceived their needs and rights in very different ways, conflict was inevitable in the postemancipation South. If the former slaveholders did not respond easily to the concept of free labor, neither did the freed blacks respond easily or passively to perceived limitations placed on their working lives and opportunities. They resisted contractual labor. They sought to reduce the hours they worked each day. They moved to withdraw their wives from field labor. They rejected working in gangs under white supervisors. They broke up the slave quarters. They demanded shares or wages that reflected their contribution to the making of the crop. In securing farms of their own and moving onto those farms, whether as purchasers or (more often) as renters, they achieved a certain kind of personal autonomy and forced upon the old ruling class a new organization and management of labor.[12]
    Whether expressed collectively, as in tough bargaining sessions, plantation strikes and walk outs, or individually, as in the personal struggles waged by a Ned Cobb, the efforts of former slaves and the first generations born in freedom to use their labor to force concessions from white employers marked a break with the past—an often courageous chapter in the history of the American working class. Even the sharecropping system was in many ways a compromise, since black workers achieved a semblance of autonomy while the landlord maintained control of the land. For most southern blacks, however, personal triumphs were rare, expectations were disappointed, and hopes rapidly faded. Neither the illusion of autonomy imparted by the initial experiments in sharecropping nor hard work and frugality could overcome the cycle of debt that sharply circumscribed their economic freedom. The fact remained that most black farmers enjoyed neither ownership of the land nor the full rewards of their labor.

The bargaining power wielded by black laborers proved less formidable in practice than in theory. If they held out for better terms, they faced eviction. If they left the plantation, seeking better terms, they faced arrest as vagrants. If they chose to work elsewhere, they faced the possibility of blacklisting by other planters and farmers, particularly if they had reputations as malcontents or rebels. And if they combined among themselves to better their conditions, as they did on numerous plantations, they faced the possibility of intervention by local police, militia units, or even federal troops.[13]

No matter how often the black press celebrated the few examples of black economic success and landownership, the great mass of black laborers remained a landless peasantry. The political and civil rights won by black southerners during Reconstruction failed to alter their economic lives. How long the euphoria of political participation lasted no doubt varied with each freedman, but the principal problem remained the same and persisted long after Reconstruction had ended. "Some say that politics is our greatest danger," a South Carolina black worker remarked. "But I dispute that. The greatest evil that could befall us is the failure in a crop this year. That is our great trouble."[14] Returning from the polling place for most freedmen was not unlike returning from school or church: realities that neither politics, education, nor religion seemed to be able to touch, at least not in any measurable ways, confronted them. "Wat's de use ob niggers pretendin' to lurnin?" asked a black worker on a plantation in the Deep South in 1865. "Dey's men on dis yeah plantation, old's I am, studyin' ober spellin' book an' makin' b'lieve's if dey could larn. Wat's de use? Wat'll dey be but niggers wen dey gits through? Niggers good for nothin' but to wuck in de fiel' an' make cotton. Can't make white folks ob you'selves, if you *is* free."[15]

For most it was a far cry from the kind of freedom they had envisioned for themselves and their families. Whether they listened to their leaders, to their teachers, to their ministers, or to their professed northern white friends, southern blacks after the war heard the same hopeful message of uplift and self-help, the same moral and economic injunctions. Through their industry, skill, enterprise, and frugality, they would some day enjoy the same material pleasures and rewards that abounded in the white folks' society; they would some day command a place in American society commensurate with their numbers and their weight in the economy.

From virtually every source, these same assurances were imparted and embellished. The freedmen's schools taught them to be diligent, faithful, and punctual in the work place, to respect property and authority, to cultivate the virtues of honesty, industry, and frugality. Frederick Douglass admonished them: "If you would be prosperous, you must be industrious." A freedman's newspaper advised them, "Work every day. If you cannot make a dollar, make two bits." J.M. Langston, a prominent black leader, assured them, "Money is a moral as well as material power. . . .The representatives of dollars and cents are always the most influential men in a community." The African Methodist Episcopal Church told them that the only way to win over the hearts and minds of white Americans was through their pockets: "If free black labor affects the pocket in any way, it will affect the heart." Still another influential black asked his people to emulate the Jews: "They got wealth and education and kept together; they were patient; but ever toiling, hopeful, and ever watching, economical, saving, even penurious and mercenary." If any doubts remained about the rewards of materialism and the need to emulate successful whites, the Reverend Henry Highland Garnet, a veteran black abolitionist, assured a gathering of freedmen, "The more money you make, the lighter your skin will be. The more land and houses you get, the straighter your hair will be."[16]

Even as they found their economic opportunities sharply curtailed, even as the deepening agricultural depression of the post-Reconstruction years drove thousands off the land, black men and women were asked to pay obeisance to the same materialist deities, values, and goals that motivated the larger society. They imbibed the lessons of the McGuffey Readers much as young whites did. Respectability would always gain respect. Character makes the man, not class. The greatest men, the leading capitalists began in humble employments. Success came ultimately to the hardworking, the sober, the honest, and the educated, to those who served their employers faithfully, who respected property and the sanctity of contract, who cultivated habits of thrift, cleanliness, and temperance, who led moral, virtuous, Christian lives.[17]

In the experience of black southerners, such advice was as naive and mistaken in its assumptions as it was persistent. Faithful adherence to the shibboleths of capitalism and democracy had brought them nothing. Having been told that his people needed only to improve themselves to win the respect of whites, John Randolph of North Carolina thought the evidence suggested otherwise: "It is not enough to tell us that we will be respected accordingly as we show ourselves worthy of it, when we know there are some worthy ones whose fate is just the same."[18] After all, if success came to the hardworking, why were black southerners not the most successful race on earth? How could they be frugal if they had no money to save? And if they did manage to save some money, how could they buy land if whites conspired to deny them ownership? When they sought to lead law-abiding, moral, Christian lives, they were subjected to restrictive laws and victimized by a violence that went unpunished. When they tried to help themselves, they were deemed impudent and sassy.

The Negro as a buffoon, as a menial, as a servant was acceptable.

Whites had come to accept irresponsibility, ignorance, and submissiveness as peculiar Negro traits. Those blacks who failed to fit the stereotype seemed somehow abnormal, even menacing. "The Negro as a poor ignorant creature," Frederick Douglass observed, "does not contradict the race pride of the white race. He is more a source of amusement to that race than an object of resentment. . . . If he comes in ignorance, rags, and wretchedness, he conforms to the popular belief of his character, and in that character he is welcome." While "in his downward course," Douglass perceived, the Negro "meets with no resistance," yet "his step upward is resented and resisted at every step of his progress." For blacks who aspired to better themselves, this posed an impossible dilemma.

The resistance is not to the colored man as a slave, a servant or a menial. It is aimed at the Negro as a man. . . . It is only when he acquires education, property, and influence, only when he attempts to rise and be a man among men that he invites repression. It is not to the Negro but the quality in which he comes which makes him an offense.[19]

Neither during nor after Reconstruction were black leaders able to surmount a paradox. While claiming that blacks were incapable of becoming their political, social, or economic equals, the dominant society betrayed the fear that they might. If Reconstruction taught blacks any lesson, it was that southern whites feared black success far more than black failure. The more blacks succeeded, the more they gave any indication of learning, the more they demonstrated a capability of moving out of their place, the more likely they were to arouse white resentment and hostility. The language used to describe black participation in Reconstruction, the violence meted out to black leaders, the methods employed to undermine Radical rule, the determination to inculcate future generations with the notion of Reconstruction as a "tragic era" betrayed white fears that biracial democratic government might succeed. The white South was driven to violence not because it had been dismayed by black failure in Reconstruction but by the spectacle of blacks learning the uses of political power. "There was one thing," W.E.B. Du Bois would write, "that the white South feared more than Negro dishonesty, ignorance, and incompetency, and that was Negro honesty, knowledge, and efficiency."[20] James Lynch, a black Reconstruction leader in Mississippi, suggested as much when he paraphrased white justification of racial repression: "We must proscribe the negro because he is inferior and incapable." But when blacks attempt to be successful, the same whites would say, "We must proscribe the negro, or he will equal us: he will become so refined, and strong in intellect, that he will win the hearts of our daughters and become our legislator."[21]

To grapple with this kind of paradox could be a most frustrating and debilitating experience. Thirty years after the Civil War, Booker T. Washington, articulating classic petit-bourgeois aspirations, emerged as the preeminent black spokesman. He grounded his advice to blacks on the proposition: "It is not within the province of human nature, that the man who is intelligent and virtuous, and owns and cultivates the best farm in his county, shall very long be denied the proper respect and consideration." And he insisted as well: "The Negro merchant who owns the largest store in town will not be lynched." W.E.B. Du Bois, no less a petit-bourgeois thinker at this time whatever his differences with Washington, articulated much the same position: "The day the Negro race courts and marries the savings-bank will be the day of its salvation."[22]

But such assumptions were proven false on too many occasions for blacks to maintain the faith. The violence inflicted upon blacks at times was quite selective and aimed primarily at those who had succeeded, those in positions of leadership, those who owned the largest store in town, those who had stepped out of their proper sphere—the "uppity, aloof, smart-ass niggers." Washington had only to read his own mail to gain a sense of what was happening around him. Back in 1890, Isaiah Montgomery, the only black delegate to the Mississippi constitutional convention, proclaimed his faith in economic and educational progress as the key to race progress. He approved a reduction in black voting, based on literacy and a poll tax, convinced such qualifications would encourage blacks to improve themselves. By obtaining property and knowledge, they not only would win back the franchise but also gain acceptance by the dominant white society. Some fourteen years after the constitutional convention, however, Montgomery wrote a discouraging letter to Washington in which he cited several incidents in Clay County to describe "the depths to which Mississippi has descended."

Rev. Buchanan has the best appointed printing establishment of any colored man in the State, and conducts a Baptist Newspaper. . ., and was no doubt prospering, his daughter was his cashier and Book-keeper, they kept a Horse and Buggy, which the young woman used frequently in going to and from work; they kept a decent house and a Piano; a mass meeting of whites decided that the mode of living practiced by the Buchanan family had a bad effect on the cooks and washerwomen, who aspired to do likewise, and became less disposed to work for whites. [A mob subsequently forced Buchanan and his family from the town, not even permitting them to remove their possessions.]

Thomas Harvey runs a neat little Grocery, he kept a Buggy and frequently rode to his place of business, he was warned to sell his Buggy and walk. Mr. Chandler keeps a Grocery, he was ordered to leave, but was finally allowed to remain on good behavior. Mr. Meacham ran a business and had a Pool Table in connection therewith, he was ordered to close up and don overalls for manual labor. Mr. Cook conducted a Hack business between the Depots and about town, using two Vehicles, he was notified that he would be allowed to run only one and was ordered to sell the other.[23]

The examples might be multiplied many times over. The Class of 1886 at Tuskegee Institute adopted as its motto, "There is Room at the Top." But in the town of Tuskegee, the danger of success was readily acknowledged by black residents. "I know men who won't keep a horse. If they get one they will sell it. If you ask such a one why he sold his horse, he very likely will say: 'A white man see me in dat 'ere horse, he look hard at me. I make my min' a mule good 'nugh for a ole nigger like me." A black farmer in Alpharetta, Georgia, knew that he "better not accumulate much, no matter how hard and honest you work for it, as they . . . well you can't enjoy it." In Mississippi, in the early years of the twentieth century, mobs singled out for attack and murder black field hands and sharecroppers who had managed to purchase small plots of land with money they had saved.[24]

Few understood better than Ned Cobb, the Alabama sharecropper, the limits placed on black advancement and how whites feared and resisted any evidence of black success. Through persistence and hard work and by drawing on his inner strength and refusing to submit to the whims of white men, Cobb managed to accumulate some property. But to keep it was a continual struggle:

I had men . . . didn't want to see me with anything. Soon as I got to where I . . . was makin somethin . . . then they commenced wantin to make trades with me.

Nor did Ned Cobb's white neighbors appreciate his resourcefulness in stocking up an impressive supply of meat on his place:

They didn't like to see a nigger with too much; . . . and it caused em to throw a slang word about a "nigger" havin all this, that, and the other.

The sight of Ned Cobb driving about town in a buggy infuriated local whites even more. That was because, Cobb explained, white people "hated to see niggers livin like people." For blacks to accumulate property or money was to make them independent, and whites feared rather than admired such independence.

The idea—"keep the dollar out the niggers' hands"—these white folks went rock bottom with that. . . . The white people was afraid the money would make the nigger act too much like his own man.

For some blacks, as Cobb came to realize, the way to survive in the

South was not to accumulate enough to arouse white resentment. He described his own father as such a man.

> He had money but—whenever the colored man prospered too fast . . . they worked every figure to cut your britches off you. So, . . . to his way of thinkin it weren't no use in climbin too fast . . . if they was goin to take everything you worked for when you got too high.

Neb Cobb's brother seemed to have worked precisely in that spirit. "He made up his mind that he weren't goin to have anything and after that, why, nothin could hurt him."[25]

Whatever extraordinary efforts made by black southerners after emancipation to educate themselves, to assume political responsibilities, and to provide for their families, whatever the speeches of black leaders, the manifestos adopted by black meetings, the uplifting sermons, the editorials of outrage, the clashes over programs and ideologies, to the great mass of black men and women, trying to work out their lives on the farms and plantations owned by whites, the effort was futile. The examples cited by an Isaiah Montgomery or by a Ned Cobb seemed to suggest that there was no way to win. To survive was to conform to white expectations, to accommodate. "They'd have dealins with you, furnish you what you needed to make a crop, but you had to come under their rulins," Cobb recalled. "They'd give you a good name if you was obedient to 'em, acted nice when you met 'em and didn't question 'em 'bout what they said they had against you. You begin to cry about your rights and the mistreatin of you and they'd murder you."[26]

Neither accommodation nor the accumulation of property guaranteed blacks their civil rights or even their physical survival. How many black southerners were lynched, beaten, flogged, mutilated, or quietly murdered will never be known. Nor could any body count reveal the barbaric savagery and depravity that characterized assaults on black men in the name of restraining their savagery and depravity—the severed ears and entrails, the mutilated sex organs, the burnings at the stake, the open display of skulls and severed limbs as trophies. The degree, the intensity, the quality of the racial violence at the turn of the century made a mockery of the notion that racial progress would win the respect and recognition of whites. In the Wilmington race riot of 1898, as in the Atlanta riot of 1906, the brunt of mob violence appeared to fall on property-owning blacks, on the most industrious, the most respectable, the most law-abiding, the most accommodating, the most educated—teachers, physicians, lawyers, clergymen, merchants, businessmen, editors. Albion Tourgee observed of the Wilmington riot that education had obviously failed to reduce racial tensions; on the contrary, knowledge was resented in the black man or used by the whites to rationalize, refine, and strengthen exploitation.[27]

For four days in 1906, white mobs in Atlanta lynched, murdered, and assaulted blacks and plundered their homes and shops. "I knew then who I was," recalled Walter White, then a youth of thirteen. When the mob threatened to burn down his house, they shouted, "It's too nice for a nigger to live in!"[28] Much of the violence fell on those blacks who had succeeded, who had faithfully adhered to the Washingtonian faith. The middle-class neighborhood in which they lived became a convenient target of the mob, the place to teach those "uppity, aloof, smart-ass niggers" lessons they would never forget. Among those driven from their homes was Dr. W. F. Penn, a prominent black physician, a graduate of Yale University, a man who commanded influence in the community. "What shall we do?" he asked Atlanta whites in the aftermath of the riot:

We have been disarmed: how shall we protect our lives and property? If living a sober, industrious, upright life, accumulating property and educating his children as best he knows how, is not the standard by which a coloured man can live and be protected in the South, what is to become of him? If the kind of life I have lived isn't the kind you want, shall I leave and go North?

When we aspire to be decent and industrious we are told that we are bad examples to other coloured men. Tell us what your standards are for coloured men. What are the requirements under which we may live and be protected? What shall we do?"[29]

The question defied any easy answer. No matter how many whites condemned lynching and white terrorism, the dominant racial views that had fed the violence remained unchanged. Historians provided a version of Reconstruction that dramatized the need to repress blacks. The newly emerging social sciences provided scholarly footnotes to traditional racist assumptions about the character and capabilities of blacks. Those assumptions in turn encouraged and explained still further oppressive racial practices, the need to insure the subordination of blacks by legal segregation, disfranchisement, and economic proscription. With equal forcefulness, dehumanizing portraits of black men and women were imprinted on the white mind in the commercial products sold to white America, in caricatures that exaggerated and distorted the physical appearance of blacks and made a mockery of their aspirations. The "picturesque" Negro, replete with banjo eyes, saucer lips, and an obsequious smile, was promoted as a suitable household adornment, even as racist tracts and political demagogues dwelled on the brutal instincts and unrestrained savagery of blacks. In southern literature, in the press, in daily conversations among whites, it also became customary at the turn of the century to contrast the "old time darkeys" and the "New Negro" in ways that suggested a renewed threat to white supremacy. The contrast also suggested the need to impress upon the new generations of blacks who had never known enslavement and were flocking to southern cities and towns after being squeezed off the land that there were significant restraints on their freedom and aspirations.

If black southerners found it difficult to control their own destiny, even their daily working lives, they still waged a continual struggle to overcome illiteracy, to develop their own community institutions, to shape a culture that would impart personal pride and self-respect and provide the inner resources necessary to survive in a hostile society. If they were forced to accommodate, they did not necessarily submit. There was a difference, as Ned Cobb suggested:

I've gotten along in this world by studyin the races and knowin that I was one of the underdogs. . . . I got tired of it but no help did I know, weren't nobody to back me up. I've taken every kind of insult and went on . . . but I didn't believe in this way of bowin to my knees and doin what *any* white man said do. Still, I always knowed to give the white man his time of day or else he's ready to knock me in the head. I just aint goin to go nobody's way against my own self. First thing of all—I care for myself and respect myself.[30]

The success ethic inculcated into the minds of generations of postemancipation black southerners persisted into the twentieth century as "race uplift." In the black press, editors still insisted that "money power will stop lynchings quicker than all our oratory and protest meetings combined." But the great mass of southern black men and women, no matter how hard they worked to uplift themselves, remained landless agricultural workers, trapped in an exploitative economic system that encouraged neither initiative nor hope. If some still clung to a belief in self-help, even as they were denied the tools by which to help themselves, most struggled as best they could, tried to suck whatever joy they could out of a bad situation, and raised a new generation of blacks, many of whom chose to look elsewhere for the chance to realize the dreams and aspirations denied their parents and grandparents.

The face of the South that I had known was hostile and forbidding, and yet out of all the conflicts and the curses, the blows and the anger, the tension and the terror, I had somehow gotten the idea that life could be different, could be lived in a fuller and richer manner. . . . True, I had lied. I had stolen. I had struggled to contain my seething anger. I had fought. And it was perhaps a mere accident that I had never killed. . . . But in what other ways had the South allowed me to be natural, to be real, to be myself, except in rejection, rebellion, and aggression?[31]

And so, in 1927, at the age of nineteen, Richard Wright boarded the train that would take him to Chicago, as it had tens of thousands of southern black migrants in the preceding decade.

Each migrant carried with him or her experiences and stories, many of them passed on from generation to generation; some were expressed in song, some in folk tales, some in humor, some in shouts, and in the North the songs and stories were likely to be reshaped to deal with new realities and to reflect urban folkways. The common theme remained the betrayal of black expectations in a white-dominated society. Few contemporary speeches or editorials made the point more tellingly than did the story of how God had sent the white man, the Mexican, and the Negro on a mission.

After the Lord had created the Earth, he created the white man, the Mexican, and the Negro. So one day he told them, "Go out and get you some rocks." The white man, being industrious, went out and got a huge rock. The Mexican got a middle-sized rock, and the Negro, being lazy, got a pebble. Later on that evening, the Lord said, "I'm going to turn these rocks into bread." As a result, the white man had a lot of bread, the Mexican had a sufficient amount, but the Negro only had a crumb, and he stayed hungry. So the next day, the Lord again told them the same thing. This time the white man got a great big rock, the Mexican got a little smaller rock, but the Negro brought back a whole half of a mountain. That evening the Lord stood before them and said, "upon this rock, I will build my church." The Negro said, "you're a mother-fucking liar, you're going to make me some bread."[32]

To succeed was only to fail. The paradox was a familiar one in the black experience. The story suggests a perception of white America as unbeatable. There is no way to assimilate. There is no way to separate. Like Ralph Ellison's protagonist in *Invisible Man*, indoctrinated with the success myth, there remains only the illusion of progress as he tries to deal with a society that denies him his very identity.

For all the rhetoric of the recent "black revolution," for all the strides made by the civil rights movement, for all the legislation enacted and the court decisions handed down, many of the same frustrations and anxieties persist—the same sense of powerlessness, the same desperate struggle for survival and recognition, the same indifference by those who command power. In *Dusk of Dawn*, W.E.B. Du Bois warned his people that they faced not simply "the rational, conscious determination of white folk to oppress us" but "age-long complexes sunk now largely to unconscious habit and irrational urge."[33] The warning retains much of its forcefulness today, more than a century after emancipation. What is suggested by the deepening economic disparities between whites and blacks, the controversies over busing and affirmative action, the deteriorating quality of public education, the revival of the Ku Klux Klan, the reduced commitments to the working poor, and the rhetoric and implementation of Reaganism is that the commitments to racial equality and equal opportunity made in previous decades are being revised, compromised, diluted, permitted to erode, or abandoned altogether to accord with new priorities and ideologies and with old and still popular and deeply held convictions—with those "age-long complexes sunk now largely to unconscious habit and irrational urge."

When Richard Wright reached the "Promised Land" in 1927, he learned the same lessons previous southern migrants had been taught in the North: that racial oppression knew no Mason-Dixon line, nor did it always manifest itself in lynchings, Jim Crow laws, or disfranchisement.

Slowly I began to forge in the depths of my mind a mechanism that repressed all the dreams and desires that the Chicago streets, the newspapers, the movies were evoking in me. I was going through a second childhood; a new sense of the limit of the possible was being born in me. What could I dream of that had the barest possibility of coming true? I could think of nothing. And, slowly, it was upon exactly that nothingness that my mind began to dwell, that constant sense of wanting without having, of being hated without reason. A dim notion of what life meant to a Negro in America was coming to consciousness in me, not in terms of external events, lynchings, Jim Crowism, and the endless brutalities, but in terms of crossed-up feeling, of psyche pain. I sensed that Negro life was a sprawling land of unconscious suffering, and there were but few Negroes who knew the meaning of their lives, who could tell their story.[34]

Notes

1. George P. Rawick, ed., *The American Slave: A Composite Autobiography*, 19 vols. (Westport, Conn., 1972), 15, N.C. Narr., pt. 2, pp. 117-23.

2. Paul Murray, *Proud Shoes: The Story of an American Family* (New York, 1956), pp. 159-60.

3. Joseph LeConte, *'Ware Sherman: A Journal of Three Months' Personal Experience in the Last Days of the Confederacy* (Berkeley, 1938), p. 125.

4. Rawick, ed., *The American Slave*, 7: Okla. Narr., pp. 165-67.

5. See Leon F. Litwack, *Been in the Storm So Long: The Aftermath of Slavery* (New York, 1979), especially chap. 5, "How Free is Free?"

6. Rawick, ed., *The American Slave*, 4, Texas Narr., pt. 2, p. 204; 17, Fla. Narr., p. 182; 7, Okla. Narr., p. 209. For other examples, see 2, S.C. Narr., pt. 1, p. 335; 4, Texas Narr., pt. 1, pp. 153, 262; 5, Texas Narr., pt. 3, pp. 153, 161; 8, Ark. Narr. pt. 1, p. 105; 12, Ga. Narr., pt. 1, p. 8, pt. 2, p. 279; 13, Ga. Narr., pt. 3, pp. 65, 293; 14, N.C. Narr., pt. 1, p. 460; *Christian Recorder*, 16 January 1864; M. Waterbury, *Seven Years Among the Freedmen*, 3d ed. (Chicago, 1893), p. 76; David Macrae, *The Americans at Home* (1870; reprint ed., New York, 1952), pp. 133, 210, 213; Whitelaw Reid, *After the War: A Southern Tour, May 1, 1865, to May 1, 1866* (Cincinnati, 1866), pp. 272-73; J. T. Trowbridge, *The South* (Hartford, 1867), p. 151.

7. Mrs. William Mason Smith to Mrs. Edward L. Cottenet, 12 July 1865, in *Mason Smith Family Letters, 1860-1868,* Daniel E. Huger Smith, Alice R. Huger Smith, and Arney R. Childs, eds. (Columbia, S.C., 1950), p. 221.

8. Rawick, ed., *The American Slave,* 2, S.C. Narr., pt. 1, p. 22. For freedmen and freedwomen who remained to assist former owners, see Litwack, *Been in the Storm So Long,* p. 330. For the postwar experiences of white women forced to assume household tasks, see Litwack, *Been in the Storm so Long,* pp. 354-58.

9. Lacy Ford, "Labor and Ideology in the South Carolina Up-Country; The Transition to Free-Labor Agriculture" (Paper presented at The Citadel Conference on the South, April 25, 1981), pp. 16-17. I am grateful to Mr. Ford for permission to use his source.

10. "To the Freed People of Orangeburg District," in Captain Charles Soule to O. O. Howard, 12 June 1865, Records of the Subordinate Field Officers for South Carolina, Bureau of Refugees, Freedmen and Abandoned Lands, Microcopy 752, Roll 17, National Archives, Washington, D.C.

11. Theodore Rosengarten, *All God's Dangers: The Life of Nate Shaw* (New York, 1974), p. 108. Nate Shaw is the fictitious name of Ned Cobb, who died on November 5, 1973. The author chose to use the alias "as a measure of protection and privacy." Shaw's real identity was subsequently revealed and in future references in this essay Nate Shaw will appear as Ned Cobb.

12. See Litwack, *Been in the Storm So Long,* especially pp. 392-99, 420-25, 430-45.

13. Ibid., especially pp. 437-43.

14. *New York Times,* 2 June 1867.

15. Reid, *After the War,* p. 510.

16. S. S. Ashley to Col. N. A. McLean, 7 February 1866, American Missionary Association Archives (Freedmen's Schools), Amistad Research Center, Dillard University, New Orleans, La: *The Black Republican* (New Orleans), 29 April 1865 (F. Douglass); *The Free Man's Press* (Galveston), 14 January 1868 (freedman's newspaper); *Christian Recorder,* 25 August 1866 (J. M. Langston), 18 August 1866 (AME Church), 17 March 1866 ("The Jew and the Black Gentile"), 30 September 1865 (H. H. Garnet).

17. For advice to the freedmen, see, in addition to the preceding, *The Black Republican,* 15 April 1865 ("The Duty of Colored Men in Louisiana"); *The Colored American* (Augusta, Ga.), 30 December 1865 ("What is a Man?"), 6 January 1866; *The Free Man's Press,* 1 August 1868 ("Learn a Trade"); *Christian Recorder,* 8 April 1865 ("What Shall We Do To Be Respected?"), 3 June 1865 (R. H. Cain), 26 August 1865 (R. H. Cain), 9, 16, 23 December 1865 ("Advice from the Editor. . .To the Many Freedmen Throughout the South"), 3 February 1866 (J. C. Gibbs), 10 March 1866 ("Trying Moment for the Colored People"), 24 March 1866 ("Emigration of Colored People") 21 April 1866 (R. H. Cain), 19 May 1866 ("Get Land"), 26 May 1866 (Bishops of the AME Church, "Address to the Colored People"), 22 September 1866 ("Our Great Need"), 5 January 1867 (editorial), 14 September 1867 (J. M. Langston), 30 November 1867 ("Self-Reliance the Key to Success"); *The Louisianian* (New Orleans), 6 April 1871 ("Self-Reliance").

18. *Christian Recorder,* 21 May 1864.

19. Philip S. Foner, ed., *The Life and Writings of Frederick Douglass,* 4 vols. (New

York, 1950-55), 1:414; 4:195, 378; Waldo E. Martin, Jr., "The Mind of Frederick Douglass" (Ph.D. diss., University of California, Berkeley, 1980), pp. 397-99. I am grateful to Dr. Martin for calling my attention to the extract.

20. W.E.B. Du Bois, "Reconstruction and Its Benefits," *American Historical Review* 15 (1910): 795.

21. *Christian Recorder*, 3 March 1866.

22. Booker T. Washington, *Future of the American Negro* (Boston, 1899), p. 176; Robert L. Factor, *The Black Response to America* (Reading, Mass., 1970), p. 253; Francis L. Broderick, *W.E.B. Du Bois: Negro Leader in a Time of Crisis* (Stanford, 1955), p. 66.

23. Louis R. Harlan and Raymond W. Smock, eds., *The Booker T. Washington Papers*, 11 vols. (Urbana, 1972-81), 8: 61-63.

24. C. Vann Woodward, *Origins of the New South, 1877-1913* (Baton Rouge, 1951), p. 218; Letter to the Editor, *Chicago Defender*, 28 April 1917; "The Money Ralley at Sweet Gum. The Story of a Visit to a Negro Church in the Black Belt, Alabama," Typescript, n.d. (circa 1912), Robert Park Papers, Box 1, Folder 10, p. 11, University of Chicago, Chicago, Ill. (I am grateful to James Grossman for bringing the last two items to my attention). On white terrorism in Mississippi, see William F. Holmes, "Whitecapping: Agrarian Violence in Mississippi, 1902-1906, *The Journal of Southern History* 35 (1969): 165-85.

25. Rosengarten, *All God's Dangers*, pp. 544, 192, 193, 264, 27, xxi.

26. Ibid., p. 545.

27. Otto H. Olsen, *Carpetbagger's Crusade: The Life of Albion Winegar Tourgee* (Baltimore, 1965), pp. 346-47.

28. Walter White, *A Man Called White* (New York, 1948), p. 11. On the Atlanta riot, see also Charles Crowe, "Racial Violence and Repression in the Progressive Era," *Journal of Negro History* 53 (1968): 234-56, and "Racial Massacre in Atlanta, September 22, 1906," *Journal of Negro History* 54 (1969): 150-73.

29. Ray Stannard Baker, *Following the Colour Line* (New York, 1908), pp. 19-20.

30. Rosengarten, *All God's Dangers*, p. 545.

31. Ronald G. Walters, "The Negro Press and the Image of Success: 1920-1939," *Midcontinent American Studies Journal* 11 (Fall 1970): 44; Richard Wright, *Black Boy: A Record of Childhood and Youth* (New York, 1945), pp. 226, 227.

32. Roger D. Abrahams, *Positively Black* (Englewood Cliffs, N. J., 1970), p. ix.

33. W.E.B. Du Bois, *Dusk of Dawn* (New York, 1940) p. 296.

34. Richard Wright, *American Hunger* (New York, 1977), p. 7.

2

LABOR AND IDEOLOGY IN THE SOUTH CAROLINA UP-COUNTRY: THE TRANSITION TO FREE-LABOR AGRICULTURE

Lacy Ford

Perhaps the supreme yet most subtle irony of the American Civil War was that both North and South fought to defend dramatically different visions of the perfect republican society, visions that were themselves destined to become casualties of the war. Politicians and ideologues in both regions used the inherited republican tradition that had so animated American politics during the late eighteenth century as a prism through which to refract their respective visions of the good society and in the process of doing so sometimes badly distorted republicanism itself. As Eric Foner has demonstrated, the emergence of the Republican party in the North during the 1850s marked the triumph of an ideology devoted to the principles of "free soil, free labor, and free men." This free-labor ideology was a dynamic version of republicanism adjusted to the peculiarities of early commercial capitalism. According to free-labor ideology, the good society was one dominated by independent, property-holding, petty producers, who were free to attain self-sufficiency and pursue the main chance in an expanding market economy. This ideal North of the free-labor enthusiasts was a veritable republican utopia composed of "family farms, small shops, and village artisans"—a competitive society of petty capitalists, where labor knew neither the oppression of alienation from capital nor the degradation of competition with slavery.[1]

However shortsighted the proslavery theorists of the South were in other matters, they were prophetic critics of the northern social order. As early as 1850 they predicted the unrelenting and violent struggle between labor and capital that scarred the North during the Gilded Age. These southern thinkers saw that the North was not heading toward a free-labor millennium of prosperous producers but rather toward an unfettered capitalism of rapacious robber barons, belligerent wage-laborers, and corrupt government officials. Antislavery spokesmen usually dismissed the prewar southern criticism of northern society as simply a *tu quoque* response that was designed to bury the fundamental issues of the slavery debate beneath a flurry of sectional charges and counter-charges. Nevertheless, after the Civil War, the free-labor landscape, peopled by independent producers, did begin to disappear behind the smoke of giant factories.[2] In 1850, South Carolina planter William Henry Trescot warned the North of the dangers inherent in the use of free labor. "History teems with rebellion of free labour . . . against class privilege" he noted, as he advised the North to "abandon the palpable inconsistency of free labour and a privileged class."[3]

Despite their skepticism of free labor, southerners, especially pros-lavery theorists, considered themselves the true champions of republi-canism. Throughout the period of sectional conflict, southern leaders argued that the southern experiment in slave-labor republicanism had better prospects for continued success than did its northern free-labor counterpart. "[N]o social state, without slavery as its basis, can per-manently maintain a republican form of government," asserted Iveson Brookes, an Edgefield minister, in 1849.[4] As its advocates in South Car-olina saw it, slave-labor republicanism was simply the "country ideol-ogy" of the Revolutionary era that had matured to accommodate the needs of expanding staple agriculture. Free-labor republicanism could succeed, they argued, only in a static, hermetic economy in which self-sufficiency was the height of economic ambition. In a dynamic economy blessed with seemingly inexhaustible natural resources, such Spartan frugality must succumb quickly to the republican urge for progress. Ultimately, the pursuit of wealth would lead to the accumulation of large amounts of capital by a few individuals and the emergence of a prop-ertyless laboring class. In a free-labor society, proslavery theorists claimed, the alienation of labor from capital produced mutual antagonism, polit-ical hostility, and class conflict. In a slave society, the dependent labor force was defined out of the body politic. It would remain forever beyond the reach of scheming demagogues, even as its material needs were supplied by an enlightened master class whose honor was staked in stewardship.[5]

William Henry Trescot aptly summarized the proslavery position on the labor question when he wrote in 1850:

There is one relation, lying at the basis of all social and political life, the shifting character of which fairly indicates the national progress in wealth and civiliza-tion—the relation of labor to capital . . . the history of all that is great in achieve-ment . . . proves that the best interests of humanity require, first, that labour should be subordinate to, and controlled by capital; and second, that the interests of the two should by that very dependence be as closely as possible identified. It may be safely asserted . . . that the interest of labour and capital can never be permanently or properly reconciled, except under the institution of slavery; for it stands to reason, that wherever the political theory of government rec-ognizes the equality of capital and labor, while the great reality of society shews the one in hopeless and heartless dependence on the other, there will exist between the two a constant jealousy and a bitter strife, the weaker demanding its rights with impotent cursing, or enforcing them with revolutionary fierceness.[6]

Slavery, based on racial differences, Trescot contended, prevented such problems from arising in the South.

The appeal of slave-labor republicanism extended beyond the planter class. The yeoman world view also was infused with the slaveholding ideal. For southerners, the prosperous planter represented the virtues of the independent yeoman writ large. Waxing eloquent at an agricultural society meeting in 1855, Edgefield planter Arthur Simkins explained the kinship of yeoman and planter through their common zeal for independence:

The commonest cottager, on his hundred acres of pine land, looks upon his little possession around him as his own . . . in the enjoyment of which he is safe from intrusion . . . while many a Southern planter, as he surveys his broad acres and passes in review of his hundreds of slaves, feels the pride of a baron of olden times. . . . Each man is master within his own domain and has no rival there. . . . he jostles no one and no one jostles him.[7]

In a slave society, this zeal for personal independence developed some peculiar manifestations. As slavery and staple agriculture spread across the South, the southern definition of independence grew to require not only individual autonomy but also mastery over others. Models for both labor control and family structure were drawn from the imperatives of possessive individualism, which required the independent patriarch to maintain absolute control over his dependents.[8] Therefore mastery, which was defined simply by South Carolina Governor James H. Hammond as the desire "to control and scorn to be controlled," became accepted in the South as an elaborate form of republican independence, a higher expression of individual liberty. The psychological appeal of mastery reached yeoman farmers as well as slaveholders. The presence of black slaves allowed an entire race of would-be masters without slaves to enjoy certain caste privileges and to flaunt a certain instinctive sense of natural mastery. White skins made men masters, even if they actually owned or controlled barely anything.[9]

In the hot and uncertain months of the summer after Appomattox, planters and yeomen in the South Carolina up-country found their mastery destroyed, their vision of a well-ordered slave republic forever shattered by defeat and emancipation. While up-country leaders were quick to note that "might" and not "right" had decided the issue of slavery, they nonetheless realized that up-country agriculture would have to be reorganized with free labor.[10] In fact, Reconstruction turned the South Carolina up-country into something of a practical laboratory for experiments in novel free-labor systems. Up-country landowners hoped for a system that would be a close approximation of slavery, thus allowing them tight control of black labor. The freedmen, on the other hand, sought to give their new freedom full expression by acquiring as much independence from whites and as much control over their own work routine as possible. In this atmosphere, pervaded with racial animosity and tinged with sectional bitterness, the Bureau of Refugees, Freedmen and Abandoned Lands, created in June of 1865, attempted to convince both landowners and freedmen of the advantages of a free-labor system. O. O. Howard, the bureau's chief, advised his agents in South Carolina that "the Negro shall understand that he is really free, but on no account, if able to work, should he harbor the thought that the government will support him in idleness" and that "demand and supply shall regulate the whole subject of labor."[11]

The practical implementation of Howard's ideas proved difficult. In the summer of 1865, the Freedmen's Bureau accepted the thankless task of attempting to salvage damaged or abandoned crops already in the field. Most bureau agents urged white landowners to divide the crop into shares, usually allowing freedmen no more than one-third of the crop. Although they were desperate for harvest labor, white landowners nevertheless resented being forced to divide a short crop with former slaves. At the same time, many freedmen, like those in the southeastern portion of Union district, refused to sign share contracts, preferring to wait for the rumored redistribution of property or to rely on their own wiles for subsistence. Up-country whites, of course, had their own view of such black recalcitrance. "Freedom for the black," moaned the Yorkville *Enquirer*, "means to live a life of idleness and barbarism—to live like the beasts of the field." No barn, no corncrib, no smokehouse, and no poultry yard was safe from thieving freedmen, according to up-country whites.[12]

Despite the problems they encountered in late 1865, free-labor advocates within the Freedmen's Bureau believed that they could get better results in 1866. Robert K. Scott, newly appointed assistant bureau commissioner for South Carolina, admitted that whites "all agreed that the only way a Negro can be induced to work would be under a system of forced labor," but he also maintained that "the difficulties which have been faced . . . have been the natural disinclination of all the human race to labor, unless compelled to do so. This inclination is shared by freedmen in common with other races of men and so far as my observations extend, to no greater extent."[13] Another bureau official characterized white planters as "desirous to comply in good faith with the wishes and orders of the Government" and willing "to make the best of a system of labor in which . . . they thoroughly disbelieve." In the early weeks of 1866, the Freedmen's Bureau supervised bitter negotiations between landowners and freedmen. A variety of labor arrangements emerged from these negotiations, but none proved entirely satisfactory to all the parties involved.[14]

Planters generally preferred to hire freedmen on a straight cash basis for plantationwide work under the close supervision of the planter. Using these laborers in gangs allowed planters to return to large-scale commercial agriculture while making a modest accommodation to emancipation. Many planters, however, did not have enough liquid capital on hand to pay cash in 1866. Paper currecy had always been scarce in the up-country and much of what circulated there had been exchanged for worthless Confederate bills. To make matters worse, many up-country farmers were unable to pay old debts. Before and during the war, credit was extended on the basis of collateral in land and slaves, but emancipation and the short crop of 1865 left many debtors woefully short of both cash and assets. To circumvent this cash shortage, a system of paying wages in kind developed. Some labor contracts specified fixed payments-in-kind to be made at the end of the year. Landowners, however, were generally reluctant to contract for specific payments to laborers whose work habits they distrusted. As a result, over one-third of all up-country labor contracts made for 1866 specified the payment of some fraction of the crop as a wage to black laborers (see table 2.1).[15] The share-wage system provided laborers with a limited incentive to increase output, and allowed the landowner to share the risks of a poor crop with his laborers. The share-wage system differed markedly from share-tenancy. Under the share-wage system, the landlord retained control of the crop but paid his employees a share of the crop as a wage. The sharecropper, a wage hand, had no legal interest in the crop except as an agricultural laborer's lien for wages, and he worked under the supervision of the landowner. Under share-tenancy, a form of land tenure not uncommon among whites during the antebellum period, the tenant supervised his own crop, usually furnished his own animals and agricultural implements, but paid his landlord a share of the crop as rent.[16]

In 1866 in the lower Piedmont, where specialized plantation agriculture had been more prevalent before the Civil War, planters used cash and share wages to reestablish large-scale commercial agriculture. Lower Piedmont planters required wage laborers to work on a plantationwide basis and to perform certain noncrop tasks, such as fencing and ditching, essential to plantation upkeep. Wage-labor plantations were less common in the upper Piedmont, where involvement in the cotton economy had been traditionally rather limited. Upper Piedmont landowners agreed to more individual share-wage contracts, paying freedmen to work a tract of land about the size of a small family farm and requiring no plantationwide work. Although frustrated at their inability to achieve

Table 2.1
LABOR CONTRACTS IN THE SOUTH CAROLINA UP-COUNTRY, 1865-1868 (IN PERCENTAGES)

	CASH WAGES	FIXED KIND WAGES	SHARE WAGES		SHARE TENANCY	NUMBER OF CONTRACTS
			GROUP	*INDIVIDUAL*		
1865						
Newberry	0.0	4.0	96.0	0.0	0.0	(23)
Union	0.0	12.0	88.0	0.0	0.0	(25)
1866						
Anderson	32.0	12.0	30.0	26.0	0.0	(25)
Chester	50.0	16.3	33.3	0.0	0.0	(12)
Greenville	40.0	12.0	16.0	32.0	0.0	(25)
Newberry	48.0	12.0	32.0	4.0	4.0	(25)
Spartanburg	25.9	4.0	44.0	25.4	0.0	(27)
Union	40.0	26.4	40.0	4.0	0.0	(27)
1867						
Anderson	32.0	12.0	20.0	36.0	0.0	(25)
Chester	46.1	0.0	53.8	0.0	0.0	(26)
Union	68.0	8.0	28.0	0.0	0.0	(25)
1868						
Chester	24.1	6.8	34.5	34.5	0.0	(29)

Source: Sample of Labor Contracts, South Carolina Subordinate Field Offices, Records of the Bureau of Refugees, Freedmen and Abandoned Lands, RG 105, National Archives, Washington, D.C.

Note: This sample selected twenty-five labor contracts from each up-country district from which contracts were extant for each year from which contracts survived. In a few instances the total number of labor arrangements for a particular district exceeded twenty-five because more than one type of arrangement was specified on a single contract.

greater autonomy, freedmen seemed to prefer share wages to fixed wages, feeling that share wages established them as "partners" in the crop. Freedmen also preferred individual share-wage arrangements to gang labor and plantationwide work.[17]

Despite concessions to reality from both landowners and freedmen, the free-labor experiment won few converts during 1866. White landowners like Andrew Baxter Springs, a prominent Fort Mill planter, complained that freedmen would not work without the threat of corporal punishment to spur them to industry. Reports from the Freedmen's Bureau also testified to white eagerness to use force. "Just as soon as those who are disposed to treat freedmen cruelly learn that I do not fine them as did my predecessor," noted A. P. Caraker, bureau agent for the Union District, "they put on the lash more freely. I am of the opinion that if troops were withdrawn. . .the freedmen could not live here."[18] To complicate matters even further, some white landowners deliberately tried to cheat freedmen out of their shares of the crop, particularly as a summer drought, the most severe in South Carolina since the 1840s, began to take its toll on up-country crops. Planter R. N. Hemphill of Blackstock admitted that whites schemed to defraud freedmen in August of 1866. "A large number of farmers," Hemphill wrote, "put off to Chester with some frivolous complaint to the Provost Court and have their hands discharged. Consequently the country is inundated with idle darkies wandering about without home or employment."[19] Some planters claimed that freedmen worked only sporadically, often ignoring the crop at critical points of the growing season. In a report solicited by the Freedmen's Bureau, James Lowry, a farmer, testified to the problems of agricultural reconstruction in the Chester District. The acreage under cultivation in Chester was less than one-sixth of prewar levels, Lowry noted, while cotton production in 1866 was likely to be only about one-fourth of the 1860 output. Moreover, for the first time in decades, the Chester District would not be self-sufficient in foodstuffs. Lowry claimed that production was down because "the freedwomen have all abandoned the fields" and "nine freedmen will not do the work of six slaves."[20] In any case, the catastrophic drought turned the Freedmen's Bureau's chore of supervising crop divisions into a nightmare. Greenville bureau agent J. W. DeForest explained the problem of dividing the short crop:

It is usually impossible to render a decision satisfactory to both parties. . . . The share of the negro is eaten up by what has been advanced to him, and the share of the employer hardly replaces what he has advanced.[21]

DeForest's observation pinpointed one of the central problems facing the up-country in 1866 and 1867: the question of how to finance agricultural production. When the drought damaged the crop of 1866, many debt-ridden up-country landowners again found themselves unable to pay out. Appeals to the state legislature for debt relief largely went unanswered, and by the end of 1866 the up-country found itself in a financial straitjacket. Early in 1866 the Freedmen's Bureau and military officials had allowed landowners to receive advances on the security of the crop to be raised in that year, a de facto crop lien. In September the South Carolina legislature passed the state's first crop lien law. In a desperate effort to make credit available to South Carolina farmers, the new law gave anyone—merchant, landlord, or both—who furnished the necessary agricultural supplies for production a prior lien on the crop to the extent of the advances, provided that the lien agreement was in writing and properly recorded with the registrar of mesne conveyance.[22] The Freedmen's Bureau supported the lien law's efforts to loosen credit in the up-country but insisted that the laborer's wage should be paid before the supply lien was satisfied. The new lien law underscored the differences between sharecroppers and share-tenants. As wage laborers, sharecroppers could not encumber the crop with a lien because they did not control the crop. As a result, sharecroppers were forced to depend on landowners for supplies. As renters, share-tenants qualified as "owners of the crop" and were allowed to give liens, independent of the landlord, in order to obtain supplies. Freedmen quickly recognized that the new lien law gave tenants an important source of independence from landowners, and they renewed their agitation to rent rather than to work as laborers.[23] Of course, the lien law also produced new problems. James H. Rion, a Winnsboro lawyer, agreed that "without advances our farmers are ruined," yet he maintained that South Carolina "merchants and capitalists will not make advances without additional sureties." Rion wanted the military authorities to make reneging on a lien a misdemeanor punishable by imprisonment.[24] J. L. Neagle, a white Republican merchant from Rock Hill, also complained about the difficulty of enforcing the lien law. "Everyone seems disposed to keep what he has. . .and pay nothing," noted Neagle, "parties now in possession of large tracts of land and owning horses, mules, cattle, hogs, cotton, and large quantities of plantation supplies . . . refuse to divide with me."[25]

Regardless of short-term enforcement problems, the lien law certainly enhanced the importance of the supply merchant in up-country agriculture. From 1866 through 1874, the merchant's lien for advances, if recorded, was superior to all liens except the laborers' lien for wages. It is particularly significant that a merchant's lien for advances on a tenant's crop was superior to any rent contract between landlord and tenant. This preferred lien allowed merchants to deal directly with the multiplying tenant population, thus bypassing the landlord and superseding his claim for rent.[26] Nevertheless, with the labor situation unstable and agricultural output down dramatically, the up-country merchant plied a risky trade. Indeed, most men who entered the mercantile trade during the early years of Reconstruction soon fell by the wayside. For that small coterie of merchants who began or reopened businesses on solid financial footing, the Reconstruction was a profitable era. The career of the Chester mercantile firm of C. H. Smith and G. W. Melton was atypically successful. Both Smith and Melton had been quarter-masters in the Confederate army and had made some money by buying and selling cotton on their own accounts during the war. In 1866, Smith and Melton began a general mercantile business in the town of Chester and involved themselves heavily with liens and cotton buying. In 1868 alone they acquired over $25,000 worth of the most valuable farmland in Chester from indebted and distressed farmers. The performance of Smith and Melton in 1869 was even more incredible. In that year the firm traded several thousand bales of cotton, bought more than $100,000 of Chester real estate, and reportedly extended cash advances to Chester farmers in amounts totaling tens of thousands of dollars.[27] A less spec-tacular, but perhaps more typical, success story was that of the Abbeville firm of G. M. Miller and J. F. Robertson. Miller and Robertson had been a leading mercantile firm before the Civil War and were able to settle amicably with their northern creditors early in 1866. They quickly re-sumed business and became the largest supply merchants in Abbeville. Starting virtually from scratch in 1866, the firm was worth over $60,000 by the early 1870s.[28]

However infrequent such merchant success stories were, they still impressed beleaguered landowners. The year 1867 was not a good year for farmers. Gully-washing rains and accompanying freshets damaged crops throughout much of the up-country, and continued racial hostility compounded labor difficulties. Late in 1867, when blacks began to reg-ister to vote under the provisions of congressional Reconstruction, racial tensions in the up-country increased. "Trouble," J. W. DeForest ob-served, "may be anticipated from the unwillingness of many planters to have their employees join the Union League." The freedmen, on the other hand, buoyed by the prospect of political power, demanded more concessions from white landowners, who were themselves strapped by a third successive year of short crops. This combination of increased black recalcitrance and continued financial losses by white landowners made 1868 a pivotal year for property and labor in the up-country. In 1868, the proportion of individual sharecropping agreements, calling for freedmen to work small tracts of land, increased even in the most plan-tation-oriented districts. Moreover, for the first time, significant numbers of blacks were allowed to rent land. David Wyatt Aiken, one of the up-country's leading planters, recalled that "in 1868, hands could not be hired for any amount . . . and I had to yield, or lose my labor." R. N. Hemphill also observed that after 1867 freedmen became "rent crazy."[29]

Indeed, by 1868, the complex arrangements between agricultural labor and capital that would persist in the up-country until World War II were already settling into place. Attempts by planters to establish plantations worked by free laborers on the gang system had been abandoned for the most part. In place of plantations, a new system of commercial agriculture emerged in which most blacks worked either as individual sharecroppers, paid and supplied by the landowner and working under his supervision, or as share-tenants, paying a share of their crop as rent while they controlled their own work place and made their own arrangements for supplies. Of course, racial hostility and labor unrest lasted throughout Reconstruction and beyond. The Ku Klux Klan's reign of terror in the up-country in 1871 and the violence and intimidation of the Red Shirt Campaign in 1876 are only the two most spectacular examples. Even as late as 1882 respected South Carolina journalist James C. Hemphill observed that, "The great question which lies at the root of agricultural prosperity in South Carolina is that of labor."[30]

Everyone involved in the adjustment to free labor learned some bitter lessons from the experience. Northern free-labor enthusiasts learned first hand about the white South's "antipathy to the colored race and desire that the free labor system and its accomplishments of intelligence, thrift, and self-respect shall prove a failure."[31] Freedmen learned the harsh truth that was contained in the warning given to them by northern military captain Charles Soule in 1865:

You are free, but you must know that the only difference you can feel yet, between slavery and freedom, is that neither you nor your children can be bought or sold. You may have a harder time . . . than ever before; it will be the price you pay for your freedom.[32]

Planters generally continued to insist that the "edifice of republicanism" was "crumbling to decay," even as they occasionally showed signs of accepting free labor. One up-country newspaper admitted that "though by no means as effective as the old-fashioned 'nigger', it must be admitted that the freedman has done, as a general rule, better than was expected of him." More important, one South Carolinian revealed a growing knowledge of free-labor discipline when he asked: "Can not freedmen be organized and disciplined as well as slaves? Is not the dollar as potent as the lash? The belly as tender as the back?"[33]

The most important change wrought by the Civil War and the transition to free labor lay hidden beneath the furor over labor discipline. The shift to free labor and the use of crop liens to secure credit allowed a reconstituted merchant class to establish an important role for itself in the financing and marketing of up-country agricultural products. This merchant class became the heart of an indigenous bourgeoisie that would change the face of the up-country in the fifty years after Reconstruction.[34] As this dramatic transformation of the up-country economy proceeded, many propertyless up-country laborers, white as well as black, judged for themselves the truthfulness of James Henry Hammond's famous prewar assertion that the man "who has to put out his labor in the market, and take the best he can get for it" is essentially a slave.[35]

Notes

1. Eric Foner, *Free Soil, Free Labor, Free Men: The Ideology of the Republican Party before the Civil War* (London and New York: Oxford University Press, 1970), especially pp. 11-72, and "The Causes of the American Civil War: Recent Interpretations and New Directions," *Civil War History* 20 (September 1974): 197-214; Michael Holt, *The Political Crisis of the 1850s* (New York: John Wiley and Sons, 1978), pp. 219-59.

2. Foner, "The Causes of the American Civil War," pp. 213-214; An outstanding example of the southern critique of free labor is James Henry Hammond, "Speech on the Admission of Kansas, Under the Lecompton Constitution," in *Selections from the Letters and Speeches of the Hon. James H. Hammond*, with an introduction by Clyde N. Wilson (Columbia, S. C.: Southern Studies Program, 1978), pp. 301-22.

3. William Henry Trescot, *The Position and Course of the South* (Charleston: Walker and James, 1850), p. 10.

4. Iveson Brookes, *A Defense of the South Against Reproaches and Incroachments of the North* (Hamburg, S. C., 1850), pp. 45-47.

5. Trescot, *Position and Course*, pp. 10-11; Brookes, *A Defense*, pp. 46-47; Drew Gilpin Faust, *A Sacred Circle: The Dilemma of the Intellectual in the Old South, 1840-1860* (Baltimore: The Johns Hopkins University Press, 1977), pp. 87-111; Robert M. Weir, "The South Carolinian As Extremist," *South Atlantic Quarterly*, (Winter 1975): 86-103. For a survey, see David Brion Davis, "Slavery and the Idea of Progress," *The Bulletin of the Center for the Study of Southern Culture and Religion* 3 (June 1979): 1-9; and Howard Temperly, "Capitalism, Slavery, and Ideology," *Past and Present* 75 (May 1977): 94-118.

6. Trescot, *The Position and Course*, pp. 9-10.

7. Arthur Simkins, *Address before the State Agricultural Society of South Carolina* (Edgefield: The Advertiser Office, 1855), pp. 1-2.

8. Excellent discussions of the meaning of independence in southern thought can be found in J. Mills Thornton III, *Politics and Power in a Slave Society: Alabama, 1800-1860* (Baton Rouge: Louisiana State University Press, 1978), 54-58; and Steven Howard Hahn, "The Roots of Southern Populism: Yeoman Farmers and the Transformation of Georgia's Upper Piedmont, 1850-1890" (Ph.D. diss., Yale University, 1979), especially pp. 119-87; C. B. MacPherson, *The Political Theory of Possessive Individualism: Hobbes to Locke* (London and New York: Oxford University Press, 1962), pp. 137-59.

9. James Henry Hammond, "Anniversary Oration of the State Agricultural Society of South Carolina. . .25th November, 1841," in *Proceedings of the Agricultural Convention of the State Agricultural Society of South Carolina from 1831 to*

1845 (Columbia: Summer and Caroll, 1846), p. 183; Kenneth Vickery, *"Herrenvolk* Democracy and Egalitarianism in South Africa and the United States South," *Comparative Studies in Society and History* 16 (January 1974): 309-28.

10. Two fine monographs on South Carolina during Reconstruction have blazed a trail for all who follow. See Francis Butler Simkins and Robert H. Woody, *South Carolina During Reconstruction* (Chapel Hill: University of North Carolina Press, 1932) and Joel Williamson, *After Slavery: The Negro in South Carolina During Reconstruction, 1861-1877* (Chapel Hill: University of North Carolina Press, 1965). Two excellent studies of up-country counties that deal with many of the issues discussed herein with greater specificity are Lewis J. Bellardo, "A Social and Economic History of Fairfield County, South Carolina, 1865-1871" (Ph.D. diss., University of Kentucky, 1979), and Orville Vernon Burton, "Ungrateful Serv-ants? Edgefield's Black Reconstruction: Part I of the Total History of Edgefield County, S.C." (Ph.D. diss., Princeton University, 1976). On the particular issue of labor control, see Lewis C. Chartock, "A History and Analysis of Labor Contracts Administered by the Bureau of Refugees, Freedmen, and Abandoned Lands in Edgefield, Abbeville, and Anderson Counties in South Carolina, 1865-1868" (Ph.D. diss., Bryn Mawr College, 1974), *passim.*

11. Circular letter No. 1 of O. O. Howard, 16 May 1865, Records of the Bureau of Refugees, Freedmen and Abandoned Lands (hereinafter BRFAL) Microcopy 742, Roll 1, National Archives, Washington, D. C.

12. Labor contracts, Union District, 1865, BRFAL, Record Group 105, Series 3358; Yorkville *Enquirer,* 22 December 1865.

13. Rufus Saxton to O. O. Howard, 20 November 1865, Registers and Letters Received, BRFAL, Microcopy 752, Roll 24.

14. Much of the discussion of labor arrangements in this essay is based on a sample drawn from over 13,000 labor contracts for South Carolina found in the Records of the BRFAL. Patterned after the path-breaking contract analysis found in Chartock, "Analysis of Labor Contracts," this sample attempts to achieve wide geographic coverage, using twenty-five contracts per year from each district for which they are available. For a complete explanation of Chartock's procedure, see Chartock, "Analysis of Labor Contracts," pp. 116-21. Further information about differences between this sample and that of Chartock is available from the author. Hereinafter this sample will simply be cited as Sample of Labor Contracts, South Carolina Subordinate Field Offices, BRFAL, Record Group 105; Charles C. Soule to General O. O. Howard, The Papers of the Commissioner of BRFAL, BRFAL, Microcopy 752, Roll 17.

15. Sample of Labor Contracts, South Carolina Subordinate Field Offices, BRFAL, Record Group 105.

16. Roger L. Ransom and Richard Sutch, *One Kind of Freedom: The Economic Consequences of Emancipation* (Cambridge: Cambridge University Press, 1977), pp. 56-105; Harold Woodman, "Post-Civil War Agriculture and the Law," *Agricultural History* 53 (January 1979): 319-37; Gavin Wright, *The Political Economy of the Cotton South: Households, Markets and Wealth in the Nineteenth Century* (New York: W. W. Norton and Co., 1978), pp. 158-84; Oscar Zeichner, "The Legal Status of the Agricultural Laborer in the South," *Political Science Quarterly* 55 (September 1940): 412-28.

17. The differences between upper and lower Piedmont were quite important.

Table 2.2
DISTRIBUTION OF BLACK POPULATION—THE UP-COUNTRY, 1850-1880 (IN PERCENTAGES)

	1850	1860	1870	1880
LOWER PIEDMONT				
Abbeville	52.7	64.6	64.9	67.7
Chester	55.6	60.8	66.5	68.3
Edgefield	58.6	60.7	59.8	65.0
Fairfield	66.9	71.1	70.9	75.2
Laurens	51.4	55.8	56.0	60.0
Newberry	64.0	58.1	64.1	68.9
Union	53.0	55.8	54.7	56.2
UPPER PIEDMONT				
Anderson	35.4	37.5	39.8	44.2
Greenville	33.6	33.1	32.0	38.7
Lancaster	46.6	48.6	49.0	52.9
Pickens	22.4	21.9	24.7	25.8
Spartanburg	30.6	31.1	32.6	34.7
York	41.8	47.3	51.9	54.1

Source: Julian J. Petty, *The Growth and Distribution of Population in South Carolina* (Columbia, S.C., 1943), Appendix F.

The lower Piedmont was a belt of relatively flat districts that included Edgefield, Abbeville, Newberry, Fairfield, Laurens and Union, lying just above the fall-line. These districts had black majorities by 1850 and were highly specialized in cotton production. See tables 2.2 and 2.3. Landowners in the lower Piedmont, where plantations had been more numerous before the war (see tables 2.4 and 2.5), tried to revive the gang-labor system during Reconstruction. The upper Piedmont, a rim of districts lying in the rolling red clay hills along South Carolina's border with North Carolina and Georgia, was over 65 percent white and considerably less specialized in cotton than the lower Piedmont. Gang labor and large plantations never had been common in the upper Piedmont, so landowners found the transition to individual sharecropping and share-tenancy a bit easier to make. To put this another way, where farm units tended to be smaller to begin with, the decentralization process was not as difficult as it was in regions previously dominated by plantations.

18. A. B. Springs to James L. Orr, December 1865, Governor Orr Papers, South Carolina Department of Archives and History, Columbia, S.C.; A. P. Caraher to Colonel H. W. Smith, 29 June 1866, Unionville, Register of Letters Received, BRFAL, Record Group 105, Series 3361.

Table 2.3
COTTON PRODUCTION AND SPECIALIZATION IN 1850

	BALES OF COTTON	BUSHELS OF CORN	COTTON-CORN RATIO
LOWER PIEDMONT			
Abbeville	27,192	1,054,233	10.3
Chester	17,810	573,070	12.4
Edgefield	25,880	1,155,489	9.0
Fairfield	18,122	529,461	13.6
Laurens	15,842	895,291	7.1
Newberry	19,894	664,058	12.0
Union	14,156	655,078	8.6
UPPER PIEDMONT			
Anderson	6,670	820,549	3.3
Greenville	2,452	637,784	1.5
Lancaster	8,661	352,218	9.8
Pickens	1,357	634,011	0.9
Spartanburg	6,671	873,654	3.1
York	9,986	690,447	5.8
TOTALS			
Lower Piedmont	138,896	5,526,680	10.1
Upper Piedmont	35,797	4,008,663	3.6
Up-Country	174,693	9,535,343	7.3
South Carolina	300,901	16,264,919	7.4

Source: United States Bureau of the Census, *Seventh Census of the United States, 1850* (Washington, D.C., 1853), pp. 334-51.

Note: The cotton-corn ratio was calculated by dividing the number of pounds of cotton (400 lb. per bale) by bushels of corn.

19. Robert W. Hemphill to W. R. Hemphill, 11 August 1866, Hemphill Family Papers, Manuscript Division, Perkins Library, Duke University, Durham, N.C.

20. James G. Lowry to A. H. Hart, 30 April 1866, Chester District, BRFAL, Record Group 105, Series 3147.

21. J. W. DeForest to Colonel H. W. Smith, 31 October 1866, Greenville District, Letters Sent, BRFAL. Record Group 105, Series 3227.

22. South Carolina Statutes at Large, vol. 13. no. 4786, p. 366; *Cureton* v. *Gilmore*, 2 South Carolina 46 (1871); *Hair* v. *Blease*, 6 South Carolina 63 (1876).

23. *Hair* v. *Blease*, 6 South Carolina 63 (1876); Harris Journal, December 31,

Table 2.4
DISTRIBUTION OF FARM UNITS BY IMPROVED ACREAGE, 1860
(IN PERCENTAGES)

	0-50 ACRES	51-100 ACRES	101-500 ACRES	Over 500 ACRES
LOWER PIEDMONT				
Abbeville	14.6	23.3	53.8	8.3
Chester	14.5	19.5	53.9	12.1
Edgefield	22.6	22.3	44.9	10.2
Fairfield	4.3	12.5	62.1	21.1
Laurens	7.5	19.1	62.1	11.3
Newberry	22.8	22.4	50.6	4.2
Union	27.6	25.3	41.6	5.5
UPPER PIEDMONT				
Anderson	32.5	32.8	33.4	1.3
Greenville	33.2	39.2	26.1	1.5
Lancaster	40.7	27.9	27.8	3.6
Pickens	35.5	33.1	30.1	1.3
Spartanburg	37.5	28.7	32.9	0.9
York	19.5	23.9	53.9	2.7

Source: Manuscript Census of 1860, South Carolina, Schedules I, II, and IV. Data compiled by the Inter-University Consortium For Political Research, Ann Arbor, Michigan, available on computer disc at University of South Carolina, Columbia, S.C.

1866, David Harris Farm Journals, Southern Historical Collection, Wilson Library, University of North Carolina at Chapel Hill, Chapel Hill, N.C.

24. James H. Rion to General Canby, 31 December 1867, Letters Received, Department of South Carolina and the South, 2nd Military District, 1862-1883, Records of the United States Army Continental Commands (hereinafter USACC), Record Group 393, Series 4116, National Archives, Washington, D.C.

25. John L. Neagle to Colonel A. J. Willard, 26 October 1867, Letters Received, Records of USACC, Record Group 393, Series 4116.

26. *Visankan* v. *Bradley*, 4 South Carolina (1873) 288. For a broader perspective on this issue see Woodman, "Post-Civil War Southern Agriculture and the Law," pp. 324-33.

27. R. G. Dun and Company Collection, South Carolina, vol. 9, p. 179J, Baker Library, Harvard University Graduate School of Business Administration, Cambridge, Mass.

28. Ibid., vol. 2, p. 20.

29. J. W. DeForest to Edward L. Deane, 31 July 1867, Greenville, Letters Sent,

Table 2.5
RATIO OF PLANTERS TO TOTAL FARMS IN 1860

LOWER PIEDMONT

Abbeville	.251
Chester	.173
Edgefield	.227
Fairfield	.343
Laurens	.143
Newberry	.250
Union	.226

UPPER PIEDMONT

Anderson	.059
Greenville	.070
Lancaster	.092
Pickens	.028
Spartanburg	.063
York	.092

Source: Julian J. Petty, *The Growth and Distribution of Population in South Carolina* (Columbia, S.C., 1943), appendix F.

BRFAL, Record Group 105, Series 3227; David Wyatt Aiken, "Does Farming Pay in the South," *Rural Carolinian* 12 (March 1871): 323-24; R. N. Hemphill to W. R. Hemphill, 15 November 1869, Hemphill Family Papers.

30. James C. Hemphill, *Climate, Soil, and Agricultural Capabilities of South Carolina and Georgia* (Washington: Government Printing Office, 1882), p. 31; Sample of Labor Contracts, South Carolina Subordinate Field Offices, BRFAL, Record Group 105. On continued labor unrest and racial violence see J. C. A. Stagg, "The Problem of Klan Violence in the South Carolina Up-country, 1868-1871," *Journal of American Studies* 8 (December 1974): 303-18, and Lacy Ford, "One Southern Profile: Modernization and the Development of White Terror in York County, South Carolina, 1856-1876" (M.A. thesis, University of South Carolina, 1976), pp. 71-102. Ralph Schlomowitz, "The Origins of Southern Sharecropping," *Agricultural History* 53 (July 1979): 557-75, suggests that the use of labor "squads" was important in the transition from the gang system to individual sharecropping. In the sample used for this paper, only one labor contract specifying the use of squads was found. Squads may have been used more frequently in other parts of the state, but there is little evidence indicating use of squads in the up-country.

31. Annual BRFAL Report from South Carolina, quoted in Chartock, "Analysis of Labor Contracts," pp. 45-46.

32. Speech of Charles C. Soule to Freedmen of Orangeburg District included

in Soule to General O. O. Howard, The Papers of the Commissioners of the BRFAL, BRFAL, Microcopy 752, Roll 17.

33. Yorkville *Enquirer*, 3 January 1867; Anderson *Intelligencer*, 3 June 1868; "The Question of Labor in the South," *Rural Carolinian* 2 (July 1871): 572-74.

34. An excellent study of the role of the new middle class in industrial development is David L Carlton, *Mill and Town: The Cotton Mill Workers and the Middle Class in South Carolina, 1880-1920* (Baton Rouge: Louisiana State University Press, 1983).

35. Hammond, "Speech on Kansas," p. 319.

3

"NO MORE MUD WORK": THE STRUGGLE FOR THE CONTROL OF LABOR AND PRODUCTION IN LOW COUNTRY SOUTH CAROLINA, 1863-1880

John Scott Strickland

When Port Royal fell to Union forces in late 1861, many rice and cotton planters south of Charleston abandoned their homes and fled to safer regions. They took with them those of their slaves they could coerce, leaving their plantations to the blacks who remained behind and seized their chance for freedom. As the war dragged on, some of the low country whites north of Charleston followed their neighbors to safety in the upper parts of South Carolina. Thus, as federal soldiers gradually occupied the coastal areas of the state in early 1865, they found numerous rice and sea island cotton plantations under the control of those African-Americans who had toiled for generations to make the low country plutocracy one of the richest ruling classes in the world.[1] These historical circumstances fused with the traditionally unique rice and long-staple cotton labor system and the aftermath of Sherman's Field Order Number 15 to assure that the social and economic transition from slavery to freedom would become a particularly dramatic struggle between blacks and whites for control of the coastal regions.

Both current and past scholarship on the first years of emancipation have been concerned exclusively with the short-staple cotton areas of the southern uplands. Historians working from such a vantage point have offered generalizations about the entirety of the revolution in labor relations that was wrought by the abolition of slavery. They, therefore, have tended to homogenize the emancipation experience and have neglected the great diversity found in the contest between black and white to determine what the nature of freedom would be in the era of Reconstruction.[2] Specific attention to the low country of South Carolina reveals the inadequacies of broad explanations that are based on short-staple cotton agriculture. The struggle of the freed people in the coastal areas to shape their social and economic futures was dramatically different from that of the freed people elsewhere in the state and the South. Only the combined efforts of northern and southern whites and decisive blows struck by the weather prevented a thorough transformation of power in the low country. Although the struggle fell somewhat short of its initial revolutionary potential, the story of Reconstruction in the low country should note the remarkably unique culture and social heritage of coastal South Carolina blacks.

Despite substantial differences on almost every important issue, whites on both sides of the war wanted to create some order out of the chaos that prevailed in low country South Carolina during the spring and summer of 1865. To avert disaster and reap even a small harvest northerners and southerners alike knew they had to act quickly and they knew the only sure way to do this was to compel blacks to return to work on the plantations.[3] Toward this end, the infant Freedmen's Bureau formed commissions in each of its districts to assess the situation and to create a system of work contracts that would foster regular and peaceful change to a free agricultural labor system.

The intent of these commissions, indeed the entire mission of the bureau during its tenure in South Carolina, was best stated by Captain Charles Soule of the 55th Massachusetts Volunteers early in the summer of 1865. Soule reported that "affairs were found to be in a very unsettled state." The blacks were, he continued, "excited by the prospect of freedom" and there was "every prospect that the crops would be neglected." Soule dispatched his subordinates throughout the countryside to explain the new relationship between black and white, and he assumed as his personal mission the task of ensuring that freedom would not tip the balance of power too far in favor of the freed people. The course of black liberation, he felt, should be shaped and directed by the hands of capital, not by the desires and expectations of labor. Much to his dismay, Soule found blacks believing that "besides receiving their food, clothes, the free rent of houses and gardens, and the privilege of keeping their hogs and poultry, they are to take for themselves all day Saturday and Sunday, and to receive half the crop." He felt that such expectations rendered even the best freed people "idle, insolent, vagrant, and thievish." He argued that the main objective of the bureau should be to prevent "so low, uneducated and inefficient a class of labor" from receiving "more pay than northern farm laborers," for if this were to happen, "the relation between capital and labor would be disturbed, and an undue value placed on the latter, to the prejudice and disadvantage, in the end, of the laborers themselves."

Throughout the spring of 1865, Soule toured the plantations of the low country to admonish the freed people to work hard and to accept the authority of the planters. The whites had a right to this authority, he told them, because they were rich. "Some people," Soule contended, "must be rich to pay the others, and they have the right to do no work except to look after their property." Everyone had a place, he said, and "he must stick to it." Plantation laborers should remember that all their "working time belongs to the man who hires you," and they therefore should remain on the plantations. Reunions of widely dispersed families could wait until the end of the contract year. Only by following these admonitions, Soule proclaimed, could order prevail and disaster be averted.[4]

One of the principal impediments to the early realization of Soule's goals appeared as soon as the countryside was safe for travel. The freed people, who had spent their lives confined to the boundaries of plantations except when they could steal away to visit friends or family or on those rare occasions when they gained permission to move about, immediately asserted their right to unrestrained mobility. The fundamental structure of low country plantation agriculture, however, required a stable labor force of predictable size to perform the daily tasks of rice and cotton cultivation. If only a portion of the working hands could be counted on at any given time, the planter could not expect a profitable crop. For this reason, those blacks who seized their right to go where they pleased when they pleased generated considerable anxiety. The superintendents of contrabands on Port Royal during the war had realized the disruptive effects of mobility. As A. S. Hitchcock wrote from Beaufort in August 1864, "Had I the control of the negroes, the first thing I would endeavor to do, and the thing I think of most importance to be done is to keep all the people possible on the farms or plantations at *honest steady* labor. Young women particularly flock back and forth by scores to Hilton Head, to Beaufort, to the country simply to while away their time, or constantly to seek some new excitement." He found the freed people most comfortable with employment that provided minimum support, which in turn allowed them time to go where they wished. "This getting a precarious livelihood by a little at this and a little at that," Hitchcock bemoaned, "is the very curse of the freedpeople."[5]

When emancipation came to blacks elsewhere in the low country, they grasped their chance for mobility. In some cases, all the hands on a plantation would choose the same moment to travel.[6] As they began to realize the dimensions of freedom in the summer of 1865, blacks moving from place to place stimulated others to follow their example.[7] When the first free harvest neared completion, low country blacks seized the opportunity for mobility in ever greater numbers. The danger of losing crops became apparent and bureau officials came to the aid of planters by arresting the freed people who were "strolling about the country doing nothing."[8] The police action was only partially effective. By exercising their options to travel, blacks continued to revolt against northern and southern white efforts to reimpose the vestiges of slavery.

However significant geographical mobility was for the freed people's control over their labor, it was not a part of the struggle for autonomy that was unique to the South Carolina low country. Blacks throughout the South enjoyed the new opportunities to move about that came with emancipation.[9] There were, however, things singular to the history of coastal African-Americans that allowed them to counter the efforts of whites to impose a new labor system. One hundred and fifty years of black majority, a tradition of large, stable plantation communities, the prevalence of intergenerational continuity in slave families, the long-established practice of absentee proprietorship, and wartime experience were significant factors in black resistance during the first years of Reconstruction. They combined to create a social identity that countervailed the concerted white effort to dictate the nature of freedom. Nevertheless, none of these was as important in giving blacks a heritage supportive of their postemancipation contest as the mode of work organization that characterized rice and sea island cotton cultivation.

In the antebellum South, there were two ways of organizing slave labor: the gang system and the task system. The gang system, used in the cultivation of short-staple cotton and thus characteristic of the upland regions, demanded that slaves labor as a unit, working side by side in the crop rows, simultaneously executing the same job. Often an overseer or a driver set the pace, and all hands worked to that pace for the entire day with only mealtimes as respites. Labor was regimented, directed, and closed to essentially all personal initiative. In contrast, the task system allowed significant individual control of the work pace. Task labor had evolved in the Carolina low country during the eighteenth century as the natural outgrowth of the development of rice culture in which the fields were marked off in regular squares by the ditches and trunks essential for irrigation. These squares, usually one-fifth to one-quarter of an acre in size, provided the units for measuring labor time. When long-staple cotton became an important crop in the same parts of South Carolina during the early nineteenth century, whites yielded to the social and cultural precedents of the rice region and applied task labor to its cultivation. By the end of the century's second decade the system had become so routinized that the size of rice and cotton tasks were standardized throughout the low country.

Under the task system, each worker had an assignment that was keyed to a type of work and to his or her personal ability. Full hands were the most stalwart workers on the plantation, and their abilities set the limits of the maximum accomplishable. Other slaves, unable to achieve the productivity of full hands, received ratings of three-quarters, one-half, or one-quarter depending upon their physical strengths. The system allowed a laborer to finish a day's assignment at a chosen rate. A rice or cotton worker could concentrate on the day's duties and be out of the fields by noon; if, however, he or she desired a less demanding pace, or if the collective experience of work was a primary objective at a given time, the laborer could stretch the task out over the entire day.

In the event that they finished before sundown, hands sometimes were given extra duties beyond their basic tasks and compensated for them with cash or goods. The experience of working tasks thus helped to fashion a perspective that prized the virtues of independence, autonomy, self-determination, and personal achievement. The low country work ethic entailed the expectations that labor would be both individually controlled and predictable. Consequently, when northern and southern whites attempted to fashion a free-labor system after their own ideals, they encountered a work force long accustomed to independent labor and control over the pace of production.[10]

Bureau officials quickly realized the significance of the task system in traditional patterns of labor. While negotiating contracts in 1865, they saw the futility of the planters' efforts to exclude task organization in order to gain better control of their free work force. A Georgetown agent wrote that the blacks on rice plantations "have been accustomed to working by task which has always given them leisure to cultivate land for themselves, tend their stock, and amuse themselves, and therefore, very correctly, I think, that with such a change in the march of labor all their privileges will go and their condition will be less to their taste than it was when they were slaves."[11] For this reason, despite planter efforts to the contrary, the majority of plantation work agreements in the low country recognized the tradition and included tasks in their stipulation of laborer responsibilities.[12]

By demanding deference to traditional ways, blacks forced both planters and bureau officials to relinquish considerable control over the rate of production in the new labor system. As one agent complained, "the Freedpeople generally do not perform more than ten compasses daily getting through their tasks at or before noon and nothing can induce them to perform more." In this manner, blacks refused to turn a large profit for their employers and worked just enough to provide the necessities of life. As the agent ruefully noted, "the crop raised will be small, probably just sufficient to subsist them for the year."[13]

Each successive year brought no diminution in the power of the task system to control the rate of production. Another bureau official bitterly complained in 1867 that although a season's responsibility for a full task worker was generally set at eight acres, "a smart hand can cultivate nearly twice that amount."[14] One of South Carolina's major rice planters lamented the power he had lost in acquiescing to the task system after emancipation. Things had gotten so out of hand that he could command only half the work he had extracted on his plantations under slavery.[15] Two contracts later, he was still frustrated by his dilemma. For the coming year he resolved to try to do something to enhance his control over task labor by hiring a white overseer to lay out the squares and keep an accurate time book of his hands' performance. Pay in shares of the crop, he asserted, would for once strictly correspond to the execution of tasks.[16] Despite such efforts to exert control over the task system, it remained a primary factor in black labor patterns and thus black life throughout the nineteenth century.

In the early fall of 1865, low country planters and bureau agents confronted the type of plantation work in which the task system and its tradition of independence created major difficulties for the smooth transition to a free-labor economy. In this and each successive autumn and winter, blacks mounted an aggressive resistance to postharvest and preplanting tasks. Rice culture particularly required some of its most unpleasant jobs after the old crop had been milled and shipped to market and before another round of planting began in mid-March. Ditches and canals had to be cleaned of debris, their banks mended, and their bottoms dredged of accumulated mud. Trunks and gates needed repair. Often, new squares had to be constructed by digging ditches and canals. All of this demanded work in both mud and water during the coldest and dreariest parts of the year. Although less distasteful, the preparatory work of sea island cotton was also tedious and difficult.[17] There were numerous reports from Georgetown that the contract hands for 1865 refused to do what they felt contributed only to the 1866 crop. Although their contracts stipulated such tasks, one agent reported that blacks universally maintained "they never intended to contract for anything beyond the harvesting and division of the growing crops." The agent believed that workers saw the possibility of being forced into labor arrangements that discarded the task system once they had invested in a future crop by preparing the fields.[18] Planters and agents joined in arguing that failure to perform work in the rice fields allowed water to stagnate and created a public health hazard from which both whites and blacks would suffer. Such pleas, however, did not induce hands to return to the cold, wet fields.[19]

As the end of the next season approached, low country blacks again refused to perform work not directly related to the crop. Reports came from Mount Pleasant that whites were anxious about the prospects for fall tasks as early as August. "Most of the crops are now 'laid by'," the agent stated, "and the freedmen suppose they are not obliged to make fences, repair roads, etc."[20] Confronted with such worker solidarity, one planter tried the ploy of telling hands that "by doing in the Fall, the work mentioned, they who contracted another year, would be far better off than they were this year."[21] The freed people would have no part of these tactics, however; they joined workers from other plantations in hiring their time for cash to different landowners while they waited for the crops to mature.[22] The solution to this particular problem came only when the planters agreed to pay additional wages for tasks unrelated to the crops.[23]

Contention over work in the rice fields was not dispelled so easily. In February of 1867, Arnoldus Vanderhost received reports from his overseer that the hands on Chickessee "positively refused" to perform work in the ditches.[24] Although Vanderhorst eventually struck a deal with his employees, the resolution was only temporary. By the next autumn, hands up and down the coast were again refusing to enter the cold rice fields. Not only did they reject the work, they even resisted combined planter and bureau efforts to force them off the plantations.[25]

The struggle to exact maintenance tasks reached one of its more dramatic moments on the long beleaguered Keithfield estate of Confederate General James Trapier. When Francis S. Parker, the executor of the Santee River property, found hands reluctant to work in the ditches, he unwisely turned to force and intimidation to accomplish his ends. Parker should have relented, as he had nearly lost his life in another dispute with Keithfield laborers a year and a half earlier, when he had tried to impose a particular black overseer on the estate only to find his choice rejected by the laboring community. He pressed his case further only to be driven from the plantation, along with a supporting unit of U.S. troops, by blacks brandishing rocks, sticks, and farm implements. Now in the late fall of 1867, he again failed to assert his will successfully. During a visit to the plantation, Parker met a redoubtable opponent in the person of Israel Lance, one of the leaders of the hands, who stepped forward to take charge. Lance proclaimed that "no more mud work was to be done on that plantation after today—that no charge [of] forfeit could be enforced against the gang of laborers." Parker again turned to Union assistance, this time with greater success: only the arrest and incarceration of Lance cooled things at Keithfield. It is not known whether or not Parker accepted the black leader for another year's work, as the bureau agent recommended.[26] Even if he did, and even if Israel Lance labored peacefully at distasteful "mud work" thereafter, the resistance to tasks not directly related to the crops continued to be a factor in low country life during Reconstruction and after.[27] In fact, the black struggle in this realm directly contributed to the demise of the plantation system in the low country. As one planter remembered, by the late 1870s it had become the practice to transport Irish and Italian men from New York in December when the cold weather had thrown them out of work. They cleaned the ditches and canals in the freed people's stead.[28]

The tradition of independent labor in the coastal regions of South Carolina challenged more than just the acceptability of postharvest tasks. Indeed, the very control of plantations frequently was a matter of ardent contention between blacks and whites. James F. Ferguson, like many other planters, found just how vigorous the struggle could be when he sought to make contracts with the hands occupying his property on the Cooper River in January 1866. When he asked if they would be willing to begin working under some sanctioned agreement, the freed people shouted back that "they would not work for any rebel son of a bitch." He responded by saying they would have to leave, "whereupon two or three addressed the crowd saying 'the Yankees had placed them there and there they would stay if they had to fight for it.' "[29] Whole areas of the low country became so suffused with the spirit of resistance that no plantation group signed a contract. As one sympathetic bureau agent said, "It is really wonderful how unanimous they are, communicating like magic, and now holding out, knowing the importance of every day in regard to the welfare of the next crop, thinking that the planters will be obliged to come to their terms."[30]

As each new calendar year approached, laborers would gather in various locales throughout the coastal region to search for some means of standardizing terms for the coming year. In some cases, as on James Island in early 1867, the sense of these meetings was so strong that the participants would pledge violence to anyone who contracted on a basis less favorable than their collective agreement.[31] Other occasions found committees from these gatherings going to plantations where bargains already had been made to encourage the freed people to renege.[32] Blacks in the Kingstree area gathered and marched 200 strong under a red flag in an effort to make their opinions felt by the laboring community.[33]

Even in the places where labor resistance was not coordinated between plantations, the refusal to contract constituted a major threat to sustained white efforts to control agricultural labor. The initial bargains of 1865 were hastily reached measures that were directed at forestalling disaster by saving the small crop the freed people had already planted. In many cases, especially in the Port Royal and Santee River areas, native whites had failed to return to the low country until late 1865 or early 1866. Contracts for 1865, therefore, were generous in their terms for the workers. Recalcitrance among bureau agents and planters was not an issue. But as the first year of freedom neared its end, blacks demonstrated their resolve to control their own labor. As one agent noted, there had never been any conception of the worth of rice and cotton tasks under slavery, and the terms for the present crop were merely a negotiated stopgap. Planters and hands held widely disparate notions of the value of tasks, and consequently there was "little progress . . . towards contracts for the coming year."[34] Reports from throughout the low country confirmed the general indisposition to contract.[35] The end of March 1866 found the situation little changed from the South Carolina side of the Savannah River to north of Georgetown.[36] Some planters were told that the hands occupying their estates refused "to contract or work for any white man."[37] Others, like Williams Middleton, were warned that they "had better not come on the plantation" to attempt negotiation.[38] Those who finally reached agreements found the crop season so far advanced that they gave far more liberal terms to the freed people than they had intended. As the Georgetown bureau official recounted, "Planters who for a long time insisted on giving a third have yielded and close their contracts for one half."[39] Many whites, however, found that they could reach no agreement at all; the freed people in numerous instances were content to squat on plots in the woods and pine barrens, planting a few acres of provision crops and living in a basically subsistence economy.[40] Blacks working independently on expropriated plots of land continued to plague planters and agents throughout Reconstruction largely because the coastal areas provided rich opportunities through hunting and fishing to supplement agricultural products.[41]

During 1867 and 1868 the Freedmen's Bureau also encountered resistance in making contracts with the freed people.[42] Neither year, however, found opposition as intense as in 1866. One reason for the more obstinate refusal to contract in 1866 arose from the almost universal anticipation among coastal blacks that they would receive title to land. The old saw of "forty acres and a mule" that has come down through history trivializes the real, indeed, the millennial, expectation that conquering Yankees would turn the world upside down by making every freedman a freeholder. The role of landownership in the settlement of labor is far too complex to address fully here, but it should be said that in 1866 low country African-Americans ardently believed that land would be theirs and therefore refused to contract in great numbers.[43]

Throughout the tenure of the bureau in South Carolina, agents found that both the promise of land and the proper belief among the freed people that they should have the right to control their own labor had transcended the singular matter of negotiating contracts. From 1865 through 1868, single plantations and whole areas of the low country were consumed by undeclared war between blacks and whites. One might argue with little exaggeration that some of the prolonged incidents in various locales were on the brink of tipping the balance of power into the hands of the black majority. Along the Santee River in 1865 and 1866, whites were so slow in returning to their homes that the freed people established virtual control of numerous plantations. When the former masters tried to reassert their power, they met violent resistance. The troubles of Francis Parker were just one example of the difficulties that faced Santee area whites.[44]

At the southern extreme of the South Carolina low country, Langdon Cheves's Savannah Back River plantation, Delta, was the scene of a violent struggle between blacks and whites throughout Reconstruction. In 1865 and 1866, the hands seized control of Delta and refused to work on any terms that involved direction by whites. They broke the plantation into plots that were farmed as family units. When the Cheveses regained ownership, blacks demanded and received the right to farm

Delta as renters. A year later, in 1867, efforts to extend white control met violent resistance. Gun battles erupted leaving both blacks and whites, including bureau agent O. T. Lemon, wounded.[45]

In between the two perimeters of the low country, other areas periodically erupted into open rebellion. Harriet Beecher Stowe's younger brother, Colonel James C. Beecher, discovered the limits of the humanitarian spirit that had led him to serve with the U.S. Colored Infantry sorely tested by blacks in the Combahee River area. Their refusal to conform to his notions of proper free-labor behavior drove Beecher to totalitarian acts of coercion and violence.[46] On the nearby islands, laborers resisted white dominance with incredible strength. Former Governor William Aiken encountered an armed force that opposed his attempt to regain control of the island plantation Jehossee. African-Americans on Edisto, Johns, Wadmalaw, and James islands struggled to maintain their independence. On numerous occasions, their sentries prevented northern and southern whites from landing on the islands to negotiate labor terms. Along the Cooper and Ashley rivers and north to Georgetown, troops were necessary to subdue rebellious plantation communities.[47]

However vigorously blacks asserted their rights, they did not wholly determine the social and economic contours of low country South Carolina after 1865. The shape of things emerged dialectically from the struggle for the balance of power between former slaves and one-time masters during the final third of the nineteenth century. Consequently, although low country African-Americans mounted an intense struggle to define the nature of their freedom, they did not entirely realize their goals. Unlike the up-country where native whites used unrestrained violence to thwart the drive for independence, coastal planters struck alliances with the military and Freedmen's Bureau to counter black initiatives. The army acted quickly to subdue the most revolutionary incidents at Keithfield, Delta, and elsewhere. The initial rejection of Sherman's Field Order No. 15 and its commitment to land redistribution struck a heavy blow to the creation of an autonomous black yeomanry based on property ownership.

In the daily course of events, federal officials acted to subvert black independence in dramatic ways. From the beginning, the military and the bureau strove to sustain the old order. While they worked to stamp out the vestiges of slavery and opposed the thermidorian black codes, bureau agents sought to impose their own vision of a free-labor society, which placed capital decidedly in control. When the 1866 growing season approached, federal agents traveled to trouble spots in their districts to deal with those laborers who refused to come to terms. The military commander of the Georgetown area, for example, selected the leaders of any resistance on plantations and punished them in front of the forcibly assembled community. He reported that this usually had the desired results.[48] A great deal of James C. Beecher's correspondence with headquarters concerned his almost constant travel between Summerville and the Combahee area to force blacks to sign agreements or vacate the plantations.[49] In the two subsequent years of bureau activity in South Carolina, African-Americans assented to contracts more readily than in 1866; nevertheless, the agents continued to police coastal people by seeing that laborers were faithful to their contracts. As one bureau official wrote to a Walterboro planter, "Tell the freedmen that they will be made to comply with the terms of the contract or punished for the neglect."[50]

Although force and intimidation were basic tools for whites in their search for postemancipation labor control, they did not always have to resort to such extraordinary measures. Both northern officials and local planters received unexpected assistance from the destitution and starvation that prevailed in the low country throughout Reconstruction. From the beginning of the era blacks often found their progress toward independence from plantation agriculture thwarted by critical shortages of the basic necessities of life. Evolving federal policy exploited these natural circumstances to preserve, at least for a while, large-scale productive units. In the turmoil of the summer of 1865, Rufus Saxton, a federal official, made a critical decision that helped to disrupt black objectives. He authorized his agents "to issue rations to white refugees and freedmen in case of extreme destitution, when the plainest dictates of humanity demand it. To those who are able to work and provide for themselves and fail to do it no rations should be issued."[51] At the same time, military officials ordered their subordinates to cease supplying emergency aid to all workers "that are able to earn their food by labor."[52] When the harvest of 1865 proved to be insufficient for the low country population, federal relief policy took on an added significance for blacks struggling for independence from plantation agriculture. In 1866 Union authorities amended their regulations and further circumscribed black alternatives. The new policy allowed for the issuing of rations on credit to "special cases" of "resident freedmen on Plantations through the owners thereof."[53] This action clearly favored the former masters in their struggle to prevent the fragmentation of their holdings into small, single-family farms. As one agent claimed, "This arrangement will enable many planters to carry on their plantations more extensively and some to plant crops who could not have done so without such assistance."[54] Federal relief practices combined with the retreat from land redistribution had a major impact on the contours of low country society and economy, especially after the disastrously small crops of 1866 and 1867.[55]

It is impossible to measure exactly the extent to which Union policy undermined the coastal African-Americans' achievement of independ-

Table 3.1
LABOR TERMS IN THE SOUTH CAROLINA LOW COUNTRY, 1865-1868 (IN PERCENTAGES)

BRFAL DISTRICT	CASH WAGES	WAGES IN FIXED KIND	SHARE WAGES—"GANG"	SHARECROP-PING	TENANCY	(TOTAL N)
BARNWELL						
1865	12	20	68			(25)
1866	8	8	76	8		(25)
1867	4	8	80	4	4	(25)
1868		3	68	26	3	(31)
BEAUFORT						
1865	68	4	11	14	4	(28)
1866	30		28	23	19	(43)
1867	4	2	33	49	11	(45)
1868	10	7	45	24	10	(29)
BERKELEY						
1865	14		63	23		(56)
1866	10	7	57	27		(30)
1867	11	64		25		(28)
1868						
CHARLESTON						
1865		5	95	3		(20)
1866	7	7	83	3		(29)
1867	9	31	47	9	3	(32)
1868						

54

COLLETON

Year					
1865	15	4	96		(26)
1866	13	4	67	11	(27)
1867		16	71	4	(32)
1868					

GEORGETOWN

Year					
1865	4	2	98	2	(45)
1866	14	2	83	11	(47)
1867		5	83	5	(42)
1868			91		(22)

Source: Records of the Subordinate Field Officers for South Carolina, Bureau of Refugees, Freedmen and Abandoned Lands, Record Group 105, National Archives, Washington, D.C. The Labor Contracts for Barnwell, Beaufort, Berkeley, Colleton, and Georgetown districts provided the data.

Note: These data were drawn from a sample of the over 13,000 labor contracts extant for the period 1865-1868 in South Carolina. Lacy Ford and I took a stratified random sample based on the total universe of contracts for each district. The total sample comprises 10 percent of the 13,000 contract universe. In his recent dissertation, "The Transition from Slave to Freedman Labor Arrangements in Southern Agriculture, 1865-1870," (University of Chicago, Economics, 1978), Ralph Shlomowitz also samples the South Carolina contracts; he makes, however, a serious mistake in drawing his approximately 600 contracts from the total universe of contracts available in the bureau records. This leaves him with only about 60 from the low country and almost 550 from what he calls the upland region. It is our belief that such a method seriously distorts the reality of labor arrangements in the years immediately following emancipation. Taking a sample on a district basis rather than from the total population allows greater sensitivity to geographical and historical forces. We are currently executing a 48 variable analysis of these contracts that will detail labor relations much more fully than presented here.

ence in the first years of freedom. However, a close analysiş of bureau-approved contracts shows that despite concessions to the black traditions, in many instances whites were able to determine the scale of agricultural production during Reconstruction. In 1865, only Beaufort District blacks engaged in individual farming to any significant degree. Freed people in this area where the redistribution of land was extensive worked family farms as sharecroppers or cash tenants at a rate of less than 20 percent of the population. About 2 percent of Georgetown District blacks were sharecroppers, but there were no individual farmers registered with the bureau in the Barnwell, Charleston, and Colleton districts. The work agreements for 1866 showed some increase in small-scale farming, especially in Beaufort where the combined rate of crop and money rental approached 45 percent. Nevertheless, undifferentiated plantations still constituted 85 percent or more of the productive units in all districts except Berkeley. In Berkeley 23 percent of the contracting laborers were sharecroppers but there were still no black cash renters, the condition of greatest autonomy other than landownership. Low country blacks in 1867 confronted a mixed fate. Although the Beaufort, Berkeley, and Charleston districts had more renters and sharecroppers in this third year of the bureau's tenure than in either the first or second, African-Americans in Barnwell, Colleton, and Georgetown at best held their own in the struggle to escape plantation agriculture; many who had previously farmed alone found it necessary to return to work for former masters. Existing data for 1868, the final year of the federal oversight of labor agreements, underscores the efficacy of bureau policy and planter determination. Even the Beaufort and Berkeley districts experienced a downward trend in the number of sharecroppers and tenants within their borders (see table 3.1).[56]

Evidence indicates that contracting laborers accepted the necessity of plantation-based work at first, but this is only half the story. While coastal people often entered such agreements as a means of survival, they still strove to define the terms of the work and to minimize the surplus extracted from them. Before the end of the bureau's active time in South Carolina, blacks had created a pattern of labor that included tasks and extended control over the rate of production well beyond that found under slavery. The new form of plantation-based work that evolved throughout the low country was known as the "two day system." Initially the principal terms entailed two to three and one-half days devoted to the main plantation crop every week. In return for this, the planter compensated his workers with an allotment of land to be farmed as they pleased during the remaining days. The land in payment was sometimes given to individual workers in plots of two to ten acres and at other times granted in larger amounts to the whole labor force.[57] By the end of Reconstruction, the freed people had expanded the terms of the two-day system. In addition to the plots of land granted in return for work on the planter's crop, they were given cash payments for each task performed.[58] The added benefit led blacks to insist even more adamantly on the two-day system when they worked as part of a large labor force. The small payments for each task allowed them to participate peripherally in the cash economy, purchasing the few necessities they could not produce on their allotted land. As the two-day system evolved, it spread throughout the low country so that by the mid-1870s, it was the characteristic mode of work organization for the large plantations that continued to exist.[59]

Reconstruction for blacks in the low country of South Carolina, then, was a time of struggle, defeat, and triumph. They entered the era of emancipation better equipped to fight for the control of their labor than blacks elsewhere in the South, and they challenged the authority of northern and southern whites with more intensity than any other African-Americans. Soon after Appomattox, whites realized the revolutionary potential of coastal blacks and set about preserving the balance of power in their society. Although they effectively forestalled an apocalypse by the time of the bureau's demise, whites never gained full control of the freed people's work. The planter class after 1865 continually confronted the limits of this control, and on occasion, the confrontation was dramatic. In 1876, laborers in the rice fields south of Charleston reached back to the first years of Reconstruction when they struck for higher wages. As with their earlier struggles, tradition remained strong. They walked out for more pay, but more pay for each task performed.[60]

Notes

1. See Willie Lee Rose, *Rehearsal for Reconstruction: The Port Royal Experiment* (Indianapolis: Bobbs-Merrill, 1964) and George C. Rogers, *The History of Georgetown County, South Carolina* (Columbia: The University of South Carolina Press, 1970) for discussions of the flight of the planters during the Civil War.

2. The literature involving a short-staple cotton perspective is extensive and growing. Some of the most recent econometric contributions are Roger Ransom and Richard Sutch, *One Kind of Freedom: The Economic Consequences of Emancipation* (New York: Cambridge University Press, 1977); Robert Higgs, *Competition and Coercion: Blacks in the American Economy, 1865-1914* (New York: Cambridge University Press, 1977); Stephen DeCanio, *Agriculture in the Postbellum South: The Economics of Production and Supply* (Cambridge, Mass.: M. I. T. Press, 1974); and quite different from the other economic works, Jay Mandle, *The Roots of Black Poverty: The Southern Plantation Economy after the Civil War* (Durham, N. C.: Duke University Press, 1978). The main works of social history are Jonathan M. Wiener, *Social Origins of the New South: Alabama, 1860-1880* (Baton Rouge: Louisiana State University Press, 1978); Dwight Billings, *Planters and the Making of the "New*

South": Class, Politics, and Development in North Carolina, 1865-1900 (Chapel Hill: University of North Carolina Press, 1979); Leon Litwack, *Been in the Storm So Long: The Aftermath of Slavery* (New York: Alfred A. Knopf, 1979); and Lawrence Powell, *New Masters: Northern Planters During the Civil War and Reconstruction* (New Haven: Yale University Press, 1980). The most thoughtful treatment of the literature is Harold D. Woodman, "Sequel to Slavery: The New History Views the Postbellum South," *Journal of Southern History* 48 (November 1977): 523-54.

The manor literature on postwar South Carolina also tends to underplay the variation within the state. See Francis Butler Simkins and Robert H. Woody, *South Carolina During Reconstruction* (Chapel Hill: University of North Carolina Press, 1932); Joel Williamson, *After Slavery: The Negro in South Carolina During Reconstruction, 1865-1872* (Chapel Hill: University of North Carolina Press, 1965); and Martin Abbott, *The Freedmen's Bureau in South Carolina, 1865-1872* (Chapel Hill: University of North Carolina Press, 1967).

3. See the discussions in Simkins and Woody, *South Carolina During Reconstruction*, Williamson, *After Slavery*, and Abbott, *The Freedmen's Bureau* and in George R. Bently, *A History of the Freedmen's Bureau* (Philadelphia: J. B. Lippincott, 1955).

4. Captain Charles Soule to General O. O. Howard, 12 June 1865, Records of the Subordinate Field Officers for South Carolina, Columbia Office, Miscellaneous Records, Bureau of Refugees, Freedmen and Abandoned Lands, Record Group 105, Series 3169, National Archives, Washington, D. C. Hereinafter cited as SFO/BRFAL.

5. A. S. Hitchcock to James F. Call, 25 August 1864, Letters Received, Records of the Departments of the South and South Carolina and Second Military District (hereinafter DOS), Record Group 393, Series 4109, Part 1, National Archives, Washington, D. C.

6. J. J. Upham to J. W. Clous, 4 September 1865, Letters Sent, Records of the United States Army Continental Commands (hereinafter RUSCC) Record Group 393, Series 2383, Part 2, National Archives, Washington, D. C.

7. Jno. G. Lawton to Captain Upham, 8 September 1865, Letters Received, RUSCC, Record Group 393, Series 2384, Part 2.

8. Wallington Wood to S. Baker, 12 October 1865, ibid.

9. Litwack, *Been in the Storm So Long*, pp. 292-335.

10. Citations to the task system in primary sources are numerous, the earliest dating from the mid-eighteenth century. There is sufficient evidence to conclude that by this early date task labor was firmly established in the low country. As the antebellum period progressed, discussion of the ins and outs of tasking became commonplace in agricultural literature. It is clear from plantation records that the mode of labor constituted the backbone of coastal production. No historians—those of South Carolina included—have appreciated the significance of the system in structuring black life. The best appreciation and description of task labor in comparison to gang labor can be found in Lewis C. Gray, *History of Agriculture in the Southern States to 1860*, 2 vols. (Washington, D. C. : Carnegie Foundation, 1933), 1: 550-56. U. B. Phillips also discussed task labor in *American Negro Slavery* (New York: Appleton and Company, 1918). One recent study, however, does emphasize the importance of task labor in postwar rice culture

in Georgia. See Thomas F. Armstrong, "From Task Labor to Free Labor: The Transition Along Georgia's Rice Coast. 1820-1880," *Georgia Historical Quarterly* 64 (Winter 1980): 423-47.

11. A. J. Willard to George W. Hooker, 7 November 1865, Letters Received, DOS, Record Group 393, Series 4112, Part 1.

12. The labor contracts for the low country in SFO/BRFAL provide excellent evidence of the tenacity with which freed people held to the task system after emancipation.

13. S. F. Smith to H. W. Smith, 25 April 1866, Letters Received, DOS, Record Group 393, Series 4112, Part 1.

14. A. J. Willard to H. W. Smith Georgetown District, SFO/BRFAL.

15. Ralph Izard Middleton to General, December 1867, Letters Received, DOS, Record Group 393, Series 4111, Box 11.

16. Ralph Izard Middleton to H. A. Middleton, 1869, Middleton Papers, Cheves Collection, South Carolina Historical Society, Charleston, S. C.

17. See, for example, F. H. Whittier to Lieutenant Fillebrown, 4 October 1865, Letters Received, DOS, Record Group 393, Series 4112, Part 1; and J. J. Upham to J. W. Clous, 14 November 1865, ibid.

18. A. J. Willard to George W. Hooker, 7 November 1865, ibid.

19. Ben Allston, F. S. Parker, and others to Colonel Williams, 20 October 1865, Letters Sent, RUSCC, Record Group 393, Series 2392, Part 2; A. J. Willard to G. W. Hooker, 20 October 1865, ibid.; and Charles Devens to W. L. M. Burger, 13 November 1865, Letters Received, DOS, Record Group 393, Series 4112, Part 1.

20. E. F. O'Brien to A. M. Crawford, 10 August 1866, Letters Received, Mount Pleasant District, SFO/BRFAL.

21. R. Y. Dwight to H. W. Leidtke, 18 August 1866, Letters Received, Moncks Corner District, SFO/BRFAL.

22. H. W. Leidtke to Major, 31 August 1866, Records of the Assistant Commissioner for South Carolina, Records of the Bureau of Refugees, Freedmen and Abandoned Lands, Record Group 105, Microcopy 869, Reel 34, National Archives, Washington, D. C. (hereinafter cited as AC/BRFAL and reel number).

23. R. K. Scott to O. O. Howard, 22 October 1866, AC/BRFAL, reel 1.

24. J. M. Hucks from Chickessee to Sir, 4 February 1867, Arnoldus Vanderhorst Papers, South Carolina Historical Society, Charleston, S. C.

25. E. W. Everson to E. L. Deane, 31 October 1867, Georgetown District, Letters Sent, SFO/BRFAL. See also Ralph Izard Middleton to E. W. Everson, 22 November 1867, Georgetown District, Letters Received, SFO/BRFAL; J. A. McCall to G. E. Pinegree, 26 November 1867, Darlington District, Letters Received, SFO/BRFAL; and J. E. Lewis to G. E. Pinegree, 30 November 1867, Marion District, Letters Sent, SFO/BRFAL.

26. The material on Keithfield is extensive and in conjunction with events elsewhere, is worthy of an article in itself. The major outlines of the situation in 1867 can be found in Francis S. Parker to E. W. Everson, 11 November 1867, Georgetown District, Registered Letters Received, SFO/BRFAL; Everson to Parker, 24 November 1867, Georgetown District, Letters Sent, SFO/BRFAL; and Everson to W. H. Read, 11 November 1867, ibid.

27. See, for example, W. C. Daniels to H. C. Brandt, 10 February 1868, Rice

Hope District, Letters Received, SFO/BRFAL; and R. I. Middleton to H. A. Middleton, 24 August 1869, Middleton Papers.

28. Henry W. Ravenel, "The Last Days of Rice Planting," *Rice and Rice Planting in the South Carolina Low Country*, ed. David Doar, Contributions of the Charleston Museum, no. 8 (Charleston: The Charleston Museum, 1936), pp. 45-46.

29. H. F. Hawkins to Commander of the Military District of Charleston, 1 January 1866, Heyward Ferguson Papers, Southern Historical Collection, University of North Carolina at Chapel Hill, Chapel Hill, N.C.

30. H. W. Smith to Lieutenant, 21 January 1866, Letters Received, DOS, Record Group 393, Series 4112, Part 1.

31. R. K. Scott to O. O. Howard, 25 January 1867, ibid.

32. W. H. Holton to J. S. Guenther, 31 January 1867, Columbia District, Letters Sent, SFO/BRFAL.

33. James W. Johnson to A. M. Crawford, 4 February 1866, Governors' Papers, South Carolina Department of Archives and History, Columbia, S. C.

34. A. J. Willard to W. H. Smith, 13 November 1865, Georgetown District, Letters Sent, SFO/BRFAL.

35. F. H. Whittier to C. B. Fillebrown, 20 November 1865, Letters Received, DOS, Record Group 393, Series 4112, Part 1.

36. H. S. Hawkins to Charleston District Headquarters, ibid.

37. W. H. Wesson to A. B. Andrews, 7 February 1866, A. B. Andrews Papers, Southern Historical Collection, University of North Carolina at Chapel Hill, Chapel Hill, N.C.

38. B. T. Sellers to Williams Middleton, 15 February 1866, Middleton Papers, Middleton Place Archives, Middleton Place, S.C.

39. B. F. Smith to H. W. Smith, 20 February 1866, Grahamville District, Letters Sent, SFO/BRFAL.

40. B. F. Smith to M. N. Rice, 20 February 1866, Letters Received, DOS, Record Group 393, Series 4112, Part 1; H. W. Leidtke to H. W. Smith, 15 May 1866, Columbia District, Letters Sent, SFO/BRFAL; R. K. Scott to O. O. Howard, 21 May 1866, AC/BRFAL, Reel 1.

41. R. K. Scott to O. O. Howard, 20 May 1868, AC/BRFAL, Reel 2; W. C. Daniel to H. C. Brandt, 20 July 1866, Rice Hope District, Letters Received, SRO/BRFAL.

42. See, for example, A. J. Gonzales to Emmie, Summer 1867, Elliott-Gonzales Papers, Southern Historical Collection, University of North Carolina at Chapel Hill, Chapel Hill N.C.; James R. Sparkman to Ben Allston, 23 November 1866, in *The South Carolina Rice Plantation as Revealed in the Papers of Robert F. W. Allston*, J. Harold Easterby, ed. (Chicago: University of Chicago Press, 1941), pp. 224-25; R. K. Scott to O. O. Howard, 25 January 1867, Letters Received, DOS, Record Group 393, Series 4112, Part 1; J. D. Waring to G. A. Williams, 13 January 1867, Summerville District, Letters Received, SFO/BRFAL; William Nearland to William Stone, 27 February 1868, Barnwell District, Letters Sent, SFO/BRFAL; F. E. Irving to F. W. Leidtke, 14 January 1868, Moncks Corner District, Letters Sent, SFO/BRFAL.

43. For a discussion of the problems inherent in overemphasizing the importance of landownership, see Herman Beltz, "The New Orthodoxy in Reconstruction Historiography," *Reviews in American History* (March 1973): 106-13.

44. The Santee area remained unsettled for much of 1866 and after. Discussions of many incidents appear throughout the bureau and military records at the National Archives. See, for example, William B. Pringle to General D. Sickles, 18 January 1866, RUSCC, Record Group 393, Series 2392, Part 2; D. T. Corbin to H. W. Smith, 1 February 1866, AC/BRFAL, Reel 9; and C. V. J. Wilson to Major O'Brien, 18 July 1866, Kingstree District, Letters Received, SFO/BRFAL. Typical of the troubles encountered on the Santee is the comment of E. J. Parker to D. W. Jordan, who noted that in trying to get the blacks on the plantation to contract and then to work, one Isaac Reid "would not do it. . .He cut up all sorts of Shines—said he would suffer to be shot down before he would sign it—That he did not intend to do anything for any man that he had been under all his life." (29 September 1865, D. W. Jordan Papers, Duke University Library, Durham, N.C.).

45. The material on Delta is more extensive than on any other single plantation in the low country. It can be found in the bureau and military papers for South Carolina and Georgia at all levels. Newspapers also carried frequent reports of the incidents. One of my continuing projects is a full consideration of the Delta conflict.

46. The Beecher correspondence is the most extensive and expressive of a single opinion of any of the federal agents in South Carolina. It can be found in the James C. Beecher Papers, Duke University Library, Durham, N. C.; in DOS and RUSCC, and in AC/BRFAL for Summerville District, and in the Records of the Commissioner of the Bureau of Refugees, Freedmen and Abandoned Lands, Record Group 105, Microcopy 759, National Archives, Washington, D. C.

47. For example, on Jehossee see, James P. Roy to W. L. M. Burger, 1 February 1866, DOS Record Group 393, Series 4109, Part 1; D. H. Whittemore to A. P. Ketchum, 30 January 1866, AC/BRFAL, Reel 9; on Johns, T. A. Beckett to James C. Beecher, 13 March 1866, Letters Received, DOS, Record Group 393, Series 4112, Part 1; on Wadmalaw, James C. Beecher to Major Smith, 31 January 1866, James C. Beecher papers; on James, E. J. Daniels to G. S. Burger, 13 January 1866, DOS Record Group 393, Series 4109, Part 1; on Cooper, J. N. Low to R. K. Scott, 8 February 1866, AC/BRFAL, Reel 10; and on Georgetown, F. Weston to Colonel Smith, 17 February 1866, RUSCC, Record Group 393, Series 2392, Part 20.

48. A. J. Willard to G. W. Hooker, 6 December 1865, Letters Received, DOS Record Group 393, Series 4112, Part 1. Instances of the military forcing blacks to contract occurred in every area.

49. See, for example, James C. Beecher to M. N. Rice, 28 April 1868, ibid.

50. Garrett Nagle to John D. Edwards, 14 September 1866, Summerville District, Letters Sent, SFO/BRFAL.

51. Rufus Saxton to James C. Beecher, 17 August 1865, AC/BRFAL, Reel 1.

52. E. H. Jewett to James C. Beecher, 3 August 1865, RUSCC, Record Group 393, Series 2421, Part 2.

53. W. L. Burger to W. P. Richardson, 24 January 1866, RUSCC, Record Group 393 Series 2264, Part 2.

54. B. F. Smith to M. N. Rice, 4 February 1866, RUSCC, Record Group 393, Series 2389, Part 2.

55. See, for example, Charles Devens to R. K. Scott, 4 April 1866, AC/BRFAL, Reel 9. At every juncture, the authorities tried to exclude those who they felt were undeserving, thus forcing many of the destitute to turn elsewhere for support. Discussions of the measures taken to withhold provisions during 1866, 1867, and 1868, in the wake of droughts and floods, are too numerous to cite. In the face of destitution, bureau policy changed very little from that promulgated in 1865 and 1866. For an outline of the policy see Abbott, *Freedmen's Bureau*, pp. 37-51.

56. The discussion in this paragraph is based on data from Table. 3.1.

57. Discussions of the two-day system during Reconstruction are to be found in many private papers and in the bureau and military records. See, for example, E. F. O'Brien to M. C. Crawford, 1 March 1867, Mount Pleasant District, Letters Sent, SFO/BRFAL; J. E. Lewis to H. B. Clitz, 29 February 1868, Grahamville District, Letters Sent, SAC/BRFAL; and James Hemphill, *Climate, Soil, and Agricultural Capabilities of South Carolina and Georgia* (Washington, D. C.: U. S. Department of Agriculture, 1882), pp. 12-13.

58. It seems that cash wages for tasks had become common practice by 1868 and represented an effort on the part of planters to "buy" productive labor from the hands, who were all too willing to subsist on their gardens and small cash crops grown on the land provided in compensation. The evolution of this added wage in the bargain for labor power can best be traced through the labor contracts in the bureau papers. As we shall see, this transaction in the ongoing exchange between capital and labor had become an established custom by the mid-1870s.

59. Harry Hammond, *South Carolina Resources and Population* (Columbia, S. C.: State Agricultural Commission, 1883), p. 29.

60. Evidence for the rice strike of 1876 is extensive and in a variety of sources. I am currently finishing a paper that focuses exclusively on the strike.

4

BLACKS, EDUCATIONAL REFORM, AND POLITICS IN NORTH CAROLINA, 1897-1898

Richard B. Westin

Although the complexity of human history has defeated attempts to establish any "laws" by which it operates, historians still can find truisms. One is that we seldom grasp the full range of motivations behind human actions. Another is that an action, even when it is the result of purposeful planning, has consequences that are unforeseen and unintended by its initiators. In examining the historical record, it is not unusual to find cases in which differing motives have coalesced and led people to a course of action that has had ironical results. Such an occurrence can be seen in the political history of North Carolina during the turbulent years of the 1890s. It developed out of the crossing of two historical strands that previously had evolved separately. These were the growing demand for better public schools and the rising political strength of the Populist movement.

Until the 1890s the structure of public education in North Carolina had been established primarily in the 1870s by those Democrats who wrested control of the state government away from the Republicans. In 1869 the Republican-controlled legislature had mandated a statewide system of public schools for both blacks and whites that was supported by the state treasury. Each township constituted a school district and had a committee under the supervision of a county board of education that would establish schools as needed for both blacks and whites, although the schools for the two races were to be separate.[1]

In 1871 the legislature, now controlled by the Democrats, abolished the state system of financing schools and stipulated that school taxes would remain in the counties where they were collected. In the 1876–77 biennium, township school districts were abolished, and in their place each school was made an individual district. Thus, each county was divided into a series of white school districts and a separate series of black school districts. Three-man school committees were appointed for each district, and it became the custom for white committeemen to serve white school districts and black committeemen to be appointed for black districts. The legislature did not change that provision of the school code calling for monies to be apportioned equally to schools on a per pupil basis, and this equal per capita distribution of funds between white and Negro schools remained one source of discontent to many white taxpayers.

In the early 1880s the Democratic state superintendent, John Scarborough, became concerned about some of the problems that arose from such a highly decentralized school system. The law that had made each school into a separate district had created a proliferation of school districts with the result that many districts had too few pupils to be adequately funded. Scarborough explained why such a situation had developed:

The people, looking at the question of convenience only, had petitioned and were still petitioning for a division of the school districts into smaller districts, every man wanting the district school near *his* residence. About one-half of the districts were without houses and with no money to build them. This resulted in continued controversy as to where the school should be taught. A, B, and C of any given district had an unoccupied house that would do. Each urged upon the committee the importance of having the school taught in *his* house. The committee was forced to choose between them and selected the house of A; it was the best they could do in their judgment. B and C objected, became enemies of the school, threw obstacles in the way of the teacher, advised their next neighbors against sending [their children] to the school, circulated petitions for the division of the district, and presented them to the next meeting of the county board of education and demanded immediate action. Said board, recognizing the right of petition, ordered the division demanded, and the result was, the district, already too small, was divided into two, neither one of which had funds enough to continue a school for a longer term than four weeks with a very ordinary teacher.[2]

In 1883 Scarborough recommended a bill that would allow localities to vote a special tax upon themselves in order to improve their schools. In considering it, the legislature immediately came up against the question of what would constitute a locality. Would it be a township? If so, would it be fair to hold back a school district within a township whose voters wanted a special tax because voters in other districts in the township did not desire the tax? If the privilege of local taxation were given to each individual school district, a white district might vote a tax upon itself, while a Negro district occupying the same geographical area might have no special tax.

By granting each school district the power to vote a special tax upon itself it was possible to answer the demand that white taxes be used for white schools and Negro taxes for Negro schools. The Local Assessment Act of 1883 gave the county commissioners the power to submit the question of a special school tax to that district's voters upon the petition of ten voters from a school district, either white or black. If a white district voted the tax, it would be collected only from the white voters and would be used exclusively for the white school. Conversely, a Negro district voting the tax would have black residents within the district taxed for their school. The first statewide school law that discriminated monetarily between white and Negro schools was passed with this act.

If the law were upheld by the courts, the state might have been set upon an educational path that would have resulted in a proliferation of small special tax districts and a gradually widening educational gap between well-to-do school districts and poor ones. Almost all Negro districts would probably fall into the latter category. The answer came in the case of *Puitt and Pasour* v. *Commissioners of Gaston County* in 1886.[3] The State Supreme Court declared the local assessment act unconstitutional on two counts: first, it did not provide for uniform and equal taxation on all property, and second, it made a racial discrimination in the application of school funds.

The 1885 legislature did not try to rewrite the special tax bill, but it did modify the method of apportioning county school funds. Under the modification county boards of education, using the old per capita basis, were to apportion two-thirds of the school fund to the districts. The remaining one-third was to be used to equalize school terms among all districts in the county as far as "practicable." Any unexpended balance in a district would be returned to the county's general fund. This law made it possible for county boards of education that believed that white taxes should be used for white schools to give a disproportionate share of the equalization fund to white schools.

This method of distributing school funds accelerated the existing trend toward a proliferation in the number of school districts. Districts with few students could now call on the equalization money to keep operating for as long as larger districts. Other district committees quickly discovered that they could pay their teachers more and then use equalization funds to keep their school operating for the prescribed term, if the county board would permit it.

These were a few of the complexities faced by the state school system as the depression decade of the 1890s approached and brought with it a mounting cry of economic pain from the state's financially squeezed small farmers. By 1890 many citizens had joined the Farmers Alliance movement. After 1892, when the Democratic legislature failed to respond to their concerns, many of these Alliance members joined the Populist party.

The rise of the Populist party was especially traumatic for Democrats in North Carolina. In 1894 a fusion ticket of Populists and Republicans was able to gain control of the state legislature, and in 1896 it won control of the executive offices, including those of governor and superintendent of public instruction. In 1897 the Populist state superintendent of schools, Charles H. Mebane, George Butler, the Populist state senator, and Charles D. McIver, chairman of the white state teachers association's committee on legislation, suggested revisions in the state school law. Several of their recommendations were passed including one that used the townships as school districtsd—a system the Republicans had used during Reconstruction. Thus, the school organization the Democrats had adopted in the 1870s in which each school was a separate district with its own three-man committee was replaced by one in which there was a single five-man committee to set the salaries and appoint the teachers for all schools within a township.[4]

At the annual meeting of the North Carolina white teachers association in June 1897, Senator Butler explained why the townships had been made the school districts.[5] He noted that people had long wondered why the length of school terms had failed to increase proportionately as the school taxes were increased. In 1880 the state had set the minimum school tax rate at eight and one-third cents on property as well as a poll tax of twenty-five cents. These revenues had provided a statewide average school term of ten weeks. Despite four increases which had brought the minimum school tax to eighteen cents on property and fifty-four cents on the poll, the average length of the school term had increased to only about twelve weeks. In other words, a school tax increase of over 100 percent had lengthened the school term less than 30 percent, and understandably the taxpayer was impatient to see greater results. The situation truly was perplexing in that neither an increased school population, nor increased teacher salaries, nor a rise in the expense of school administration could explain the discrepancy. Teacher salaries actually had shown a slight decrease during the period.

Butler found the answer in the increase in the number of school districts. Every additional district meant an added schoolhouse to be maintained and a teacher to be hired, but the increase could not be attributed to additional children attending school. In fact, while there had been an increase in average daily attendance in the 1880s there had been an actual decrease during the depression years of the 1890s. There were 1,000 fewer children in classrooms in 1896 than in 1888. Meanwhile, despite the decreasing attendance, the number of school districts continued to increase from 6,755 in 1888 to 7,249 in 1897.[6]

The result, Butler pointed out, was a constant weakening of the school districts, as divided districts had fewer pupils and less money to pay competent teachers or to build decent schoolhouses. He attributed the increase in districts to the 1885 law that allowed one-third of the school fund to be used to equalize the length of term between schools. This had allowed districts with few students and little money to call for extra help in order to operate for a longer term. The problem of obtaining competent school committeemen had been aggravated by the proliferation of districts and the result was "incompetency and confusion." Butler explained:

The County Commissioners, only three men, are chosen to manage the finances of a county, and why four hundred and fifty school committeemen should be required for one county . . . is not easily understood, and many counties have a greater number than this. In 1896 there were 6,918 licensed public school teachers in North Carolina. There were 22,680 public school committeemen to supervise the work of these teachers and this large number does not include the County Boards of Education, and the County Superintendents. . . . Five carefully chosen committeemen in each township district with the assistance of the County Board of Education and the County Supervisor, will be sufficiently ample to protect and promote the school interest of the county.[7]

The legislature accepted Butler's reasoning and made the township the smallest unit of school management.

Butler foresaw several advantages for the new township system. It would result in fewer and larger schools with better wages and better teachers. It would end the "constant petitioning" to change district boundaries and to transfer children from one school to another. Under the new system longer and more uniform terms would be obtained, and under a section of the law allowing the funds of two or more districts to be combined, "a central High School could be established if people so desire." Also, the new system would give more permanency to the teaching force of the state.[8] Finally, the new law would provide for the school fund "to be apportioned to the township per capita, but to each school according to its grade, thereby preventing unjust discrimination against higher grade schools."[9] A question of vital importance to blacks was whether or not white schools would be regarded as the "higher grade schools," since the township school committees now had control over the distribution of the funds to all schools within the township.

This provision that school funds were no longer to be apportioned to the schools on a per capita basis was of prime significance. By law the township committees were to distribute the money "so as to give each school in their district, white and colored, the same length of school term, . . . and in making such apportionment the said committee shall have proper regard for the grade of work to be done and the qualifications of the teachers required in each school, white and colored, within their districts."[10] There was now only one absolute criterion for equal school provisions for the two races: equal term length. All other criteria were open to the interpretation of local officials. The new law, while halting a drift toward the proliferation of school districts, accentuated the use of a disproportionate amount of school funds for white schools.

Although Charles McIver later claimed that the 1897 law had been designed specifically to place the apportionment of funds in the hands of the five-man school committees, which whites would dominate and therefore could insure that white schools received an "equitable" share, Superintendent Charles Mebane showed no awareness that the law might be so used.[11] Bertie County Superintendent Rhoden Mitchell assumed that whites and blacks would serve together on the township committees. He praised the law in the Populist newspaper, the *Caucasian*, saying:

This plan will bring white and colored men together to inspect the white schools, and the amount expended, also white and colored men to inspect colored schools and the amount expended for them. All tax payers should be pleased with this plan as the enterchange [*sic*] of opinion must result to good to both races.[12]

Criticism of the new law was mild, until it went into effect.

To encourage local taxation, the 1897 legislature also passed a bill requiring every township in the state to hold a special tax election in August. Townships voting such a tax were to receive matching funds from the state up to $500. Indications that the composition of the five-man township committees would cause what the Raleigh *News and Observer* editor, Josephus Daniels, called "a storm of resentment" and thus interfere with the tax election soon became apparent. As early as May, S. M. Hill of Faison, North Carolina, outlined the problem. He told Mebane that the new school law was more objectionable to blacks than any "since the war." Previously, they had controlled their own schools. While the new law did not exclude Negroes, whites were not willing to have them on the committees that were to have charge of schools for both races, and blacks were dissatisfied if they had no representation. Hill warned Mebane that this racial dilemma over school committeemen was overshadowing all other questions. Mebane did not appreciate its seriousness. He patiently explained to Hill that the township system would consolidate small, weak schools into fewer but stronger schools and said that the race question should not cause any difficulty because wherever there were "qualified" blacks, they should have representation on the township committees.[13]

By July Mebane had become aware that the passion of the white community in many areas was such that it was not expedient to have Negroes on the committees. He wrote that there was nothing to prevent them from serving but that county authorities had to "use prudence" and that "it would generally be the better thing to do, to appoint 5 *good* white men and let the colored make their wants and wishes known to these 5 men." He added that Negro grievances always could be appealed to the county board of education and, if necessary, to the state board.[14]

The special tax election was scheduled for August 1897. By early summer the white teachers association had enlisted some of the state's most prominent people and most of the leading newspapers behind the campaign. Unfortunately, despite the efforts of the state's educational leadership, the election became a political issue with many Democrats working actively against the so-called fusion law. Animosity was great, and a wide variety of tactics were used to defeat the proposed taxes. Upon receiving reports of irregularities, Mebane could only encourage supporters not to allow such things to "hinder the election." But the efforts of proponents were in vain; the election was a resounding failure. Only eleven townships throughout the state voted for the tax.[15]

Although many fusionists attributed the defeat to the Democrats, Mebane was informed that dissatisfaction with the school law was also a cause. J. R. McCrary, a lawyer from Lexington, told Mebane that "the main trouble with the popularity of the law in this section is the fact that the negroes and whites are not allowed to manage their own schools." G. L. Beaman, the registrar of deeds for Montgomery County, reported that the special tax lost in every township in his county almost solely because of one defect in the new school law.

It is this, that five Committee [men] shall have control of both White & Col. Schools, the More ignorant Class both White and Colored are very much displeased with that and they are not only displeased but they seem to be enraged and mad so much so that they will not listen to reason. Nothing that Could be done would . . . induce the Colored people to vote for the Tax unless They could be assured the controll of their Schools[.] That is that their race Controll their Schools and the Whites above mentioned are no less dissatisfied with the Colored having Something to say in regard to the white schools.

Mebane admitted that the issue of Negro committeemen did work against the school tax but believed: "the politicians . . . did more to kill the measur[e] than anything else."[16]

On August 19 the editor of the *Caucasian* criticized the Raleigh *News and Observer* for saying that the school tax issue was "dead as a doornail" and that a cause of its demise was the issue of Negro committeemen. He accused the *News and Observer* of merely trying "to pump life into the 'nigger' question" instead of telling the whole story. He then explained:

When the negro school committees were abolished and all the white and colored schools in a township put under the management of one committee, and where a colored man has been put on, it was done so he could look after the interests of the colored schools of the township.

The News and Observer knows that there is not a white school in North Carolina under the "control" of a negro board.

Resentment against the fusion school law did not abate with the failure of the tax election. G. L. Hardison, a Populist state senator, warned Mebane that people were thinking of returning to the Democratic party in order to return to the old school law. He cited one township that had run a six-month school term for twelve years but now was forced to run only a four-month term. Hardison, irritated because the law called for equal length of terms for white and Negro schools, complained that whites "pay all the taxes nearly" but the Negroes get most of the money.[17]

An opposite view was presented by D. P. Allen, a teacher at Lumberton, who claimed that the fusionist school law was the only one that had been used to discriminate against blacks. He explained that in his area the white and Negro populations were about equal but that there had been more white schools. When funds had been distributed on a per capita basis, each white teacher had received less. If some white teachers would not accept low salaries, there had been others ready to teach at the prevailing price. The fault lay with the parsimonious white committees who hired teachers who could afford to take a lower salary because they had other jobs and to whom teaching had been merely a sideline. Because teaching was their main occupation, teachers in black schools, however, had received more money, and "many of the country people would almost go into *spasms* to see a teacher of color getting more money than their teachers could get." Under the fusionist law the Negro schools had been turned over to white committees to "milk," too. The result was that in a township with 480 black children and 470 white children, the Negro schools got $325 and the white schools, $650. Allen concluded that the Democrats often tried to make the law "odious" in order to discredit it as a product of the Populist and Republican legislature.[18]

Not all persons, however, were dissatisfied with the new township school system. Many young professional educators saw it as a progressive step toward greater efficiency and honesty. They also viewed the system as a way to alleviate the discontent of whites who believed that much of their tax money was being wasted, particularly upon black schools. During a meeting of superintendents in Raleigh in December 1897, Superintendent Street Brewer of Sampson County defended the system and pointed out the advantages to be gained through efficient management, especially in the grading of teachers.

The little district, as we have had heretofore, was a territorial unit not only too narrow, but too variable to serve either as the basis for a wise distribution of school funds or for efficient supervision of the schools. Chance, caprice, sometimes the interests of a single family, or an insignificant village rivalry, sometimes, also, the prejudice or carelessness of a single man, would determine the fate of a locality in regard to its public school. The old district system has been tried; it was not liberty, but chaos.

However, he warned, the township system could fail too, if the proper grading of teachers were not carried out. Lack of systematic management had been a major difficulty under the old district system, and good management was complicated by the fact that the Negro was "an important factor" in the schools.

Their interests must be jealously guarded and cared for, as well as the interests of the whites. Under the district system, when the colored schools were controlled entirely by colored committees, they were very extravagant in paying their teachers, therefore it requires a double discretion to grade satisfactorily.

As an example Brewer mentioned that:

In one colored district in my county in which the average attendance was less than a dozen, the teacher received a salary of $35 per month. That school now, under the "grading system" is being taught at a salary of $18 per month, a saving of $17 per month in one school. . . . One instance came to my attention a few years ago, where a young lady was teaching a public school with only two pupils, at a salary of $20 per month. She carried her crocheting, and one of the pupils her knitting, to the schoolhouse, and the State paid for their household work. I could cite other cases equally as ridiculous. . . .

Under the township system Brewer could solve such problems by meeting with the township committees, grading the teachers on the basis of Superintendent Mebane's instructions, and then setting salaries on the basis of that grading. This, he said, had allowed $2,500 to be saved for the county, and the school term was thereby increased by three weeks in the white and four weeks in the Negro schools. Brewer mentioned that among other advantages such grading prevented dishonest and unprincipled committeemen from receiving bribes or part of the teacher's salary as sometimes had happened under the old district system.[19]

Despite its supporters, the township system faced mounting criticism, and Mebane eventually concluded that the law would have to be revised. In reply to the charge by partisan newspapers that Negroes were being given charge of white schools in eastern North Carolina, Mebane replied that there were no white schools under Negro control since three whites on a five-man township committee could control white schools and Negro schools as well. He was aware that "in many of the eastern counties" three whites and two Negroes composed the township committees, but he denied that there were any black county superintendents. However, since the present system allowed opponents "to create prejudice against Public Education," he concluded that it would be better to have a six-man committee for each township with three white and three black members to supervise the white and Negro schools respectively. When the school fund was to be divided between the races, the county superintendent could be the presiding officer of this committee.[20]

Mebane recommended that the next legislature provide for six-man township committees, and went on to suggest that when qualified Negroes could not be found, all-white committees should be appointed. Individuals wishing to be appointed to the committee should be aware of the importance of having a good teacher and be willing to select the best without regard to family ties or political party. Only men who could write their own name should be considered, he emphasized.[21]

Mebane knew that some townships were disregarding the law by setting up separate committees for the white and Negro schools. Believing it futile to promote racially mixed committees, he acquiesced in such arrangements and defended his position by stating that it was necessary to avoid racial prejudice. "The mixed Committees cause trouble and dissatisfaction, and, in my opinion, always would, if retained. The very instinct of our Anglo-Saxon race is against the idea of a colored man, either directly or indirectly, having authority over them. We must remove all the objections we possibly can in operating our public schools."[22]

In time both astute educators and Democratic politicians came to realize that the township system with its white majorities could control the money spent for Negro schools and thus remove the white complaint that white taxes went to educate Negroes. Men such as Street Brewer continued to use this as an argument for the township system. He admitted that having whites and Negroes on the township school committee had resulted in "prejudice and complaint against" the township system. He said that in his county the one Negro committeeman in each township had not tried to interfere with the white schools, but, as the law was written, that committeeman could do so if he desired and there would be no legal means to prevent him. If there were to be Negro committees, Brewer recommended that they should be separate and so defined by law. "Beginning with my boyhood days," Brewer said, "the greatest and most unceasing complaint of the white people has been and is now, 'the paying of taxes for support of the negro schools.' " The township system, he maintained, was the answer and should not be condemned for one defect. In his own county, under the old district system with its apportionment of school funds on a per capita basis, one township that had twice as many Negro children as white, had not been able to keep the white schools running as long as the Negro schools. Negro schools ran one-third again as long as the white schools and sometimes twice as long. Under the township system with its apportioning of school money so that every school in a township ran an equal length of time, the "white tax payers can control their money and give general satisfaction to both races."[23]

The year 1897 had marked the high tide of fusion politics. Plagued by a lack of harmony from within and by strong Democratic attacks from without, the fusionists were unable to hold their support in the elections of 1898. The Democrats, under the able leadership of State Chairman Furnifold Simmons, conducted a campaign unprecedented in its organization and effectiveness. They depicted the state as threatened by Negro domination, which, they warned, would bring about an anarchic condition of disorder and violence. The campaign was known as the Red Shirt Campaign because the Democrat whites attempted to intimidate Negroes and Republicans by dressing in red shirts and parading, heavily armed, on horseback through Negro communities and at political rallies. The Democrats made "white supremacy" the issue, and the Populists were hopelessly split. While a few stayed with the Republicans, many drifted back into the Democratic ranks. In addition, many Negroes did not vote. The result was the election of 134 Democratic legislators and only thirty Republicans and six Populists.

The legislature of 1899 appointed in each county a new three-man county board of school directors, which in turn appointed in each township a committee of three trustees. As under the 1897 law, these trustees were to apportion the school funds to each school to give each the same length of term, while having "proper regard for the grade of work to be done and the qualifications of the teachers required in each school for each race."[24] Thus, the township trustees were to fix the maximum salary for each school. The Democrats essentially retained the fusionist township school system and its method of apportioning school funds in which equal terms were the sole statutory criterion for equal education.

The Republicans and Populists who had wrested control of the state from the Democrats and then attempted to solve the state's educational problems had devised a school law that created racial friction, helped to defeat an election for increased school taxes, and helped to defeat themselves at the polls in 1898. At the same time they provided the Democrats with a way to end the long-standing irritant among whites who believed their taxes were being used to provide black children with schools. The removal of that irritant did cause many whites to be more amenable to the public schools and thus helped spur the educational revival that occurred in the state under Democratic Governor Charles B. Aycock in the first decade of the twentieth century. In turn, the revival helped to give both the governor and the state a reputation for progressive southern leadership. Ironically, it was a leadership derived in part from the fusionist action in which blacks were deprived of financial control over their schools. This deprivation, which was the result of a reform aimed at improving the quality and efficiency of education, did help to improve schools but only white schools.

Notes

1. For the introductory material concerning the development of school legislation during the 1870s and 1880s in this and the eight succeeding paragraphs see Richard B. Westin, "The State and Segregated Schools: Negro Public Education in North Carolina, 1863-1923" (Ph.D. diss., Duke University, 1966), pp. 43-44, 51-53, 59-72.

2. North Carolina, *Biennial Report of the Superintendent of Public Instruction for the Scholastic Years 1881-1882* (Raleigh, 1882), p. 6 (hereinafter cited as *Biennial Report of the S.P.I.*).

3. *J. C. Puitt, Eli Pasour and others* v. *Commissioners of Gaston County*, 94 N. C. 709 (1886).

4. North Carolina, *Public Laws and Resolutions of the State of North Carolina Passed at Its Sessions of 1897. . .*(Raleigh, 1897), Ch. 421 (hereinafter cited as P.L. with the appropriate date and chapters). See also *The Caucasian* (Raleigh) 28 January, 4 March, and 11 March 1897.

5. *The Caucasian*, 1 July 1897.

6. Ibid.

7. Ibid.

8. Ibid.

9. Ibid.

10. P.L., 1897, Ch. 108, Sec. 11.

11. William E. King, "Charles McIver Fights for the Tarheel Negro's Right to an Education," *North Carolina Historical Review* 14, no. 3 (July 1946): 360-69.

12. *The Caucasian*, 29 July 1897.

13. P.L., 1897, Ch. 421; Josephus Daniels, *Editor in Politics* (Chapel Hill: University of North Carolina Press, 1941), pp. 252-53; S. M. Hill to C. H. Mebane, 17 May 1897, and Mebane to Hill, 24 May 1897, Correspondence of the Superintendent of Public Instruction, North Carolina State Archives, Raleigh, North Carolina (hereinafter cited as Correspondence of the S.P.I.).

14. Mebane to Fernando Ward, 20 July, 1897, Correspondence of the S.P.I.

15. *The Caucasian*, 1 July, 29 July, 12 August, and 26 August 1897; Mebane to James J. Coley, 3 August 1897, Correspondence of the S.P.I.

16. J. R. McCrary to Mebane, 12 August 1897, Correspondence of the S.P.I.; G. L. Beaman to Mebane, 12 August 1897, ibid.; Mebane to J. L. M. Curry, 24 August 1897, ibid.

17. G. L. Hardison to Mebane, 16 February 1898, ibid.

18. D. P. Allen to Mebane, 15 February 1898, ibid.

19. *Biennial Report of the S.P.I.*, 1896-98, pp. 259-65.

20. D. D. Crisp to Mebane, 12 August 1898, and Mebane to Crisp, 15 August 1898, Correspondence of the S.P.I.

21. *Biennnial Report of the S.P.I.*, 1896-98, pp. 11-14.

22. Ibid.

23. *Biennial Report of the S.P.I.*, 1898-1900, pp. 234-36.

24. P.L., 1899, Ch. 732.

5

WAITING IN LIMBO: A RECONSIDERATION OF WINSLOW HOMER'S THE GULF STREAM

Peter H. Wood

A number of recent books about slavery and emancipation have carried pictures of blacks on their covers, but almost without exception, historians have used these illustrations to attract readers and to ward off dust; they rarely invite detailed consideration of the painting.[1] At the same time, art historians, whose bread and butter is the careful analysis of creative works, frequently seem oblivious or disdainful of the historical context in which these works were created. All of us are the poorer for this gap between art criticism and historical study. Although interesting works have begun to fill the void, such as the new book by Loren Partridge and Randolph Starn, *A Renaissance Likeness: Art and Culture in Raphael's Julius II*, there is not yet a standard label or format for what I wish to attempt here: the discussion of a single work of art from the cultural historian's perspective.

I originally intended to concentrate upon artistic images concerning blacks and freedom from the 1850s through the 1870s, such as Eastman Johnson's *A Ride for Liberty—The Fugitive Slaves* (1863) or Theodor Kaufmann's *On to Liberty* (1867). Pictures such as Eyre Crowe's *Slave Market in Richmond, Virginia* (1852) or Thomas Moran's *Slaves Escaping Through the Swamp* (1863) are more competent, varied, and intriguing than most people realize. One person particularly interested me: the gifted American painter, Winslow Homer, born in Boston on February 24, 1836. As I had admired this self-taught and versatile artist since my childhood, when I wore out our old volume of Civil War reprints from *Harper's Weekly*, I was pleased to find that his images of blacks from that era (including his remarkable but little-known oil painting *Shackled Slave* [1863]) are now coming under closer examination.[2]

At the same time I was amazed to discover that the historical context and implications of Homer's most famous picture of a Negro—indeed one of the most renowned black images in all of American or Western art over the past century—have scarcely been examined at all. That painting, *The Gulf Stream*, was created by Homer in 1899 at the age of

The Metropolitan Museum of Art, Wolfe Fund, 1906

Winslow Homer (1836-1910), *The Gulf Stream*. Oil on canvas, 28⅛ × 49⅛ in., dated 1899.

sixty-three. It remains, despite generations of faint praise from experts, the single most popular and well-known work of this prolific master, and it presently hangs in a corner of the new American wing of the Metropolitan Museum in New York.[3]

For Alain Locke, the distinguished intellectual of the Harlem renaissance, *The Gulf Stream* represented "the artistic emancipation of the Negro in American art," for it shattered what he called "the-cotton-patch-and-back-porch-tradition" well-known in such paintings as Eastman Johnson's *Old Kentucky Home* (1859) and in hundreds of lesser works.[4] But in this view, as in much else, Locke was far ahead of his culture. Since Homer's death in 1910, none of his paintings has been so widely reproduced and admired as this one, yet almost no one has commented on *The Gulf Stream*'s complex and paradoxical meanings in the Afro-American experience.

From the time it first went on display in 1900, *The Gulf Stream* aroused anxious and conflicting emotions in its viewers. Indeed, despite the prominence of its creator, the work went unsold for more than six years. Two women on the board of the Worcester museum vetoed its purchase because of the picture's "unpleasantness," and it drew nervous laughter from visitors to the National Academy exhibition in Philadelphia in 1906, where the Metropolitan acquired it for $4,500. From some, the composition received impressive praise. The *Evening Post* called it "that rare thing in these days, a great dramatic picture," and the New York *Herald* cited it as "an unusually strong canvas, even for a Winslow Homer."[5]

The muralist Kenyon Cox liked "the dramatic force of the composition," the "admirable mastery of design, and the consequent perfection with which it renders the helpless sliding of the boat into the trough of the sea." According to Cox:

There is not an inch of any of the innumerable lines of the magnificent wave drawing that does not play its part in a symphony of line. What the reproduction cannot render is the superb depth and quality of the blue of the water, of such wonderful passages of sheer painting as the distance, with the ship driving by under full sail, or the dash of spray from the tail of the nearest shark.[6]

Homer's biographer, Lloyd Goodrich, applauded "the color, the most brilliant in any oil so far, especially the varied range of blues in the water," adding that "the variety and power of its brushwork made it one of his greatest technical achievements."[7]

But there were criticisms as well. Cox noted "a certain hardness of manner in the painting of the whole canvas,"[8] and others found fault with "the stocky boat and the figure of the downcast sailor."[9] The New York *Sun* critic called the work "huddled in composition" and "too crowded with naturalistic melodrama." He found the picture "less fantastic than cruel" and saw "the quality of the paint as neither pleasant nor translucent."[10] Homer's initial biographer reports that,

> Mr. Riter Fitzgerald, in the Philadelphia "Item," attacked the work savagely, calling it a unique burlesque on a repulsive subject, "a naked negro, lying in a boat while a school of sharks were waltzing around him in the most ludicrous manner." The same writer thought that the artist had painted it with "a sense of grim humor," and that its proper place was in a zoölogical garden.[11]

The critic concluded that a favorable review of the picture in the *American Art News* must have been written tongue-in-cheek, and he offered his own alternative title for the work, *Smiling Sharks*.[12]

Modern authorities have continued to find fault with *The Gulf Stream*. Barbara Novak speaks vaguely of its "illustrative deficiencies" and calls it "one of the most famous but least plastically satisfying of Homer's paintings."[13] In his book on American seascapes, Roger B. Stein says bluntly, "it is not Homer at his best, despite the painting's continuing appeal." He finds it, "Poorly painted, harsh in color, melodramatically overstated and terribly derivative in both its symbolism and its structure."[14]

In spite of the picture's troubling subject, or perhaps because of it, most commentators in the past eighty years have spent inordinate amounts of time debating the painting's stylistic attributes—color, composition, technique. In doing so, they have engaged in what John Berger, a compelling critic of art critics, calls "mystification. . .the process of explaining away what might otherwise be evident."[15] Comments on form, such as those quoted, whether early or recent, positive or negative, have been used by both writers and viewers to avoid the stark content of the picture. Yet one must assume that if the painting's stylistic achievements are so debatable, then its persistent power over American audiences must derive from something compelling or resonant in the subject itself.

No amount of preoccupation with pigments, patterns, and brushstrokes can divert critics entirely from Homer's subject matter. Over the years they apparently have offered two basic interpretations of *The Gulf Stream*. Both are logical and plausible as far as they go, but whether taken separately or together they strike me as inadequate, unsatisfying, and incomplete. Let me review both of them briefly and propose one additional interpretation, which, when fully developed in a longer study, may help expand our understanding of *The Gulf Stream* and the end-of-the-century world in which it was created.

There is no older or richer artistic image than that of a boat and its occupants at the mercy of the mighty sea. The Greek Homer used the device, and in Western painting it has been a constant theme, shifting in emphasis and meaning according to the times. In late nineteenth-century America, overtones of "tragedy and apocalypse" surround this genre, reflecting the fin de siècle anxiety over social and cultural drift in the face of a remote deity and overwhelming nature.[16] Albert Pinkham Ryder, Homer's New York contemporary, epitomized this mood in such seascapes as *Jonah and the Whale* or *The Flying Dutchman*. In 1896 he completed *Constance*, which was based on Chaucer's "The Man of Law's Tale" in *The Canterbury Tales* about a mother who is put to sea in a rudderless boat and survives the long ordeal only through her Christian faith.[17] It was in 1899 as Homer was painting *The Gulf Stream* that Stephen Crane composed a small untitled poem on the widely felt theme of universal indifference to mankind's precarious condition:

> A man said to the universe:
> "Sir, I exist!"
> "However," replied the universe,
> "The fact has not created in me
> A sense of obligation."[18]

The first and most obvious interpretation of Homer's painting for art critics then has been as a universal statement on the human situation. The artist, the viewer, all of us, are adrift in the ocean without a sail, a rudder, or a companion. We are lost at sea in the modern world with as much hope of controlling our fearful destiny as this luckless mariner. Like *Jonah* and *Constance*, it will take Divine Providence to save us. In dismissing the picture, Roger Stein summarized this interpretation:

> *Gulf Stream* is a curious pessimistic melange of [Copley's] *Watson and the Shark* and [Allston's] *The Rising of a Thunderstorm at Sea*. The sharks, the dismasted boat, the lonely and exhausted black man, the bloody water, the distant spout to the right and ship to the left (so mechanically balanced) shout at us in the older romantic rhetoric about how much humans are at the mercy of the sublime.[19]

In this interpretation it is a universal fish story with a Caribbean setting, a precursor to *The Old Man and the Sea*. But like Hemingway's metaphorical tale of his old age, Homer's symbolic statement also lends itself to a very literal reading. Therefore, a second and almost opposite interpretation of *The Gulf Stream* sees it explicitly as a story about a man caught in a storm off Key West, just as Copley's *Watson and the Shark*, America's first dramatic current events painting from 1778, dramatizes an incident in Havana Harbor. (Copley showed young Brooke Watson, who survived to become Lord Mayor of London, in the foreground and local landmarks, including Morro Castle, in the background.) Homer was no stranger to portraying anecdotes from life. After all, he had cut his artistic teeth as a wartime illustrator sketching Union army scenes, and more than once he recorded specific maritime disasters. At Tynemouth, England, in 1881 he had witnessed and sketched the wreck of the *Iron Cross* and later turned his sketch into a studio picture.[20] In 1903 he watched the tragic breakup of the schooner *Washington B. Thomas* on the rocky shore near his studio in Prout's Neck, Maine. Five years later the incident became *The Wrecked Schooner*, now in the St. Louis Museum. It is thought to be his final water color and one of his most powerful.[21]

Homer also knew tropical storms. He had, as he boasted, traversed the Gulf Stream ten times when he painted *Hurricane, Bahamas, 1898*. Earlier in the mid-1880s, when he first visited Key West, Cuba, and the Bahamas, he had recorded other tempests. His 1885 watercolor, *Tornado, Bahamas*, appeared as an engraving entitled *A Hurricane* in the *Century Magazine* of February 1887.[22] It was on these initial trips to the Caribbean (apparently in Cuba in 1885) that Homer first sketched the elements that would later figure in *The Gulf Stream*.[23] Between then and the time he composed the final picture in 1899, the artist easily could have heard some specific anecdote that sparked his imagination. In 1888 Lafcadio Hearn published a story in Homer's old magazine, *Harper's*, on a Gulf Coast hurricane, and in 1894 Joel Chandler Harris wrote a two-part illustrated report for *Scribner's*, entitled "The Devastation" and "The Relief," following the famous storm that ripped along the coast above Savannah in August 1893 and took from 3,000 to 6,000 lives in Charleston and the Sea Islands.[24] At Key West, a place Homer could claim to know "quite well," a whole fleet of small boats known as "wreckers" regularly put out in bad weather to assist larger ships caught in rough seas, and harrowing stories about the fate of such sloops and their crews must have been common.[25]

By this second interpretation, then, *The Gulf Stream* is a simple, if horrifying, anecdote underscoring the power of the ocean over all those who go to sea. Homer's first biographer, William Downes, called the picture "elaborately literary. . .frankly a story-telling piece of work."[26] The unusual focus upon a black man trapped in a powerful dilemma, rather than some simple or humorous problem, threw many white critics off balance. One expert spoke of the "sullen laziness" of the central figure; another saw him as "waiting apathetically." The art critic of the Indianapolis *News* wondered why the deck was not wetter and how the sailor kept himself from slipping off the listing hulk.[27]

The central figure and his story made prospective buyers anxious. They pressed Roland Knoedler, Homer's New York dealer, to ask the artist for more details about the figure and what became of him. In 1902 the taciturn and ironic Homer responded in his best deadpan, down-east style:

You ask me for a full description of my picture of the "Gulf Stream." I regret very much that I have painted a picture that requires any description. The subject of this picture is comprised in *its title* & I refer these inquisitive schoolmam'ms to Lieut Maury. I have crossed the Gulf Stream ten times & I should know something about it. The boat & sharks are outside matters of very little consequence. *They have been blown out to sea by a hurricane.* You can tell these ladies that the unfortunate negro who now is so dazed & parboiled, will be rescued & returned to his friends and home, & ever after live happily.[28]

At least one critic has taken Homer's sardonic description of *The Gulf Stream* at face value and claims that this passage suggests Homer "quite frankly didn't give a damn what happened to the dazed and parboiled man."[29] Did Homer give a damn about this Negro, or about blacks generally? I believe that he did, and I believe that an understanding of where his sympathies lay opens up an obvious but unrecognized interpretation of this painting. *The Gulf Stream*, besides serving as an anecdotal rendering of a Key West sailing accident and a universal statement about the human dilemma, can be interpreted as a rich portrayal of both the historical and the contemporary situation of blacks in Homer's America.

There is little in Homer's life to contradict this approach, and much to support it. Born in antislavery Boston in 1836, he was named for the minister who succeeded Lyman Beecher.[30] In May of 1856, while still a lithography apprentice, he executed the one overtly political picture of his career—a half cartoon, half re-creation of the caning of Massachusetts Senator Charles Sumner by Representative Preston Brooks of South Carolina. Perhaps significantly, the young Homer used a quotation from Henry Ward Beecher across the top: "THE SYMBOL OF THE NORTH IS THE PEN; THE SYMBOL OF THE SOUTH IS THE BLUDGEON."[31]

Late in 1859, about the time that John Brown was hanged for his raid on the arsenal at Harper's Ferry, Homer became an illustrator for *Harper's Weekly*. His reaction to the incident is unknown, but another dramatic event occurred several months later that hardly could have escaped his attention. In the spring of 1860 the bark *Wildfire* with 510 enslaved Africans aboard from the Congo river was captured in the Gulf Stream off Cuba and brought into Key West, Florida, for violation of the 1809 law prohibiting the further importation of slaves. The incident was a stark public reminder of both the plight of the Afro-American and the political state of the nation. On June 2, *Harper's* covered the story and ran an engraving entitled *The Africans of the Slave Bark, "Wildfire,"* which was based upon a daguerreotype made aboard the ship.[32]

This startling image, linking blacks on shipboard in the Gulf Stream off Key West with the "middle passage" of previous generations and the impending breakup of the union, may or may not have made a conscious impression on Homer at the time. But later in the year events came unavoidably close to home. On December 3, 1860, a year and a day after John Brown's death, the black abolitionist Frederick Douglass joined others in calling for "a dissolution of the union" at a rally in Boston. "I shall be glad of the news, come when it will, that the slave States are an independent government," he told the audience. "In case of such a dissolution, I believe that men could be found . . . who would venture into those States and raise the standard of liberty there." An early Homer engraving for *Harper's*, entitled *The Expulsion of Negroes and Abolitionists from Tremont Temple, Boston, Massachusetts, on December 3, 1860*, depicts a black orator, not unsympathetically portrayed, as the central figure.[33]

Ten years and an entire Civil War later, when Homer summarized the decade for *Harper's* in a circular montage entitled *1860-1870*, he passed over Lee's surrender and Lincoln's death as obvious midpoints for the eventful decade and placed the Emancipation Proclamation in the place of highest honor. At the lower right he introduced the positive theme of integrated education, which was continued through his hopeful images of adolescence and growth that were painted before the demise of Reconstruction.

In the decade after the war numerous artists rediscovered, rather predictably, the small and innocent pleasures of childhood in America, and Homer was more engaging and less saccharine than most in his invocation of barefoot children inside and outside the classroom, as *The Country School* (1871) and *Snap the Whip* (1873) well illustrate. But Homer, more than his contemporaries, included blacks in his paintings of youthful discovery. Even when they appeared in such stereotyped scenes as in the 1875 paintings, *The Watermelon Boys, Contraband*, and *A Sunflower for the Teacher*, they preserved a confidence, individuality, and seriousness that was unusual for Negro images of the time.

Consider the subject, tone, and implications of *Weaning the Calf*, another rural scene painted in 1875. The calf, which is being drawn into the foreground away from its mother, is linked to a young Negro boy, still in the shadows, who seems to be holding his own before skeptical white onlookers. Weaning from old ways is difficult and awkward, but it is also logical, necessary, and possible. In 1875 there is still hope that newly freed blacks, like newly weaned calves, will be able to stand on their own.

Two years later things looked very different, as a careful examination of *The Carnival*, completed in 1877, will reveal. Though often described by critics as a carefree holiday scene, this ambiguous picture is best understood through its full title, *Dressing for the Carnival*. In contrast to the alert youths eyeing the horizon, paying attention to their teachers, or testing their strength against a heifer, the central figure here is a more mature but less natural and independent man who casts his eyes downward while two thoughtful older women—as solid, knowing, and classical as Homer's later fishing women—stitch him into his holiday costume with as much seriousness as if they were weaving his shroud. He may be proud of his bright garment, but it is uncertain exactly why he is "dressing like a clown" and why the children, while impressed and fascinated, are hardly filled with glee.

One explanation for the picture, which has never been offered so far as I know, is that it symbolizes, consciously or unconsciously, the end of Reconstruction. Since one boy holds an American flag and since the picture derives from Homer's return to the South (Petersburg, Virginia) in 1876, some scholars have surmised that it illustrates the Fourth of July celebration of the centennial year. But blacks in the South had little to celebrate. On that Fourth of July Negroes, parading in Hamburg, South Carolina, dressed proudly in their official uniforms as militiamen and postal employees only to be harassed by whites. Several days later a number were killed in the nationally publicized Hamburg Massacre. The ugly incident set the tone for the notorious Red Shirt Campaign that culminated in the November election of the Confederate "redeemer," Wade Hampton, as South Carolina's governor. The national election that same fall ended in the fateful Hayes-Tilden compromise, which brought the withdrawal of federal troops from the South and the end of the hopeful Reconstruction years for blacks in the region. From 1877 onward they would find themselves increasingly segregated and cut off, forced to fulfill the roles of clowns and minstrels when they paraded in public. In this light, the bright costume, the strong women, the watchful children, and the closed gate all take on added meaning.

In charting Homer's development as an artist, biographers have often stressed his visit to Tynemouth on the North Sea in 1881-1882 as the turning point that inspired the images of robust women with their baskets and coastal sailors in their oilskins that reoccur in later seascapes. But the shift away from the distinctive Homer girls of *Harper's* toward stronger, more patient, and hardworking women began in the mid-1870s, as did experiments with watercolors (his mother's medium) in which he later proved imaginative and gifted. While Homer's impressive pictures from the 1870s, such as *A Visit From the Old Mistress* (1876), often echo in composition some of his best work from the 1860s, such as *Prisoners from the Front* (1866), they also revive with greater subtlety some of his earlier themes concerning blacks. The artist ruminates again with increased ambiguity and solemnity (and sympathy that borders occasionally on sentimentality) on such matters as labor—*Cotton Pickers* (1876)—and education—*Sunday Morning in Virginia* (1877).[34]

Suffice it to say that Negroes, like women, children and mariners, received recurrent and sensitive treatment in Homer's work. I do not wish to claim that his numerous paintings of blacks (patronizingly and misleadingly described as "Negro genre scenes") were *consciously* designed as direct statements on the Afro-American condition, but, like that somewhat older American, Herman Melville (whose important literary works were scarcely known), Homer had the ability to empathize with the black experience, to see its centrality to the American drama, and to translate it into rich and enigmatic images and stories. As with Melville, this trait confused and dismayed his white audience, a fact that bred in the artist an increasing disdain and hostility toward an obtuse public. The very fact that such a subconscious sensitivity in Homer has been minimized or denied by most of his critics makes it worthwhile to examine *The Gulf Stream* as something larger than a sailing accident and more specific than the plight of mankind.

In discussing this well-known but little understood picture from a cultural and historical perspective, it would be possible to dwell at length on the small details that are often overlooked or misinterpreted: the rope that binds the man to his boat; the title "Anne—Key West" on the rudderless stern; the flecks of red in the water; the scarcely visible flying fish that absorb the man's attention as they skim the water beside the boat like so many souls ascending to heaven. In this discussion, however, I shall focus on two important foreground elements—the unobtrusive sugar and the overpowering sharks.

The long stalks of sugar cane that rise out of the dark hold and trail down into the shark-filled waters make up one of the central, but least observed elements of the picture. Sugar cane was a common sight aboard small boats in the Gulf Stream, both as a cargo and a source of nourishment, and Homer observed it on his first trip to the tropics. Stalks of cane appear in several of his watercolors from the 1880s, such as *Sea Garden, Bahamas* (1885) and *The Gulf Stream* (1889), where the elements— still unrelated—of shark, sailor and possible storm make their tentative appearance. In Homer's *Study for the Gulf Stream* painted a decade later, the color and pattern of the cane stalks on the sloping deck prefigure the final painting almost exactly.[35]

No word has a deeper resonance in the black past than "cane." The Portuguese introduced cane from Madeira to São Tomé in 1485, and plantations on these Atlantic Islands were exporting sugar to Antwerp by the time Columbus sailed west. Once profit-seeking planters had established sugar cane in Brazil and the West Indies, their system sucked workers out of Africa voraciously and sealed their fate in the New World. The crop that enslaved Africans could also sustain them—the drifting sailor is undoubtedly chewing cane to stay alive.[36] For centuries the dark brown juice of the cane was refined into white, cone-shaped sugarloaves for export to Europe, while the thick molasses was distilled into rum for export to Africa, where it was used in the purchase of more slaves to grow more sugar.

Young Phillis Wheatley (1753-1784), brought from Africa in 1761 at the age of eight and sold to a Boston merchant named John Wheatley, was in a position to observe this English alchemy firsthand. Mastering the art of poetry and sensing the dynamics of racism at an early age, she became the first of many Afro-American writers to link cane in the fields with Cain in the Bible:

> Some view our sable race with scornful eye,
> "Their color is a diabolic die."
> Remember, *Christians, Negroes,* black as *Cain,*
> May be refined, and join th' angelic train.[37]

In Genesis, chapter 4, Cain offers up the fruit of the earth, is rejected by God, and marked to be "a fugitive and a vagabond in the earth." The echo of his name raises up the question from verse 20: "Am I my brother's keeper?" No wonder the black writer, Jean Toomer, used *Cane* as the title for his collection of stories about the pain and tribulation of Negro life in the South.[38]

Sharks, too, have special connotations for Afro-Americans. Homer, who throughout his career reversed images of hunter and hunted, linked a black man with the dangerous fish in his watercolor entitled *Shark Fishing,* which probably was painted in Nassau in the mid-1880s. The picture, which also appeared as a woodcut in *The Century Magazine* in February 1887, uses the same portrayal of a shark that appears in the 1889 watercolor of *The Gulf Stream.* Mrs. Septima P. Clark, the distinguished South Carolina educator, born in Charleston in 1898, told me recently that she could recall from her childhood the cry of the fishmen on Saturdays: "Shark steak don't need no gravy."[39] The tables could be turned; the ancestors of those who dined on shark steak had often themselves, in the parlance of the slave trade, been made into "shark bait." The expression "to be thrown to the sharks" had its origins in the gruesome practices of the Middle Passage.

In 1693, as the English slave trade underwent rapid expansion, Captain Thomas Phillips reported sharks devouring blacks who jumped overboard in African waters:

> We have . . . seen divers of them eaten by the sharks, of which a prodigious number kept about the ships in this place, and I have been told will follow her hence to Barbadoes, for the dead negroes that are thrown over-board in the passage. I am certain in our voyage there we did not want the sight of some every day, but that they were the same I can't affirm.[40]

Another slave trader, setting out from West Africa for Antigua in 1714, reported,

We caught a great many fish in ye passage, especially Sharks. Our way to entice them was by Towing overboard a dead Negro, which they would follow till they had eaten him up. They are good victuals if well dress'd, tho' some won't eat them, because they fed upon men; ye Negros fed very heartily upon them, which made us salt up several of them to save ye Ship's provision.[41]

In the entire diaspora of the Atlantic slave trade over four centuries, more than 12 million persons were thrown into the maw of the voracious New World plantation system, but several million dead or dying Africans were also thrown overboard in the course of the Middle Passage. Devouring sharks, like hungry slave buyers, are key elements in the initial chapters of Afro-American history, and this powerful image of Africans caught between the devil and the deep blue sea was not lost on American artists. In *Moby Dick* Melville describes how the *Pequot*'s old black cook, Fleece, in preaching a mock sermon to the sharks at the insistence of Stubb, addresses them ironically as "Cussed fellow-critters!" and exhorts them to "Kick up de damnest row as ever you can." As Stubb devours whale meat and mocks the cook, Fleece departs muttering, "Wish by gor! Whale eat Stubb, 'stead of him eat whale. I'm bressed if he ain't more of a shark dan Massa shark hisself."[42] Homer, like Melville, was sensitive to the powerful historic links between shipboard blacks and Atlantic sharks in ways that modern critics may not be, and in his case it is possible to trace at least one line of artistic descent through which he inherited this telling image. The lineage is worth tracing in brief detail.

In 1732 a popular English travel anthology published Barbot's "Description of the Coasts of North and South Guinea" with a vivid description of the shark:

It swims incredibly swift, and great multitudes of them usually follow our slave-ships some hundred leagues at sea, as they sail out from the gulph of Guinea; as if they knew we were to throw some dead corps over board almost every day.

If a man happens to fall over-board, and these monsters are at hand, they soon make him their prey; and I have often observ'd, that when we threw a dead slave into the sea . . . one shark would bite off a leg, and another an arm, whilst others sunk down with the body.[43]

This passage was the direct inspiration for the poet James Thompson in 1744, when he introduced into the second edition of his phenomenally popular epic, *The Seasons*, a lurid scene with sharks, Africans, and a "circling typhon."[44] Thompson's image of the shark, "Lur'd by the Scent / Of steaming Crouds [sic], of rank Disease, and Death," was aggrandized by the international movement to abolish the slave trade. It was given notorious confirmation in 1783 when Captain Collingwood of the slave ship *Zong*, faced with an epidemic and an impending storm, threw all the sick Africans overboard, since he could claim insurance for slaves lost at sea but not for those dying of disease.

In 1840, moved by new publications of this story and recollections of Thompson's famous poem as well as recent debates over ending race slavery in British dominions, the English artist J. M. W. Turner created one of his most awesome seascapes: *Slavers Throwing Overboard the Dead and Dying—Typhoon Coming On,* or more simply, *The Slave Ship.*[45] "Is this picture sublime or ridiculous?" asked the awed William Thackeray. "Indeed I don't know which." "I believe," wrote John Ruskin in *Modern Painters,* "if I were reduced to rest Turner's immortality upon any single work, I should choose this." The picture's style prompted eloquent commentary and rich debate. "So great was the controversy over the merits of Turner's manner," writes one cultural historian, "that almost no attention was given to the subject-matter."[46] Thackeray called it "the most tremendous piece of colour that ever was seen," and Ruskin, whose father bought the picture for him as a gift, effused over "the power, majesty, and deathfulness of the open, deep illimitable sea!" As recently as the 1970s an introduction to *The Slave Ship* explained, "The focal point of the heroic seascape is not the ship but the setting sun, and the overriding drama is the symphonic display of sky and sea, not the account of man's bestiality."[47]

Whatever the seascape's true focal point, Ruskin eventually found the picture "too painful to live with." In selling it he set in motion the dealings that would eventually take the painting on a middle passage of its own across the Atlantic to a port much like London for its powerfully entwined traditions of slave trading and abolitionism. In the late 1890s Turner's painting was on loan to the Museum of Fine Arts in Homer's hometown, and in 1899 Boston purchased the picture with considerable fanfare through the Henry Lillie Pierce Fund. When William Morris Hunt, the prominent Boston architect, was asked whether the picture was worth $10,000, he replied, "Well, I see a good many ten thousands lying about, but only one *Slave Ship!*"[48]

In 1899 the Museum of Fine Arts (which had purchased *The Fog Warning* five years earlier) bought Homer's *All's Well* and four of his watercolors, including *Leaping Trout,* but there were no "ten thousands" lying about for the American artist. Although he lived comfortably and earned more than most of his contemporaries, he still felt undercompensated for his painstaking studies, which he considered "quite different from posing a successful lawyer in one's studio light & rattling him off in a week's time to the tune of $3,000." When the prominent dealer-collector Thomas B. Clarke sold 372 American paintings at a four-day sale in 1899, the average price was only $630, and 30 pictures by Winslow Homer brought only $22,345, or an average of $745. "Find out if possible," he wrote his New York dealers the following year, "if there is any market value to anything I can do."[49]

The Gulf Stream went unsold for seven years before the Metropolitan bought the picture, so commercial success, though a steady concern, hardly would seem to have been Homer's primary motive, whatever the publicity surrounding the Turner purchase. At some level a competitive sense of professional pride, both individual and national, may have stirred America's foremost seascape painter to undertake an updated, New World interpretation of the old romantic theme of African facing shark in the stormy Atlantic. At another level, there must also have been purely personal concerns involved. The sixty-three-year-old artist's forceful and aged father had died the preceding year, and Homer had not painted in oil for eighteen months before beginning *The Gulf Stream*. It is hard to measure the degree of personal grief and artistic release that his father's death brought to the constrained New England painter, but there may have been considerable subconscious identification with the isolated sailor who has survived a sudden storm and is now adrift in familiar but dangerous waters.[50]

A further level of meaning and explanation exists on the horizon of Homer's consciousness and the painting itself. In the distance, oblivious of the black man's condition, a merchant vessel presses on under full sail, reminiscent of the emblematic ships that pass by the *Pequot* in Melville's *Moby Dick*. Can the captain see, as we can, that he is heading straight for a Caribbean storm? And what is that storm? In a subsequent essay I shall suggest that it has to do with the Cuban independence movement, which Teddy Roosevelt and his Rough Riders turned into a splendid little imperialist war. If true, that might explain why the black sailor's expression is quizzical, perhaps even hopeful.

Notes

1. See, for example, Theodore Géricault's *Portrait of a Negro* on Peter H. Wood, *Black Majority: Negroes in Colonial South Carolina from 1670 through the Stono Rebellion* (New York, 1974), or John Singleton Copley's *Head of a Negro* on Jeffrey J. Crow, *The Black Experience in Revolutionary North Carolina* (Raleigh, 1977), or the separate pictures on the hardbound and paperback editions of Leon F. Litwack, *Been in the Storm So Long: The Aftermath of Slavery* (New York, 1979). Examining the covers of books on slavery from *Uncle Tom's Cabin* to the present reveals a good deal about authors and publishers, as well as their public. The use of first-rate paintings—as opposed to racist woodcuts, links of chain, or simple black ink—is recent and hinges on more than refinements in the art of printing.

2. Karen M. Adams, "Black Images in Nineteenth-Century American Painting and Literature: An Iconological Study of Mount, Melville, Homer and Mark Twain" (Ph.D. diss., Emory University, 1977); Michael Quick, "Homer in Vir-

ginia," *L. A. County Museum of Art Bulletin* 24 (1978): 60-81; Mary Ann Calo, "Winslow Homer's Visits to Virginia During Reconstruction," *American Art Journal* 12 (Winter 1980): 4-27. See also Sidney Kaplan, "The Negro in the Art of Homer and Eakins," *Massachusetts Review* 7 (Winter 1966): 105-20, which is based upon notes for the catalogue of an exhibition at the Bowdoin College Museum of Art in Brunswick, Maine, during the summer of 1964 entitled "The Portrayal of the Negro in American Painting, 1710-1963." See Gordon Hendricks, *The Life and Work of Winslow Homer* (New York, 1979), p. 50 for a reproduction of *Shackled Slave* and for most of the other Homer pictures cited here.

3. *The Gulf Stream* is reproduced in color with widely varying degrees of accuracy in most general studies of Homer and many other places. From among hundreds of works created over Homer's long career, only *Eight Bells* has been published with approximately the same frequency. See Melinda Dempter Davis, *Winslow Homer: An Annotated Bibliography of Periodical Literature* (Metuchen, N.J., 1975), pp. 73-74, 82-83.

4. Quoted in Kaplan, "The Negro in the Art of Homer and Eakins," p. 112.

5. Lloyd Goodrich, *Winslow Homer* (New York, 1944), pp. 162, 187. William Howe Downes, *The Life and Works of Winslow Homer* (Boston, 1911), p. 135.

6. Kenyon Cox, "Three Pictures by Winslow Homer in the Metropolitan Museum," *The Burlington Magazine* (London), November 1907. As a competitive younger artist, Cox was frequently begrudging and ambiguous in his praise for Homer:

The tubby boat has been objected to by experts in marine architecture, and the figure of the negro is by no means faultless in its draughtsmanship. . . . But these things scarcely obscure the dramatic force of the composition, which renders it one of the most powerful pictures Homer ever painted. Nor is it merely a piece of illustration.

7. Goodrich, *Homer*, p. 161.

8. Cox, "Three Pictures." Other reviews by Cox, "Homer's perennial critic," appeared in the *Nation* and the New York *World*; see Philip C. Beam, *Winslow Homer at Prout's Neck* (Boston, 1966), p. 171.

9. Isabel Hoopes, "The Story of a Picture," *The Mentor*, August 1929, p. 34. This brief, popular commentary, written a generation later, borrows unashamedly from Cox and Downes:

Homer is often lacking in technic, but his painting of the motion of the boat—its helpless sliding into the troughs of the waves—is remarkable. Powerful too is the painting of the moisture-laden air, and of the blue sea with its ruddy flecks and white spray. The hungry sharks which dart and turn around the small craft form a contrast with the sullen laziness of the ill-fated mariner, and the distant ship that cannot possibly see its fellow in distress accentuate the drama of the situation. Like most of the oil paintings by this artist, "The Gulf Stream" is not a drawing-room subject.

10. Beam, *Prout's Neck*, p. 170.

11. Downes, *Life*, p. 135.

12. Beam, *Prout's Neck*, pp. 170-71. It is interesting to note how many of Homer's pictures have had their titles altered over time. Sometimes this is a result of honest confusion, for the artist was often cryptic or careless in this

regard. At other times, especially with paintings including blacks, Homer's own title seems to have been too stark or revealing for the sensibilities of curators, patrons, or public. A case in point is the Newark Museum's *At the Cabin Door* (1865-66). The full-length study of a thoughtful young Negro woman in apron and bandanna, looking from a doorway toward passing Confederate soldiers and their captives, takes on added meaning with its original title, *Captured Liberators*. Similarly, the title for a picture of an old black man and several children beside a dove cote, painted in Virginia in 1875, evolved from *The Dove Cote* to *Uncle Ned at Home*, to *Uncle Ned's Happy Family*, to *A Happy Family in Virginia*. The masterfully ambiguous picture from the following year, *Preparing for the Carnival* (or *Dressing for the Carnival*), loses much of its potential meaning when referred to as *The Fourth of July* or *The Carnival*.

13. Barbara Novak, *American Painting of the Nineteenth Century* (New York, 1969), p. 187.

14. Roger B. Stein, *Seascape and the American Imagination* (New York, 1975), p. 112.

15. John Berger, *Ways of Seeing* (London, 1972), pp. 15-16. Berger, an experienced art critic, concedes that the "compositional unity of a painting contributes fundamentally to the power of its image," but he rightly disparages commentary in which "composition is written about as though it were in itself the emotional charge of the painting." Such discussions, Berger contends, "transfer the emotion provoked by the image from the plane of lived experience, to that of disinterested 'art appreciation.' All conflict disappears. One is left," he protests, "with the unchanging 'human condition,' and the painting considered as a marvelously made object" (p. 13).

16. "Tragedy and Apocalypse" is the apt title of a chapter on late nineteenth-century American sea pictures in Stein, *Seascape*. See also Wallace S. Baldinger, "The Art of Eakins, Homer and Ryder: A Social Re-evaluation," *Art Quarterly* 9 (Summer 1946): 212-33. Though he does not refer to *The Gulf Stream*, Baldinger explores works of literature to show "a mind divided against itself, noted as the prevailing state in American society at the turn of the century," and finds a "visual counterpart to the state of nervous indecision . . . in both the subject and the form" of several paintings. He summarizes the fin-de-siècle malaise in words that suit Homer's picture: "Things were probably not exactly what they seemed, but who could tell just what they were or where they were drifting" (p. 233). (Incidentally, the noun "drift," which applies in nautical terms to *The Gulf Stream*, also became a popular word for social and political commentary after 1900, as in Walter Lippman's *Drift and Mastery*.)

17. Geoffrey Chaucer, "The Man of Law's Tale," *The Canterbury Tales*. Both the passage and the picture are reprinted in Corcoran Gallery of Art, *Albert Pinkham Ryder* (Washington, 1961), frontispiece and p. 42.

18. Reprinted in Stein, *Seascape*, pp. 111-12. Writing critically and suggestively about Homer's earlier painting, *The Life Line*, Stein concludes: "This chilling sense of the vast indifference of the universe to the human condition prompted both Homer and Crane into gestures of aesthetic assertiveness, to use form as a defensive ironic strategy. The aesthetic structure, the formal ordering of images on the canvas, gives what life and God and the universe withhold from man and woman" (pp. 111-12).

19. Ibid., p. 112. Both Copley's 1778 picture and Allston's 1804 painting were in the Boston Museum of Fine Arts and would have been familiar to Homer.

20. Hendricks, *Life and Work*, p. 151. Commenting on *The Wreck of the Iron Cross* (1881), Hendricks observes, somewhat gratuitously: "Homer also produced, in the studio, a turgid picture based on this *Iron Cross* disaster, proving again that reportorial pictures were not his forte."

21. Ibid., pp. 256, 258.

22. Patti Hannaway, *Winslow Homer in the Tropics* Richmond, 1973), pp. 148-49.

23. Ibid., pp. 156-69. Hannaway's book (which is totally without footnoted documentation) misdates *The Gulf Stream* as 1889 (p. 169).

24. Joel Chandler Harris, "The Sea Island Hurricanes," *Scribner's Magazine* 15 (February 1894): 229-47; 15 (March 1894): 267-84. One of the pictures by Daniel Smith entitled *Left by the Tide* (p. 236) compares to Homer's later *After the Tornado, Bahamas* (1899) in both subject and tone.

25. Hannaway, *Tropics*, pp. 261-69.

26. Downes, *Life*, p. 133. In *Seascapes* (p. 112), Roger Stein writes: "What Homer had learned in his finest work, including the moving little related watercolor, *After the Tornado*, of the same year, was to translate his sense of the sublime into radically simple, even stark, tragic pictorial statements of the brute power and force of the sea."

27. Beam, *Prout's Neck*, pp. 172-73. See also note 9.

28. Goodrich, *Homer*, p. 162. Matthew Maury, the father of American oceanography, was the author of an early study of the Gulf Stream in the mid-nineteenth century. Beam, *Prout's Neck*, p. 172, states (without citation) that when a dealer passed along comments about the "horror" of Homer's subject, the artist replied caustically:

The criticisms of the Gulf Stream by old women and others are noted. You may inform these people that the Negro did not starve to death. He was not eaten by the sharks. The waterspout did not hit him. And he was rescued by a passing ship which is not shown in the picture.

Yours truly,
Winslow Homer

As he became older Homer, like Melville, became increasingly callous toward literal-minded and sentimental artistic consumers. In 1900 he had written Knoedler about another work, "If you want more sentiment put into this picture I can with one or two touches—in five minutes time—give it the stomach ache that will suit any customer." Later he would throw up his hands and write, "What is the use? The people are too stupid. They do not understand." Goodrich, *Homer*, p. 226.

29. See the suggestive review by John Seelye of John Wilmerding's *Winslow Homer*, in *The New Republic*, 20 January 1973, pp. 27-29.

30. Hendricks, *Life and Works*, pp. 12-13. Dr. Hubbard Winslow was the popular Congregational minister at the Bowdoin Street Church, where Homer's parents were members from 1832 until 1844. One of Homer's later friends, Hubbard Winslow Bryant, was also named for the preacher. On the close affinity

between artistic New England women and their ministers in this era, see Ann Douglas, *The Feminization of American Culture* (New York, 1977).

31. David Tatham, "Winslow Homer's 'Arguments of the Chivalry,' " *American Art Journal* 5 (1973): 86-89. I am indebted to Harlan Joel Gradin for this reference.

32. Dena J. Epstein, *Sinful Tunes and Spirituals* (Urbana, 1977), pp. 11, 14; W.E.B. Du Bois, *The Suppression of the African Slave Trade in America, 1638-1870* (Cambridge, 1896), pp. 191 n, 298. *Harper's Weekly* 4 (June 2, 1860): 344, reported the sickly condition of many "passengers" and noted that the "well ones" engaged in "monotonous" songs with "words we did not understand."

33. James M. McPherson, *The Negro's Civil War* (New York, 1965), pp. 12-13. See Barbara Gelman, *The Wood Engravings of Winslow Homer* (New York, 1969), for this and other engravings. For a description of Boston abolitionist meetings by a Cambridge contemporary of Homer's, see Thomas Wentworth Higginson, *Part of a Man's Life* (Boston, 1905), pp. 17-21: "Nowhere in all the modern world could have been seen more strikingly grouped the various dramatis personae of a great impending social change than on the platform of some large hall, filled with Abolitionists. . . ."

34. See also works in note 2.

35. Hannaway, *Tropics*, plates 10, 13, 12. Hannaway dates *Study for the Gulf Stream* 1885-86 (p. 165), but Hendricks, *Life and Works* is undoubtedly correct to list 1898-99 (p. 313), for Homer wrote a friend in September, 1899, "I painted in water colors three months last winter at Nassau, & have now just commenced arranging a picture from some of the studies." Goodrich, *Homer*, pp. 161-62.

36. Sidney M. Greenfield, "Plantations, Sugar Cane and Slavery," in "Roots and Branches: Current Directions in Slave Studies," ed. Michael Craton, *Historical Reflections* 6 (Summer 1979): 115-16. Films concerning blacks in the New World have often made powerful use of the sugar cane image, as in *Plantation Boy, Burn!* and *Sounder*.

37. Sidney Kaplan, *The Black Presence in the Era of the American Revolution, 1770-1800* (Washington, 1973), p. 153. This is the last half of an eight-line elegy, "On Being brought from Africa to America," written by young Wheatley in the late 1760s. Since brown sugar is "refined" to white, she uses this color imagery for purification, conversion, and cultural loyalty in ways that intimate Rudyard Kipling's dark-skinned creation at the end of the nineteenth century, Gunga Din, who was "white, pure white inside."

38. Roger Rosenblatt observes in *Black Fiction* (Cambridge, 1974), pp. 54, 63, "*Cane* is about the search for roots, and about the penalties a people suffers by being uprooted. . . . The title refers to the idea of support as well. All of the characters in *Cane* vainly seek a cane or something to lean on. But there may be a deeper pun here, too. Cain and Abel were the sons of Eve, equal at their births except that by divine caprice or mystery Cain was automatically rejected by God and Abel was the favored boy."

In black lore, sugar (both brown and white) is alternately the staff of life and the root of evil. In the Sea Islands and elsewhere babies taken into the fields by working mothers were weaned on a "sugar-tit," a cloth sweetened with sugar. Vocalist Bessy Smith used to sing a suggestive song entitled, "Put a Little Sugar in My Bowl."

39. Interview for a book concerning important persons connected with the Highlander Folk School in Tennessee, to be edited by Eliot Wigginton.

40. George Francis Dow, *Slave Ships and Slaving* (1927; reprint ed., Cambridge, Md., 1968), p. 71 (see also pp. 11, 262).

41. "Narrative of a Voyage from London to the West Indies, 1714-1715," Add. 39946, p. 12, British Museum. I am indebted to my colleague Barry Gaspar for this reference.

42. Herman Melville, *Moby Dick*, ed. Harrison Hayford and Hershel Parker (New York, 1967), pp. 252-54. See also Edward S. Grejda, *The Common Continent of Men: Racial Equality in the Writings of Herman Melville* (Port Washington, N.Y., 1974), pp. 103-107, and Adams, "Black Images" pp. 84-85.

43. Awnsham and John Churchill, *Collection of Voyages and Travels*, 5 vols. (London, 1732), 5: 225-26.

44. James Thompson, "Disasters in Tropical Seas," *The Seasons*, rev. ed. (London, 1744), p. 97, ll. 1002-14:

> Increasing still the Terrors of these Storms,
> His Jaws horrific arm'd with threefold Fate,
> Here dwells the direful Shark. Lur'd by the Scent
> Of steaming Crouds, of rank Disease, and Death,
> Behold! he rushing cuts the briny Flood,
> Swift as the Gale can bear the Ship along;
> And, from the Partners of that cruel Trade,
> Which spoils unhappy *Guinea* of her Sons,
> Demands his share of Prey, demands themselves.
> The stormy Fates descend: one Death involves
> Tyrants and Slaves; when strait, their mangled Limbs
> Crashing at once, he dyes the purple Seas
> With Gore, and riots in the vengeful Meal.

For the link to Barbot's description in Churchill, see Alan Dugald McKillop, *The Background of Thompson's Seasons* (Minneapolis, 1942), pp. 129, 165.

45. Jack Lindsay, *J.M.W. Turner: His Life and Work* (Greenwich, 1966), pp. 189-90. "It was characteristic of Turner that he should find a great aesthetic release through an image which concentrated his social thinking and at the same time was deeply embedded in the poetic tradition he so loved." See also p. 247, note 22: "In youth Turner planned an apocalyptic *Water Turn'd to Blood*."

46. Chauncey Brewster Tinker, *Painter and Poet: Studies in the Literary Relations of English Painting* (Cambridge, 1938), p. 151. As with Homer's *Gulf Stream*, it might be equally true to state that so great was the anxiety over the subject matter of the painting that almost all attention was given to the controversy over the merits of the artist's manner.

47. Adolph S. Cavallo, ed., *Museum of Fine Arts Boston: Western Art* (Greenwich, 1971), p. 202. For Thackeray, writing as Michael Angelo Titmarsh, see *Fraser's Magazine*, June 1840; for Ruskin see Ruskin, *Modern Painters* 5 vols. (London, 1843), 1: 571-73.

48. Julia deWolf Addison, *The Boston Museum of Fine Arts* (Boston, 1910), pp. 85-86. Five figures were more than any American artist's work could command;

the Metropolitan bought George Inness's *Delaware Valley* for $8,100 that same year. The Turner purchase seemed even more extravagant because the Boston museum had just decided to move to a new site in 1899 and was collecting funds to pay for a twelve acre lot in the Fenway with frontage on Huntington Avenue, where the MFA now stands.

49. Gordon Hendricks, "The Flood Tide in the Winslow Homer Market," *Art News*, May 1973, pp. 69-71. Clarke, who had purchased *Eight Bells* for $400, sold it in the 1899 sale for $4,700. Other Homer paintings sold there included *Watching the Tempest* ($370), *Coast in Winter* ($2,725), *The Lookout* ($3,200), and *The Life Line* ($4,500).

50. No one to my knowledge has yet attempted a thoughtful psychobiography of Winslow Homer. Logical starting points would seem to be provided by the personal sketches, half-a-century apart, reprinted in Hendricks, *Homer*, pp. 19, 236. I hope to address this topic in a subsequent essay.

CLASS

Each of the five essays in this section discusses the nature of southern society and its class structure. The authors offer perspectives on the "dominant class," those who served it, the antagonisms within it, and the way in which the society helped to shape the careers of a black class of professionals.

Professor George M. Fredrickson begins his article by tracing the long debate over the nature of southern society. Some historians have seen it as an essentially aristocratic society, others have labeled it as democratic, and still others have argued that the South embraced both. Fredrickson sees a growing tension between aristocracy and democracy in the society of the pre-Civil War South. He concludes that the dominant class who were determined to maintain control in the pre- and postwar South did so by using democratic forms while appealing to a *Herrenvolk* democracy.

In the second essay Jack P. Maddex, Jr., argues that Southern Presbyterian churchmen in their ministries to slaves served the interests of the Old South's "dominant class." While they stressed the moral responsibilities of the "master class" to their slaves with missionary zeal, these same churchmen hoped to ameliorate the "peculiar institution," promote the proslavery cause, and win the world's approval of the region's social order. Emancipation disrupted their missionary efforts and ended the class system they served. "The old class rationale," Maddex concludes, "left southern white Christians no guidance for their relations with the freedmen of the postbellum South."

While the interests of the Old South's "master class"

were served by many, there were occasional individuals, themselves members of the "dominant class," whose actions and words threatened to subvert the established social order. Professor Blake McNulty has discovered one of these rare individuals in the extraordinary career of South Carolinian William Henry Brisbane, whose odyssey took him from slaveholding to abolitionism. Feeling beseiged from without, members of the "master class" feared the apostate within. A man like Brisbane became their "very worst enemy."

Besides occasional antagonisms among members of the Old South's "dominant class," itself, Professor Ronald L. F. Davis finds that there was persistent "discontent" throughout most of the South's history between the planter or farmer and the merchant. Antagonism between them waxed and waned with the changing nature of the region's marketing system. In the decades following the Civil War, a legacy of "discontent" grew into an intense hostility. Davis believes, however, that only after studies are completed on the little-known activities of the colonial merchants can we comprehend the fierce antimerchant bias of the nineteenth-century planter.

Professor E. H. Beardsley's concluding essay in this section offers a pioneering examination of early twentieth-century southern black physicians, an elite class within the black community. While he shows that a few Negro doctors "compiled a record of achievement that was as selfless as it was extraordinary," his evidence suggests that many accepted the prevailing health and medical conditions, had little interest in professionalism, refused to attend those who could not pay, and "some consciously exploited their patients." Beardsley concludes that black physicians were the products of their professional education and the racist society in which they practiced.

6

ARISTOCRACY AND DEMOCRACY IN THE SOUTHERN TRADITION

George M. Fredrickson

In popular American mythology the southern tradition has been regarded as essentially aristocratic. The civilization and legacy of the Old
South have been viewed as great departures from the dominant national
patterns of democratic aspiration and achievement. Professional historians, however, have disagreed on the validity of this conventional image. In fact, from the start of the twentieth century to the present day,
there has been continuous debate over the nature of the "real" South
of historical record. Was it an aristocracy that sometimes put up a democratic façade or a democracy with some aristocratic pretenses?

This difference of opinion can be traced back to the pioneer southern
historians of the early twentieth century—William E. Dodd and Ulrich
B. Phillips. Dodd pursued the democratic theme and venerated Thomas
Jefferson as the archtypical southerner. The antebellum retreat from the
Jeffersonian ideal of yeoman democracy was for him an aberration, a
betrayal of basic southern values.[1] In contrast, Phillips identified una-
bashedly with the great planters and dedicated one of his earliest books
to "the dominant class of the South." His works on slavery and plantation life were based on the assumption that the large slaveholders
constituted a genuine patriarchy, a ruling elite that set the tone for
southern society in general. Phillips was so preoccupied with the substantial planters that he paid scant attention to the vast majority of
southern whites who owned no slaves at all or only a few.[2]

In the 1930s and 1940s historians of antebellum politics offered a new
perspective on the issue by showing that the Old South was not, in a
political sense at least, as undemocratic as previously supposed. Fletcher
Green and Charles Sydnor in particular demonstrated that the Jacksonian movement revolutionized southern public life by extending suffrage,
removing qualifications for office holding, increasing the number of electoral offices, and creating a congenial environment for the kind of competitive party politics that drew voters to the polls in great numbers.[3]
At the same time, Frank Owsley and his students attempted to alter the

stereotypical image of antebellum society by bringing the yeoman, rather than the planter, to the forefront of southern society. Although Owsley failed to prove that "plain folk" dominated the Old South economically and socially, he did verify the presence of a large "middle class" of backcountry yeomen whose ways of life and economic conditions did not conform to the "poor white" stereotypes.[4] The same basic point was made by the Dutch historian A.N.J. Den Hollander whose important book on "poor whites" has not been translated. In an essay published in English in 1935, Den Hollander concluded that nonslaveholding farmers as a class "were honest, proud, independent, had confidence in life, had desires and usually ambition, and in a measure were substantial. In their own eyes and those of others they were respectable citizens."[5] It is difficult to view such a population of self-respecting yeomen as passively submitting to aristocratic domination.

The new generation of southern historians who contributed to Charles Sellers' collection of essays, *The Southerner as American*, which appeared in 1960, also stressed the democratic side of the southern tradition. Most of the contributors concluded that southerners in their collective heart-of-hearts had always believed in the liberal-democratic values that were enshrined in the larger American culture. Apparent deviations, such as the militant defense of slavery, produced feelings of guilt rather than a true change of convictions. According to Professor Sellers, the secession movement itself can be explained as a neurotic attempt to resolve a painful state of ambivalence—the conflict between attachment to slavery and basic liberal attitudes.[6] One notable southern historian, however, demurred from the emerging consensus. In 1963, Francis Butler Simkins, an acknowledged conservative, denied that the South had a democratic soul and argued instead that aristocracy in one form or another was what most people south of the Potomac had always wanted. To his way of thinking, the democratic tendencies and affirmations that so impressed other historians were a mere "pose."[7]

Since the early 1960s, the notion that the South, or at least the Old South, could be subsumed under a liberal-democratic consensus has been severely challenged, particularly in the work of Eugene Genovese. Genovese's view of antebellum society as precapitalist and paternalistic necessarily entails an emphasis on the aristocratic aspect. As he wrote in *The Political Economy of Slavery*, "The planters commanded Southern politics and set the tone of social life. Theirs was an aristocratic, anti-bourgeois spirit with values and mores emphasizing family and status, a strong code of honor, and aspirations to luxury, ease, and accomplishment."[8] There is no room in Genovese's view for liberal guilt. According to Genovese's brand of Marxian analysis, this precapitalist ruling class derived its power and ideology from the institution of slavery. Under these circumstances, the hegemony of its aristocratic beliefs could not survive the Civil War and emancipation. Other recent works in a neo-Marxian vein have disputed this assumption of a one-to-one relationship between chattel servitude and an "aristocratic, anti-bourgeois spirit." Jonathan Wiener, for example, has argued that with the emergence of new methods of labor coercion, planter dominance and precapitalist attitudes persisted even into the New South era.[9]

Obviously, the debate over the southern tradition as essentially aristocratic or essentially democratic remains very much alive. While the neo-Marxists have apparently agreed among themselves that the antebellum South was an aristocratic society and have moved on to quarrel about the nature of class relationships in the New South,[10] other historians have examined more closely the ideologies and patterns of power and authority that prevailed among whites in the Old South. They have discovered what appears to be a stridently *democratic* ethos. In his provocative study of Alabama politics between 1800 and 1860, J. Mills Thornton conveys an image of Jacksonian democracy in full flower. Far from demonstrating the direct rule of the large planters and the prevalence of aristocratic values, his research reveals that the politicians were responsible to an electorate dominated by plain farmers. They were successful only to the extent that they could convince these voters that they were champions of liberty, equality, and personal independence for all white males. The "republican ideology" that sustained popular crusades against aristocratic privilege and concentrated power elsewhere in the nation during the Jacksonian period appears to have been alive and well also in the Old South.[11]

For the most part, historians who have found an aristocratic ethos and those who have emphasized democracy have talked past each other. The former have based their interpretations on unequal access to productive resources and the writings of conservative intellectuals, while the latter have focused on political behavior and popular ideology. It is possible, therefore, that both viewpoints are correct and at the same time misleading, since each illuminates only part of a complex or even contradictory reality. At least two historians have refused to take sides and have embraced a dualistic perspective. W. J. Cash in *The Mind of the South* (1941) saw clearly that aristocratic aspiration and democratic assertion were both intrinsic to the white southern mentality. One of his great insights was his suggestion that certain aristocratic values in the Old South, such as the defense of personal honor, were in effect democratized.[12] More recently, David Potter has provided an eloquent statement of the dualistic perspective in his essay "The Nature of Southernism." According to Potter:

The South has been democratic as well as aristocratic, fond of "flush times" and booms as well as tradition; it has lusted for prosperity, bulldozers, and progress,

while cherishing the values of stability, religious orthodoxy, and rural life. Southerners have existed historically in a state of ambivalence, even of dualism, because they could not bear to abandon the patterns of the Old South or to forgo
the material gains of modern America.[13]

The dualistic perspective of Cash and Potter seems to encompass the
varieties of southern historical experience and consciousness better than
either of the monistic interpretations. To go beyond mere parodox, however, it is necessary to learn more about the precise relationship between
the two tendencies and, if possible, to make sense of both within a
broader, more comprehensive interpretation of southern history.

One way to transcend simple dualism is to confront the ambiguous
meaning of biracialism in white consciousness and culture. White supremacy, or a commitment to racial hierarchy, is still a plausible candidate for "the central theme of southern history," despite the fact that
it has been fifty-three years since Ulrich B. Phillips advanced this proposition.[14] It is certainly the single theme or factor that provides the most
obvious source of continuity between antebellum and postwar experiences. However they may have differed in other respects, the South's
two "peculiar" institutions—slavery and legalized segregation—shared
the common goal of white dominance and black subordination. Did the
South's enduring obsession with racial distinctions and the subjugation
of blacks promote an aristocratic ethos or a democratic one?

The answer depends in part on one's point of view and definition of
terms. The white southern tradition was clearly "aristocratic" or hier-
archical in the sense that it sanctioned social, economic, and political
inequality based on hereditary or ascriptive differences among population groups. The caste principle underlying southern race relations
was about as undemocratic a basis for the structuring of a society as it
is possible to imagine. If, however, one views the southern way of life
from the vantage point of those within the racially privileged segment
and considers blacks to be permanent aliens or subhuman creatures, a
different sense of the ideological possibilities emerges. To the degree
that blacks were regarded as nonpeople and rigidly excluded from the
community of citizens or potential citizens, a kind of in-group or *Herrenvolk* democracy could be encouraged by the sense of social status
accorded by the color line to *all* whites. A racially circumscribed affirmation of democracy and equality dominated public discourse in the
Old South and sustained a proslavery or antiabolitionist solidarity between the minority who actually owned slaves and the majority who
supported the institution primarily out of a concern for racial control
and the maintenance of *Herrenvolk* identity.[15] More recently, J. Mills
Thornton and Michael Holt have deepened and refined this argument
by relating it to the republican ideology that shaped political culture in

antebellum America. Their work suggests that an acute sense of slavery as the antithesis of liberty and equality and as a condition reserved for abject inferiors gave a peculiar edge or intensity to southern fears of northern dominance. This added intensity eventually helped to make secessionism a popular movement.[16] According to republican thinking, one was either free and equal or a slave, and those who practiced racial slavery and knew what it meant had special reasons for being militant in the defense of their own liberty and equality. The possibility that secession itself was an expression of democratic sensibilities should give pause to those who casually identify antebellum southernism with the defense of aristocracy as an ideal.

One perhaps could conclude that the traditional South was "aristocratic" only if viewed through the lens of a modern, interracial concept of democracy. Taken on its own terms, the Old South had many of the attributes of an agrarian democracy, a land of relative liberty and equality for those whom God or nature had allegedly made free and equal— namely members of the white race. But is this a fully satisfactory way of resolving the paradox? Although it has heuristic value and reflects a mainstream southern tradition of political rhetoric and ideology, such a view does less than full justice to the real tensions or conflicts in southern culture and may even obscure the differences between rhetoric and reality. In the first place, it does not take into account the full range of white opinion. Even before the modern desegregation era, a few liberals in every generation questioned the dominant view that personal liberty and legal equality stopped at the color line. As Carl Degler has shown in *The Other South*, however, men like Daniel Goodloe, John Mc-Donough, George W. Cable, and Lewis Harvie Blair were lonely dissenters who never gained a following and in fact were subjected to persecution or ostracism.[17]

Much more commonplace and respectable than their efforts to enlarge the meaning of democracy were conservative challenges to any kind of social and political egalitarianism, including the *Herrenvolk* variety. Southern intellectual history reveals a recurring conflict between elite thought and culture, which manifested genuine conservatism and a celebration of hierarchy for its own sake, and popular democratic tradition, which usually was conditioned or contaminated by a *Herrenvolk* tendency. Efforts to extend the meaning of aristocracy and hereditary privilege to justify class distinctions among whites as well as caste differences between the races culminated in the proslavery arguments of such antebellum intellectuals as Thomas R. Dew, George Fitzhugh, George Frederick Holmes, and William Harper. These thinkers offered a challenge to liberalism and the ideal of a "free society" that is almost unique in its total rejection of the American democratic consensus. The demise of slavery weakened the foundations of this kind of thinking, but a broadly antidemocratic impulse did reemerge in a variety of forms during the New South era. Such phenomena as mill-village "paternalism" for white workers and the disfranchisement of lower-class whites as well as blacks at the turn of the century, certainly owed something to the afterglow of antebellum paternalist thought. It also drew inspiration from a more general phenomenon in American culture. Historians are beginning to discover that during and after the Reconstruction period a thoroughly bourgeois form of elitism challenged the midcentury democratic ethos and sanctioned new forms of class privilege and power in the North as well as in the South.[18]

If a "class analysis" is useful for interpreting larger developments in nineteenth-century American society, it might also offer a fuller understanding of the tension between democracy and aristocracy in the southern tradition. Most previous efforts at a class interpretation, however, have tended to lose sight of the autonomous tradition of biracialism. To stimulate discussion, a working hypothesis about social relationships in the nineteenth-century South that gives due weight to a class perspective without ignoring the influence of the popular *Herrenvolk* belief is needed. An objective characteristic of southern society during this period was a substantial concentration of wealth and productive power in the hands of a minority of the white population—the large planters of the antebellum period and the industrialists, merchants, and landlords of the New South. It seems safe to assume that the economically dominant class was chronically anxious about democratic stirrings among the common whites and persistently struggled to maintain its superior social status. However, once the less dominant class had won the right to vote and internalized the antiaristocratic Jacksonian ideology, it became an invitation to class conflict for the elite to affirm its true sentiments. The great stress on race in southern ideology served the needs of economically advantaged groups by obscuring those inequalities among whites that could no longer be justified explicitly. Appeals to "democratic racism" were effective because they could tap an authentic folk tradition and mobilize it behind the status quo of power and privilege. While it might seem, then, that aristocracy was a social reality it was inhibited in its ideological expression by the practical concerns of a dominant class whose first priority was to maintain control. The substance of aristocracy, in other words, could only be achieved through democratic forms. Francis Butler Simkins' view that the South had a democratic face and an aristocratic soul remains persuasive when applied to the characteristic behavior and attitudes of the upper class. But the yeomanry of the Old South and the dirt farmers and mill workers of the New South should not be viewed only as passive victims of ideological manipulation. They struggled in their own way and according to their own lights to maintain freedom, independence, and self-esteem. The last great flowering of the grass-roots democratic tradition was the Populist insurgency of the 1890s.[19] Populism's ultimate failure was due in part to the tendency of racism to deflect southern class movements from their original objectives, but it also was turned back by the power of corporate interests at a time when monopolistic capitalism was gaining control over the American economy. Aristocratic rule through democratic forms was then, more than simply a survival of the southern past. It was a possible model for the American future.

Notes

1. See Wendell Holmes Stephenson's essay on Dodd in *The South Lives in History: Southern Historians and Their Legacy* (Baton Rouge, 1955), pp. 28-57.

2. Ibid., pp. 58-94. The dedication appears in *A History of Transportation in the Eastern Cotton Belt to 1860* (New York, 1908). Phillips' most important works were *American Negro Slavery* (New York, 1918); *Life and Labor in the Old South* (Boston, 1929); and a posthumous collection of essays, *The Course of the South to Secession,* ed. Merton Coulter (New York, 1939).

3. See Fletcher Melvin Green, "Democracy in the Old South," *Journal of Southern History* 12 (1946): 2-23; and Charles S. Sydnor, *The Development of Southern Sectionalism, 1819-1848* (Baton Rouge, 1948), pp. 275-93.

4. Frank L. Owsley, *Plain Folk of the Old South* (Baton Rouge, 1949).

5. A.N.J. Den Hollander, "The Tradition of 'Poor Whites' " in *Culture in the South,* ed. W. T. Couch (Chapel Hill, 1935), pp. 410, 403-431. Den Hollander's full-length study in Dutch is *Die Landelijke Arme Blanken in Het Zuiden Der Vereenigde Staaten* (Groningen, 1933).

6. Charles Greer Sellers, Jr., ed., *The Southerner as American* (Chapel Hill, 1960 . For Sellers' own seminal essay, "The Travail of Slavery," see pp. 40-71.

7. Francis Butler Simkins, "The South's Democratic Pose," in *The Everlasting South* (Baton Rouge, 1963), pp. 21-32.

8. Eugene D. Genovese, *The Political Economy of Slavery: Studies in the Economy and Society of the Old South* (New York, 1965), p. 28. Genovese has developed his interpretations more fully in such subsequent works as *The World the Slaveholders Made* (New York, 1969), and *Roll, Jordan, Roll: The World the Slaves Made* (New York, 1974).

9. Jonathan M. Wiener, *Social Origins of the New South: Alabama, 1860-1885* (Baton Rouge, 1978).

10. For a good discussion of the new work on the postbellum South, see Harold Woodman, "Sequel to Slavery: The New History Views the Postbellum South," *Journal of Southern History* 43 (1977): 523-54.

11. J. Mills Thornton III, *Politics and Power in a Slave Society: Alabama 1800-1860* (Baton Rouge, 1978).

12. W. J. Cash, *The Mind of the South* (New York, 1941), especially pp. 70-81.

13. David M. Potter, *The South and the Sectional Conflict* (Baton Rouge, 1968), p. 30.

14. U. B. Phillips, "The Central Theme of Southern History," in *The Course*

of the South to Secession. Originally presented as a paper to the American Historical Association, 1928.

15. George M. Fredrickson, *The Black Image in the White Mind: The Debate on Afro-American Character and Destiny, 1817-1914* (New York, 1971), especially pp. 61-71.

16. Thornton, *Politics and Power*, pp. 442-59; Michael F. Holt, *The Political Crisis of the 1850s* (New York, 1978), pp. 240-43.

17. Carl Degler, *The Other South: Southern Dissenters in the Nineteenth Century* (New York, 1974), pp. 41-46, 306-7, 313-14.

18. This conclusion would seem to follow from a number of recent works. See, for example, David Montgomery, *Beyond Equality: Labor and the Radical Republicans, 1862-1872* (New York, 1967); Eric Foner, "Reconstruction and the Crisis of Free Labor," in Eric Foner, ed., *Politics and Ideology in the Age of the Civil War* (New York, 1980), pp. 97-127; Fredrickson, *The Black Image*, pp. 204-16; J. Morgan Kousser, *The Shaping of Southern Politics: Suffrage Restriction and the Establishment of the One-Party South* (New Haven, 1974), pp. 253-57.

19. See Lawrence Goodwyn's fine study, *Democratic Promise: The Populist Movement in America* (New York, 1976).

7

A PARADOX OF CHRISTIAN AMELIORATION: PROSLAVERY IDEOLOGY AND CHURCH MINISTRIES TO SLAVES

Jack P. Maddex, Jr.

During the last forty years of the antebellum South, two developments occurred simultaneously in southern churches: an articulation of a Christian proslavery ideology and an effort to evangelize slaves and encourage humane management. Such a juxtaposition presents an intriguing paradox that challenges us to reexamine the relationship between proslavery ideas and ministry to slaves. Previous studies have noted that church leaders hoped evangelization would make slaves more loyal and thus more profitable. While such statements are undoubtedly true as far as they go, the relationship between the two developments went much deeper. It involved the very foundation of moral responsibility and shaped the theory and practice of an important church activity. This essay will explore the rationale of Presbyterian church leaders for their religious work among the slaves. Although the Presbyterians were not able to recruit a large proportion of blacks to their church, their systematic presentations won them prominence as exponents of the endeavor.

From New England to the Gulf Coast during this period, Christians found that their moral duties depended on their evaluation of the moral status of slavery. When southern ministers favored increasing attention to slaves, they presupposed the positive evaluation that was prevalent in their religious community. They viewed the master-slave relation as one of the basic legitimate relations of society, divinely authorized and morally unobjectionable, although marred by serious abuses in practice. They expresssed humanitarian concern for blacks as persons, considered abusive treatment to be an obstacle to their conversion, and recommended amelioration of plantation management. If humanitarianism and amelioration are identified with personal freedom, then the dominant religious thought of the Old South appears paradoxical, for it identified those ideals with the defense and development of slavery. Ministers who taught that slavery was "capable of reformation and indefinite improvement" were voicing the highest confidence in its fundamental morality.[1] Their commitment to amelioration was fundamentally proslavery.

Consciousness of the system of slavery and its class relations pervaded the Presbyterian missionary approach. Their writings in defense of slavery and their appeals for the instruction of slaves were not two distinct bodies of literature. Almost every important pronouncement on either subject dealt with the other as well, often at comparable length. While proponents of slave evangelization frequently appealed to humanitarian considerations they rarely appealed to a generalized humanitarianism that disregarded class and condition. "Master" and "servant" were the dominant categories of their discourse. Although they sometimes exhorted masters as "you," they habitually used the pronoun "we" for the community of Christian slaveholders and "they" for the slaves collectively. In addressing congregations that included many slaves, even ministers who did not own slaves followed that usage. In demanding service to slaves, they did not forget the roles of master and slave but rather accentuated them.

Ministers continually appealed to the master's duty—his moral responsibility for his slaves' welfare. They were not content with the simple fact that slaves were the same fellow human beings as the heathen in Asia and the poor whites at home. Duty to slaves took precedence because it stemmed from the class relation between masters and slaves. A convention of Presbyterian church officers in North Carolina described a master's responsibility to teach his slaves Christianity as "a solemn duty growing out of and inseparable from the relation. . . ."[2] The Virginia theologian Robert L. Dabney learned a secular version of that kind of duty from his brother, a thoughtful planter. Charles Dabney declined to aid a distant relative because prior moral claims required all the surplus income he felt "authorised to extract from my own pauper population, the niggers. . . ." As he explained, "My sense of duty is first to my own working people." Next came duty to his "country" as a proprietor (to improve his estate) and then the needs of his community.[3] Robert Dabney was impressed by that answer to the biblical question, "Who is my neighbor?"

Charles Colcock Jones, the great Georgia missionary to slaves, introduced an exposition of his cause with the question, *"What is their social connection with us?"* It was, he replied, one of round-the-clock, cradle-to-grave attachment. "[T]hey are not foreigners," he pointed out, "but our nearest neighbors; they are not hired servants, but servants belonging to us in law and Gospel; born in our house, and bought with our money; not people whom we seldom see, and . . . hear, but people who are never out of the light of our eyes, nor the hearing of our ears."[4] When John B. Adger began full-time ministry to Charleston slaves, he too based the slaves' moral claim on the class relationship. "They are not like the poor in Ireland, having claims on all the world," he declared, "the claim of these is on us, for we claim them as ours."[5] He went on to assert, "[N]owhere are the poor so closely and intimately connected with the higher classes as are our poor with us. *They belong to us*. We, also, *belong* to them."[6] The responsibility was a special one, unique to the social relationships of slavery.

Proslavery thinkers described slavery as a "domestic" institution, a form of family organization, and the family was a religious unit. Southern Christians knew from their Bible that the ancient Israelites had incorporated their slaves, but not their hired servants, into family rituals.[7] The Virginia minister Samuel J. Cassels classified slaves as "children of the *second* degree" to their masters.[8] "Our servants constitute a part of our households," the missionary executive J. Leighton Wilson wrote. "It is only on this ground that we can find any sanction in the word of God for the institution of slavery. As members of the family-compact, they have therefore the same claims for religious instruction that our children have."[9] Another South Carolina minister warned parishioners that God would hold them responsible for the conduct of their slaves, just as he would for that of their children.[10] The thesis provided a mandate for the instruction of slaves as well as a defense of slavery.

The dependence of slaves in the system led to the same conclusion that their attachment did. They could legitimately receive their necessities only from their masters, Cassels pointed out. "When then we consider the absolutely dependent situation of our servants," he concluded, "this should induce us not to neglect their *temporal necessities and comforts*."[11] Others applied the dependence argument to religious education. Since slaves could not organize independently, James H. Thornwell and George Howe, South Carolina theologians, taught, they "must be supplied with God's word, as they are supplied with their daily bread, by the hands of their masters."[12] That reasoning invested the slaveholder with a religious mission.

Proslavery ministers defined slavery as a right to labor service based on providential prescription, not voluntary contract.[13] They thus recognized it as a seigneurial relation of lordship with prescriptive duties for master and servant. "God does not place men under the absolute power of others," Howe held, "without binding those, under whom they are so placed, by the most stringent obligations."[14] In their ethical teachings, Southern ministers gave prominence to "relative duties," duties that were not universal but depended on vertical relationships in the social hierarchy.[15] Drawing on biblical sources, they formulated tables of the duties of masters to slaves and slaves to masters.[16] Among the masters' duties they emphasized religious instruction and paternalistic governance.

Expositions of duties were closely related to the biblical proslavery argument. Whether ministers were listing passages that taught the legitimacy of slavery or passages that commanded benevolence to slaves, they arrived at approximately the same list, by using the commandments of the Pentateuch and the *Haustafeln* of the New Testament epistles. They found in the biblical prescriptions of duties strong evidence that God sanctioned the system. "[T]he duties of masters and servants are prescribed no less than the duties of parents and children, husbands and wives," Howe argued, "and no more is said of the relation of master being wrong, than of those necessary relations of the domestic state."[17] Adger pointed out that the biblical proslavery argument and the duty of masters to slaves were inseparable. In the texts, he asserted, "these two things, this condemnation [of antislavery] and this command [of humane governance] go together. The latter is the completion, nay! the very *establishment* and *strength* of the former."[18] To enjoy the biblical sanction, southern masters should perform their duty to their slaves.

Christian paternalists went farther than any other southern intellectuals in stating the maximal concept of a master's responsibility to his slaves. Jones outgrew his youthful misgivings about slavery, but he continued to regard it (as he had once written in criticism) as "an assumption of the responsibility of fixing the life and destiny of immortal beings."[19] He and Adger called masters "almoners" of divine grace,[20] and the Georgia minister Joseph Ruggles Wilson ascribed to masters an "exalted stewardship . . . over *souls of immortal men*."[21] A slaveholder, Howe remarked, "cannnot say, Am I my brother's keeper? There is a trust committed to him."[22] In view of Protestant theological tradition, depicting the master as a channel of grace was perhaps the most extreme claim of proslavery religious thought.

In their appeals for benevolence, ministers took a maximal view of slaveholders' legitimate authority. They urged Christian masters to police their slaves' conduct rigidly and converse with them continually about their spiritual condition.[23] Calvin H. Wiley, a ministerial candidate and state school superintendent of North Carolina, insisted that a master was "not to be content with mere observation of outward acts, but to examine the hearts & consciences of his dependents, to probe in a kind & proper spirit, their inmost hopes & fears."[24] David Frierson, a minister in South Carolina, upbraided planters who worried about infringing upon their slaves' freedom of conscience.[25] When masters reported that their slaves rarely attended their family prayers, Jones exploded: "Why do you not *make* them attend?"[26] This kind of amelioration could reduce the "free space" in slaves' lives instead of increasing it. Some slaves decided that those pious and benevolent masters who conducted close surveillance and restricted Sunday activity were undesirable.

Proslavery churchmen suggested that God had ordained American slavery to benefit blacks, giving them opportunities for moral education and conversion that would otherwise be lacking. Jones invoked that teleological interpretation as an argument for evangelization. It was "in the providence of God," he contended, that the slaves "were placed under our control, and not exclusively for our benefit but for theirs also." Since elevation and conversion were the providential purposes, he concluded, God obligated slaveholders to carry them out.[27] "The servant of God, owning slaves," Wiley advised, "must endeavor to make his position one of mutual benefit to the slaves & to himself."[28] The Christian proslavery argument thus motivated the mission to slaves.

It was in the elements of this argument that Presbyterian church leaders of the late antebellum South found their mandate for the amelioration and religious education of slaves. The argument, a minister in Georgia asserted, "made the slave-holder feel that while he does not necessarily sin in holding this property, yet that God will call him to a solemn account, if he fail to do his whole duty to them."[29] As a missionary to Mississippi slaves, James Smylie stated the intended result: "Instead of hanging down his head, moping and brooding over his condition, as formerly, without action, he raises his head, and moves on cheerfully, in the plain path of duty."[30] In fact, some Southern church leaders claimed that antislavery ideas were an impediment to true amelioration.[31] For them, it was the Christian proslavery argument that motivated the mission to slaves.

In the framework of their social and religious ideology, church leaders naturally anticipated that evangelization would strengthen slavery and benefit slaveholders. When Smylie asked permission to preach to slaves, he assured the planter that the "legitimate tendency" of the gospel was "to make his slaves honest, trusty, and faithful" in service.[32] It was not hypocrisy or duplicity for these men. Smylie and his colleagues believed that slavery was a legitimate system and that God ordinarily made enlightened self-interest coincide with moral duty. "How beautifully does all duty harmonize with all human welfare and advantage," a Mississippi minister marveled.[33] Churchmen sometimes claimed that "the pecuniary interests of masters will be advanced by the religious instruction of their slaves."[34] They were as likely, however, to conceptualize masters' interests in nonpecuniary terms: "It is certainly better," Frierson preached, "to have genteel, high toned and honorable servants under your control than a number of demi savages to manage."[35] Ministers fully expected well-treated and converted slaves to serve their masters better.

They also hoped that religious instruction would diminish slave unrest and increase social stability. "Moral restraints," Adger affirmed, "are a mightier means of governing mankind than mere force."[36] If slaves understood the duties of masters and servants "from their own personal knowledge of the Scriptures," Leighton Wilson wrote, they might "be happier, more contented in their lot, and . . . far more faithful and cheerful" in service.[37] Thornwell thought that slaves would recognize the benevolence of masters who tried "to promote their everlasting good," and would "be slow to cast off a system which has become associated in their minds with their dearest hopes and most precious consolations."[38]

Presbyterian ministers pointed to the folk religion of the slave quarters as a rival influence that could become subversive if independent of proslavery church authority. Adger warned that ignorance and superstition were like "explosive material exposed to the incendiary's torch," and that to neglect church ministry would surrender slaves "to unsound and unsafe teachers."[39] Thornwell agreed: "If *we* do not furnish them with men qualified to teach them, they will provide themselves with others, who will pander to their tastes and develop the religious element of their nature in forms, it may be, incompatible with their own improvement or the interests of their masters."[40] Instruction and incorporation in the churches would counteract that danger.

Eventually, proponents hoped, evangelization and amelioration might determine the course of the international controversy over slavery. Insisting that admitted evils in southern practice were abuses separable from the master-slave relation, they hoped to prove it by removing them. If slavery could assure slaves of humane management and the amenities of religion and family life, Dabney stated, *"then it is defensible;* and the victory is ours."[41] Improving the moral and religious life of slaves would refute the strongest antislavery argument. "Go on in this noble enterprise, until every slave in our borders shall know of Jesus and the resurrection," Thornwell told South Carolinians, "and the blessing of God will attend you, and turn back the tide of indignation which the public opinion of the world is endeavouring to roll upon you."[42] Some anticipated that the ultimate result would win universal approval for the southern social system.

The mission to slaves provided the proslavery cause with a model for attaining an autonomous southern religious culture. Until the early nineteenth century many southern churchmen accepted the northern image of their region as a missionary territory that was dependent on the established Christian civilization of New England. They feared that a plantation social structure and demography were obstructing evangelization. The ministry to slaves, however, held out the hope of building a Christian slaveholding South able to challenge the moral credentials of New England through the indigenous development of possibilities in their own social order. Under this model the plantations would become not unevangelized hinterlands but centers of religious influence, and self-affirming Christian slaveholders would accomplish what northern missionaries could not.

"The Religious instruction of the negroes," Jones announced early in his career, "is the *foundation* of all permanent improvement in intelligence and morals in the slave-holding states."[43] Proponents hoped that missionaries would supply plantation districts with religious facilities and mobilize the laity in mission to their servants. Ministry to slaves, Adger told South Carolinians, "is THE WORK . . . which will raise up a SOUTHERN MINISTRY" and "fill your recently endowed seminary with students."[44] Converted, slaves would become a good instead of a bad influence on the white population. By impelling southern ministers to make stringent demands on planters, the mission freed them from the onus of moral cowardice. It gave the southern church its great mission "cause"—its equivalent to the projects of the northern "benevolent empire." A Presbyterian in Texas could now boast to northerners, "none of your clergymen have any tasks resembling these."[45] Northern religious hegemony became dispensable.

In their ministry to slaves, which called for paternalistic amelioration, southern Presbyterian leaders found assurance that Christianity and their society could go forward in mutual harmony. Under its inspiration young men saw visions, and old men dreamed dreams. Joseph Wilson predicted that "when that welcome day shall dawn, whose light shall reveal a world covered by righteousness," one of its foremost adornments would be "the institution of domestic slavery, freed from its stupid servility on the one side and its excesses of neglect and severity on the other."[46] While designing a form of church organization adapted to minister to slaves, the South Carolina minister Andrew F. Dickson went on to contemplate a "beautiful hope . . . of a Church of the Future that shall be indeed the Garden of God." "This is Utopia, no doubt," he reflected; "there is Utopia in all things good—that sweet faint perfume from the Paradise so far away!"[47] The vision invested southern slavery with the aegis of Christian idealism.

Southern church leaders, while sharing a common rationale for ministry to slaves, often differed about methods and policies for the work. In accord with their rationale they addressed slaves as slaves in the context of established southern society. A committee of the synods of Virginia and North Carolina stated the common objective: to provide instruction "in a manner consistent with the laws of the States and with the feelings and wishes of the planters."[48] Their differences emerged within that framework and reflected tensions within the slaveholding order.

Proponents disagreed about the desirability of forming separate slave congregations in cities and plantation areas. Dickson argued that common worship served to "sanctify the relation of master and servant" and that the "bond" between them was "both strengthened and softened" in common celebration of the Lord's Supper.[49] "Negroes should worship with their masters, *and not elsewhere*," Charles Dabney insisted.

Dissatisfied with the customary slave gallery, he preferred class seating arrangements that placed the slaves directly under the masters' observation.[50] In the late 1840s, however, Charleston Presbyterians concluded that a separate meetinghouse would better incorporate unsupervised city slaves into the church system. They argued that some separatism was endemic to the master-slave situation and that a white-controlled congregation of slaves would be free from seditious influence.[51] That plan, Adger claimed, actually *"brings the slave more immediately under white supervision"* than in other Charleston churches.[52] Thornwell and Howe also devised organizational plans to secure white control of black worshipping communities.[53] Proslavery considerations always motivated both sides of the argument.

The use of missionaries in specialized ministries to slaves generated similar discussions. Many saw the local congregation as the safe locus of planter control and remembered that the usual American home missionary was a rootless northerner representing a northern-dominated board. Others argued that specialized ministries under southern control suited plantation conditions better. Slaves, a Virginia minister acknowledged, were *"an imperium in imperio,—a separate class"* whose ordinary contacts with whites did not provide channels for religious communication.[54] The missionary system, Thornwell suggested, could also be *"safer"*: "Is it not an advantage that there should be some one man, . . . known to the masters—who is responsible to the country as well as to his God, for the species of instructions he imparts?"[55] Under either system, church leaders sought to assure the security of slavery.

There was still another internal debate over the use of black leadership in church work. Thornwell and Adger, applying the logic of the class system, denied that slaves could have a role in the preaching ministry. Citing church canons from the late Roman Empire, they maintained that a man whose time was under a master's control could not function as a minister.[56] Jones, in a minority on the issue, put forth social as well as theological considerations. He held up as an exemplar a black preacher who had turned over abolitionist pamphlets to civil authorities.[57] Ministers in South Carolina recognized the need for subordinate black leaders to bring slaves under effective church discipline and control. They reasoned that since "there is, from the nature of the case, a want of free and unreserved communication" between the races, slaves' "circumstances and conduct can only be intimately known by men of their own colour."[58] To assure the essential class subordination and control, all insisted that slave leaders should be selected and employed *"under the careful supervision of the established officers of the church."*[59]

The most delicate question in the ministry to slaves was whether or not the church should recognize separation through sale as altering a slave's marital status. From tenets of their common ideology, church leaders drew inferences that led to different answers.[60] Under the Confederacy, they debated whether or not to advocate legal recognition of slave marriages. The Mississippi minister James A. Lyon argued that legalization would reinforce slavery. The more fully a bondsman could enter into family relations, he contended, "the better adapted is he to become a faithful and efficient servant." A securely married slave would not be a fugitive or conspirator but "a fixture to the soil, and an interested party in the good order of society."[61] A Presbyterian legal thinker wished to prevent separations by other measures but found Lyon's proposal incompatible with proslavery social theory. To make slave marriage a civil contract, he concluded, would undermine a master's authority by intruding civil law into the master-slave relation.[62] A contradiction in proslavery ideology became for church leaders an agonizing dilemma.

Parental relations of slaves also presented questions of conflicting authority. Some ministers saw the authority of masters as a powerful remedy for parental deficiencies. In his early years, Jones thought that "if it were practicable, an *entire separation* of children & adults . . . would be the best thing that could be done."[63] Howe held that masters, as responsible guardians, were the logical baptismal sponsors for slave children,[64] and some questioned whether slave parents could assume that responsibility at all.[65] Those who took the other side of the question believed that upholding a slave's parental authority would confirm a master's authority. Describing "the family relation" as "the great school of Government," Wiley argued that in their own nuclear families slaves would "learn the necessity of authority, . . . & the mutual obligations and advantages of superiors and inferiors."[66] Proslavery Christian ideology afforded room for both viewpoints, since each developed some of its important aspects. Opinions about policy differed, but within the context of the same ideological consensus.

It was in a proslavery Christian conception of the master-slave relation that southern Presbyterian leaders found their motivation for religious ministry to slaves. They sought to apply these principles to realize the humane potential they ascribed to the system. Expecting that their efforts would ameliorate and confirm slavery and buttress the proslavery cause, they pursued in it a missionary vision that affirmed the moral legitimacy of their southern social order. Adhering loyally to their motivating principles, they shaped their mission methods and strategies accordingly.

The proslavery ideological foundation of the cause mandated a ministry to slaves *as slaves*. Most of the proponents ignored free blacks. In 1865, therefore, military emancipation disrupted their religious work along with the social order that conditioned it. While many slaves had found the white ministers' services and Sunday schools valuable, few had internalized their proslavery ideology. Social liberation brought with it religious freedom, and most freedmen quickly left the "secesh" churches to form churches that exemplified their emancipation. The end of the antebellum ministry to slaves left a void in the Christian life for many upper-class southerners. A plantation mistress who had been active in the work recalled that she had not felt then "as lonely as I have since; for there I had constant occupation which could not but be agreeable—being, as I hoped useful. Now I seem but a 'cumberer of the ground.'"[67] That nostalgia haunted southern white churches for decades.

Some white church leaders never felt a comparable responsibility to freedmen, and others persisted futilely in a "slave" style of ministry to a few blacks. Their concept of missionary duty, rooted in the social responsibilities of masters to their slaves, was not applicable to the new situation. John L. Girardeau of Charleston, one of the most successful Presbyterian ministers to slaves, continued to serve a black congregation, but he admitted that the antebellum logic now pointed to a different conclusion. "Responsibilities grow out of relations," Girardeau reminded seminary students. "The peculiar duty of the people of the South to furnish religious instruction to the negroes while they were slaves, from the nature of the case exists no longer."[68] Others came to similar conclusions.[69] The old class rationale left southern white Christians no guidance for their relations with the freedmen of the postbellum South.

Notes

1. Thomas Smyth, *North Carolina Presbyterian* (Fayetteville), 17 January 1863, p. 1.

2. Convention of elders and deacons from North Carolina, "Resolution," *North Carolina Presbyterian*, 19 March 1858, p. 1.

3. Charles W. Dabney to Robert L. Dabney, 27 December 1858, Charles W. Dabney Papers, University of North Carolina at Chapel Hill, Chapel Hill, N.C.

4. Charles C. Jones, "Address at General Assembly, Presbyterian Church in the C.S.A., 1861," *Southern Presbyterian* (Columbia, S.C.), 1 March 1862, p. 1. See also Jones, *The Religious Instruction of the Negroes in the United States* (Savannah: Thomas Purse, 1842), p. 166.

5. John B. Adger, *The Religious Instruction of the Colored Population: A Sermon. . .in the Second Presbyterian Church, Charleston, S.C., May 9, 1847* (Charleston: T. W. Haynes, 1847), p. 13.

6. Ibid., p. 6.

7. See Gen. 17:23; Exod. 12:43-45.

8. Samuel J. Cassels, *Servitude, and the Duty of Masters to Their Servants: A Sermon, Preached in the Presbyterian Church, Norfolk, Va. . . .June, 1843* (Norfolk: Press of the *Beacon*, 1843), p. 13.

9. [J. Leighton Wilson,] "Report of the Committee [of Harmony Presbytery] on the Religious Instruction of the Colored People," *Southern Presbyterian Review* (Columbia, S.C.) 14 (October 1863): 191.

10. David E. Frierson, ms. sermon, "The Sabbath," 16 August 1853, pp. 15-16, David E. Frierson Papers, University of South Carolina, Columbia, S.C.

11. Cassels, *Servitude*, p. 13.

12. James H. Thornwell and George Howe, "Report to Charleston Presbytery, April 1847," in Adger, *Religious Instruction*, p. 16.

13. James H. Thornwell, "The Christian Doctrine of Slavery," in *Collected Writings*, 4 vols. (Richmond: Presbyterian Committee of Publication, 1871-73), 4: 414; John B. Adger, "Christian Doctrine of Human Rights and Slavery," *Southern Presbyterian Review* 2 (March 1849): 581; [Charles C. Jones,] "Slavery," *Southern Presbyterian Review* 9 (January 1856): 347; Ferdinand Jacobs, *The Committing of Our Cause to God: A Sermon Preached in the Second Presbyterian Church, Charleston, S.C. on Friday, the 6th of December [1850]* . . . (Charleston: A. J. Burke, 1850), p. 6n.

14. George Howe, "The Baptism of Servants," *Southern Presbyterian Review* 1 (June 1847): 88.

15. See E. Brooks Holifield, *The Gentlemen Theologians: American Theology in Southern Culture, 1795-1860* (Durham: Duke University Press, 1978), pp. 146-49.

16. [Jones,] "Slavery," pp. 357-60; W. T. Hamilton, *The Duties of Masters and Slaves Respectively: or Domestic Servitude as Sanctioned by the Bible: A Discourse, Delivered in the Government-Street Church, Mobile, Ala.* (Mobile: F. H. Brooks, 1845), pp. 20-24.

17. Howe, "Baptism of Servants," p. 64.

18. John B. Adger, "Religious Instruction of the Black Population," *Southern Presbyterian Review* 1 (December 1847): 108.

19. Charles C. Jones to Mary Jones, September 8, 1829, Charles C. Jones Papers, Tulane University of Louisiana, New Orleans, La.

20. Jones, *Religious Instruction*, p. 157; Adger, "Religious Instruction," p. 119.

21. Joseph Ruggles Wilson, *Mutual Relations of Masters and Slaves as Taught in the Bible: A Discourse Preached in the First Presbyterian Church, Augusta, Georgia, on Sabbath Morning, Jan. 6, 1861* (Augusta: Steam Press of *Chronicle and Sentinel*, 1861), p. 20.

22. Howe, "Baptism of Servants," p. 65.

23. Jones, *Religious Instruction*, p. 245.

24. Calvin H. Wiley, mss. on slavery, long, continuously paginated draft, pp. 96-97, Calvin H. Wiley Papers, University of North Carolina at Chapel Hill, Chapel Hill, N.C.

25. Frierson, "Sabbath," pp. 14, 16, Frierson Papers.

26. Jones, "Address to General Assembly, 1861," p. 1.

27. Jones, *Religious Instruction*, p. 159.

28. Wiley, mss. on slavery, long, continuously paginated draft, p. 66, Wiley Papers.

29. C. W. Howard, *Southern Christian Sentinel* (Charleston), 16 March 1839, p. 1.

30. James Smylie, *A Review of a Letter, from the Presbytery of Chillicothe, to the Presbytery of Mississippi, on the Subject of Slavery* (Woodville, Miss.: William A. Norris, 1836), p. 4.

31. Cassels, *Servitude*, p. 3.

32. Smylie, *Review of a Letter*, p. 71.

33. E. Thompson Baird, "The Religious Instruction of Our Colored Population," *Southern Presbyterian Review* 11 (July 1859): 356.

34. Synod of South Carolina and Georgia, "Resolution, 1833," quoted in Ernest Trice Thompson, *Presbyterians in the South*, 2 vols. (Richmond: John Knox Press, 1963-73), 1: 209.

35. David E. Frierson, ms. sermon, "Masters' Duties," 7 March 1863, p. 11, Frierson Papers.

36. Adger, *Religious Instruction*, p. 12.

37. [J. L. Wilson,] "Report of Committee," p. 192.

38. Thornwell, "Christian Doctrine of Slavery," p. 435.

39. Adger, "Religious Instruction," p. 112.

40. [James H. Thornwell,] *Southern Presbyterian Review* 1 (September 1847), 146.

41. "Chorepiscopus" [Robert L. Dabney] *Semi-Weekly Enquirer* (Richmond), 29 April 1851, p. 4.

42. Thornwell, "Christian Doctrine of Slavery," p. 436.

43. Charles C. Jones to William S. Plumer, 28 June 1834, William S. Plumer Papers, Presbyterian Historical Society, Philadelphia.

44. Adger, *Religious Instruction*, pp. 12-13.

45. "Wilkinson," *The Presbyterian* (Philadelphia), 13 December 1851, p. 1.

46. J. R. Wilson, *Mutual Relations*, p. 21.

47. Andrew F. Dickson, "Our Problem," *Southern Presbyterian Review* 10 (October 1857): 462-63.

48. Committee of Synods of Virginia and North Carolina, "Report, 1834," quoted in Jones, *Religious Instruction*, p. 76.

49. Dickson, "Our Problem," p. 453.

50. Charles W. Dabney to Robert L. Dabney, 9 March 1859, C. W. Dabney Papers.

51. [Thornwell,] *Southern Presbyterian Review* 1 (September 1847): 142-50.

52. Adger, "Religious Instruction," p. 100.

53. Thornwell and Howe, "Report, 1847," in Adger, *Religious Instruction*, p. 17.

54. S. L. Graham to William S. Plumer, 7 July 1834, Plumer Papers.

55. [Thornwell,] *Southern Presbyterian Review* 1 (September 1847): 145.

56. Ibid., pp. 148-49; James H. Thornwell, "Relation of the Church to Slavery," *Collected Writings*, 4: 396-97; "Report of a Conference by [Charleston] Presbytery, on the Subject of 'The Organization, Instruction and Discipline of the Coloured People," *Southern Presbyterian Review* 8 (July 1854): 3, 9; John B. Adger, "The Divine Right of Presbyterian Church Government," *Southern Presbyterian Review* 13 (April 1860): 136n.

57. Jones, *Religious Instruction*, pp. 157-58, 215-16.

58. "Report of Conference," p. 8.

59. Dickson, "Our Problem," p. 462.

60. See discussion in "Report of Conference," pp. 15-17.

61. James A. Lyon, "Slavery, and the Duties Growing Out of the Relation," *Southern Presbyterian Review* 14 (July 1863): 30-31.

62. "A Slave Marriage Law," *Southern Presbyterian Review* 16 (October 1863): 145-62.

63. Jones to Plumer, 28 June 1834, Plumer Papers.

64. Howe, "Baptism of Servants," pp. 78-88, 92-102. Howe recognized that devout parents could sponsor their children, but he taught that masters should have children baptized even if their parents opposed it. See pp. 75-76, 87, 94.

65. See [J. L. Wilson,] "Report of Committee," p. 197.

66. Wiley, mss. on slavery, unpaginated section, Wiley Papers.

67. E. B., *South-Western Presbyterian* (New Orleans), 3 March 1881, p. 5.

68. John L. Girardeau, "The Past and Present Relations of Our Church to the Work of Foreign Missions," Address at Columbia Theological Seminary, May 11, 1868, in *The Missionary* (Richmond), 2 (August 1868): 74.

69. John B. Adger, "Northern and Southern Views of the Province of the Church," *Southern Presbyterian Review* 16 (March 1866): 409-10; *Central Presbyterian* (Richmond), 6 February 1867, p. 2. See references to that opinion in Synod of Georgia, "Resolution, October 18, 1865," *Southern Presbyterian* (Columbia), 28 December 1865, p. 4; J. M., *North Carolina Presbyterian*, 8 August 1866, p. 1.

8

WILLIAM HENRY BRISBANE: SOUTH CAROLINA SLAVEHOLDER AND ABOLITIONIST

Blake McNulty

Slavery, as several recent historians have argued, was a particularly troublesome institution in the antebellum South. White masters were determined to maintain and defend this cornerstone of their civilization according to the economic and racial imperatives of their world, yet they harbored an abiding fear of their bondsmen and held deeply engrained values that conflicted with both the concept and everyday realities of slavery.[1] By the late antebellum period Carolina masters suffered from a siege psychology, for it had become apparent just how "peculiar" their institution was. Increasingly slavery was regarded as a morally deplorable anachronism, not just in the North, but also in England and western Europe. In the minds of many Carolinians the South was a besieged section, and its defenses in the upper South had been breached by the abolitionist enemy. Governor David Johnson warned John C. Calhoun in 1848 that "there is great danger that the border slaveholding states will yield to the pressure of circumstances." He went on to wonder, "How long will Maryland, Western Virginia, Kentucky, Eastern Tennessee and even the Western part of North Carolina feel it their interest to retain slaves?"[2] Others would see in this a "domino" effect. "In Virginia, N.C. &, I may add, S.C., it is visibly on the decline," wrote William Gilmore Simms. "In 15 years Va. will be a free soil state, and will be instantly followed by N.C. S.C. will be a frontier and where?"[3] White Carolinians, therefore, could look neither to the North, nor to Europe, nor to the upper South for firm support. Moreover, even within the state nonslaveholding whites were uncertain allies. Apparently Carolina slaveholders could trust only themselves. Or could they? What if one of their own class, another Carolina master, turned abolitionist? What if the enemy had not only breached the wall but also lay unrecognized within the citadel? Whom could they trust? The story of William Henry Brisbane illustrates the panic such a perception provoked in an already apprehensive and besieged slaveholding society. As James H. Hammond observed to Calhoun, a "Southern man who falters—who apologizes—much less who denounces Slavery & regards abolition inevitable is . . . *our very worst enemy.*"[4]

In 1835 Brisbane, an ordained Baptist minister, was editor of the *Southern Baptist* and nearing the completion of his medical studies in Charleston. Scion of a prominent Beaufort planter, he counted assets of $21,000, a plantation valued at $33,000, and a large number of slaves. All avenues of success and status in the ranks of the gentry were open to him. He appeared to be orthodox on the troublesome slavery issue, for the year before in a series of articles for the Charleston *Mercury* he had written a theological defense of the institution.[5]

Yet Brisbane seemed riddled with guilt. In June 1835, he noted in his journal that he had "given my overseer a talk about using the whip with severity among my negroes," for he could "not endure that they should have their backs cut up. It is inhuman. If their conduct is so deserving of punishment, I must dispose of them to so[me] other master but I cannot assume the responsibility of severe chastisements."[6] That July, two weeks before the discovery of "incendiary" tracts in the Charleston post office threw the state into a panic and sparked a national controversy, Brisbane received an antislavery pamphlet that contained an extract from *Elements of Moral Science* by Francis Wayland, president of Brown University.[7] Initially Brisbane was "very much distressed" by Wayland's argument, but he soon was relieved to "have discovered the errors in it" so that he was "now easy on that score ag[ai]n."[8] His moral respite lasted only briefly, for within a few days, "in attempting to reply to Dr. Wayland's article," Brisbane was startled at his own argument. He discovered that Wayland's argument could be rebutted only by rejecting his own republican principles. Thus, after much prayer and struggle, Brisbane decided in violation of state law to free those slaves born into his possession and to allow them to "work for him as long as they desired & leaving when they chose."[9] He also forbade his overseer to whip his slaves and later discharged him.[10] The odyssey of William Henry Brisbane had begun.

At first Brisbane was bewildered at the "popular excitement" against him and declared that he had "broken no law of the state." "I am no abolitionist," he protested.[11] Indeed, he was not, for in the next three years Brisbane sold more than twenty-eight slaves whom he had inherited and wrote a rebuttal to Wayland in the *Southern Baptist.*[12] In fact, when his brother-in-law, whose wife was "thorough going in favor of emancipation & says slavery is wrong," expressed reservations about bondage, Brisbane advised him not "to free his slaves because it would be an injury to the family." He was "opposed to general emancipation because it would affect the prosperity of the country." Yet, he also was "opposed to Slavery because it was an evil to the slave."[13] He thought that his abolition-minded sister was "carrying the matter too far"; but he took heart that his mother "actually makes the same offer as I did to her own negroes."[14] The following summer Brisbane visited Wayland in Rhode Island and was much impressed by "this worthy man, notwithstanding our difference of opinion on the subject of slavery."[15]

Upon completing his medical studies in 1837, Brisbane returned to the small community of Lawtonville in Beaufort, a district in which 85 percent of the population was black. Here he practiced medicine, preached, and oversaw his plantation. During the course of the year, however, he began to feel "cramped & confined."[16] Finally in January 1838, Brisbane convinced his wife that they should sell their land and Negroes and "abandon the whole plantation business with slave labor forever." He rejoiced that "we are now, therefore, quite free from the care of negroes. It is our design to move to Ohio as soon as possible." Brisbane was still only partially converted to abolitionism, for he sold his remaining slaves except for two who were "reserved . . . to wait upon us" and "Old Frank" and his family who would receive wages for their services.[17]

After his arrival in Cincinnati, Brisbane's conversion was quickly completed. In October 1839, he returned to South Carolina and arranged to buy back the slaves whom he had earlier sold so that "they should have their freedom."[18] He confessed, "On this subject, I have suffered great distress of mind & since I have been in Cin [cinna] *ti* I have never remitted my anxious study of the slavery question." In early 1840, he declared:

My mind is now fully made up, not only that slavery is a wrong to man, both the slave & his master, & a sin against God having no justification in his word, but that to the principles of the abolitionists as set forth in their constitution can we alone look with any hope of success to put down the horrible system of human robbery & oppression.

He prayed "that God would awaken christians to a feeling sense of this odious sin so that they may *break every yoke & let the oppressed go free*."[19] A Carolina slaveholder had evolved into a dedicated abolitionist.

Throughout the 1840s Brisbane labored tirelessly against the "peculiar" institution. He helped to organize the Cincinnati Antislavery Society, worked with the city's black community, aided runaway slaves, and edited an abolitionist newspaper, the *Christian Politician*, which subsequently was retitled the *Western Transcript*.[20] Antiabolitionist mob violence and threats convinced him "that the slave power will destroy our liberties unless we can check it in time."[21] In 1844 Brisbane made an unsuccessful bid for Congress on the Liberty party ticket, and the following year, working closely with James G. Birney, he arranged for a Liberty party convention in Cincinnati. In 1849 Brisbane was instrumental in founding a new abolitionist organization, the Philadelphon

Society, and then served as editor of its monthly newspaper, *The Epoch*. Throughout these years he worked closely with his friends Salmon P. Chase, Levi Coffin, Joshua Giddings, and James G. Birney, as well as other less well-known abolitionists in Cincinnati. In 1846, Brisbane moved to Philadelphia where he served as a Liberty party agent and editor of the *American Citizen*, an organ of the Eastern Pennsylvania Liberty party. The next year he wrote a book on slavery, which, with the encouragement of Theodore Dwight Weld and the financial backing of Lewis Tappan, was published by the American Antislavery Society. In the fall of 1848 he returned to Cincinnati.[22]

At the national level, Brisbane was active not only in the Liberty party but also in the American Antislavery Society and on the executive committee of the American and Foreign Antislavery Society. On trips to the East he came in contact with Tappan, Weld, William Lloyd Garrison, Frederick Douglass, Horace Greeley, John P. Hale, and other notable abolitionists.[23] Of Garrison he wrote tersely: "Do not admire him."[24]

Brisbane also crusaded within the Baptist church against human bondage. After the church he pastored in Cincinnati split on the slavery issue, he formed a new one on an antislavery basis. He also labored on the executive committee of the Antislavery Convention of Western Baptists and the national Baptist Antislavery Society to rid his denomination of the taint of slavery.[25] Arguing that to join in fellowship with a slaveholder was "to partake of his evil deeds," Brisbane helped to precipitate the 1845 split between the northern and southern wings of the Baptist church.[26]

While a hard-shell teetotalling Baptist who apologized for writing "a short letter" or traveling on the Sabbath, Brisbane did have an unconventional mind. Like many abolitionists, he engaged in a wide variety of reforms and fads. Over the years he dabbled with phrenology, mesmerism, and electrology, visited and considered joining the Brook Farm experiment, worked with not only black schools and churches but also the peace movement, and the National Reform Association, and maintained a longstanding commitment to the temperance movement.[27]

Brisbane was especially interested in ridding his native state of slavery. He carried on a steady correspondence on the subject with friends and relatives in South Carolina. In the fall of 1847 he rejoiced that a visiting relative had concluded "American slavery to be sinful" and had "made up his mind to abandon slavery & emancipate the slaves over whom he has ownership."[28] In January 1848 Brisbane returned to South Carolina. Although a declared abolitionist, he was warmly greeted and hosted by friends and relatives as he journeyed from Charleston to St. Peter's Parish in Beaufort District. At Lawtonville he was even invited to conduct a service at his old church.[29] In his sermon he argued that his views were "consistent with the principles of evangelical christianity" and he prayed for "the enjoyment of life and liberty by all mankind." Brisbane toned down his remarks because slaves were in the audience, but he was certain that "the white congregation fully understood me, & for the most part were liberal or tolerant enough to pay me strict attention." One angry worshiper stormed out of the church, but after the service Brisbane "received the affectionate salutations of my old acquaintances."[30]

Nine days later there was a meeting at Lawtonville to discuss Brisbane's activities. Despite protests by a few that Brisbane was only a "liberty party man," not an abolitionist, the meeting denounced him as "an open and unscrupulous abolitionist in our midst" and resolved that "WM. H. BRISBANE was once of us, he went out from, and has turned against us, publishing at various times his reasons for becoming an abolitionist, and sending those reasons to his friends and acquaintances throughout this region." A committee was designated to inform him that he had forty-eight hours to leave the state.[31] Forewarned, Brisbane and his wife fled the state, but the circumstances of his visit and departure only exemplified the anxieties under which Carolina masters labored.[32]

Safe in the North, Brisbane wrote two pamphlets addressed to "the citizens of South Carolina."[33] In them he appealed to the class interests of nonslaveholding whites, much as Hinton R. Helper would a decade later in *The Impending Crisis of the South* (1857). In one, signed "A True Carolinian," Brisbane claimed "that even in South Carolina, there is in very many minds a private sentiment of repugnance to slavery" and asserted that *"the great mass of citizens of the State have no PERSONAL INTEREST in slaves, and they know that the benefits of the institution are confined to a very small number of the whole white population."*[34] In another, using the pseudonym of "Brutus," he warned that slavery would "forever blast the hope of elevation and prosperity to the mass of our population." While South Carolina reputedly had a republican form of government, "Brutus" charged that in fact "the great mass of the people are virtually disfranchised, their interests utterly disregarded, and their voice not heard in the Councils of the State."[35]

Brisbane's class appeal had sectional overtones, for he showed that six major slave districts in the lower part of the state, with only 20 percent of the white population, enjoyed a majority in the state senate. As a result, "Brutus" claimed, while "the upper districts may go to ruin, the rice and cotton plantations are amply protected. . . . The interests of men who have to work with their own hands are entirely unprotected." At the same time, the insatiable slaveholders were attempting to deny nonslaveholders refuge in the territories by threatening disunion if slavery was not allowed to spread there. As "Brutus," Brisbane called upon the yeomanry to "teach these masters of overgrown plantations that we cannot always endure this state of things."[36] These pamphlets were printed by the Philadelphon Society and mailed often with an unsigned letter from Brisbane to prominent Carolinians under the franks of Congressman Joshua R. Giddings and Senator Salmon P. Chase. The Philadelphon Society also sent John M. Barrett on an "agency" to South Carolina to recruit additional addresses for future mailings.[37]

In late March 1849, scores of Carolina masters stood aghast in their local post offices as they read unsigned letters enclosed with copies of the "Brutus" and "True Carolinian" pamphlets. These scenes would be reenacted many times until the flood of letters and pamphlets had slowed to a trickle in the fall and then dried up. In keeping with Brisbane's appeal to sectional antagonisms, the mailings were especially intense in the up-country districts.[38] After fifty copies of "A True Carolinian" were discovered in an up-country post office, the Spartanburg *Spartan* warned of "an incendiary attack, in our very midst . . . an effort to *raise an Abolition party in South Carolina.*" It asserted that while the pamphlet might touch off an insurrection, "the great and darling object of the incendiary author" was "to excite the nonslaveholding voters of the State to make the question at the ballot-box—assuring them that they are in the majority, and that they are themselves oppressed by the institution of slavery." The alarmed editor of the *Spartan* guessed that the pamphlet's author was living in South Carolina, "a viper that has nestled in the bosom of the State."[39] Because so many prominent Carolinians had received pamphlets and letters, it was suggested that "Brutus" had many personal contacts throughout the state, and since the letters were mysteriously unpostmarked, it was even charged that local postmasters were abetting abolitionists. Rumors were rampant, demands were made for increased vigilance, and several individuals were charged with being covert abolitionists.[40]

Meanwhile John Barrett traveled through the upper part of the state gathering the names and addresses of Carolinians, especially those of clergymen. As a secret agent he was inept, however, for he was quickly detected in Columbia and was forced to flee after a warrant was issued for his arrest. He was later stopped in Winnsboro but then released for lack of evidence. Finally, he was apprehended in Spartanburg in early June when "Brutus" pamphlets and encoded letters from "B. H. W." were found in his room. By late July it was learned that "B. H. W." was William H. Brisbane, and that he was also the notorious "Brutus." By midsummer the state was in the throes of a panic, believing that slavery was threatened from within as well as from without.[41] The Columbia *Telegraph* castigated Brisbane, Barrett, and John C. Vaughan, a former Carolina politician who was editing a free-soil sheet in Cleveland. The *Telegraph* warned that "this is one branch only of a wide-spread web of machinations directed against our peace and property by domestic renegades and foreign fanatics. A thousand evidences are around us, denoting the presence in our midst of secret spies and emissaries."[42] When Garrison's *Liberator* and other northern newspapers rushed to the defense of Barrett and "Brutus," suspicions of a plot were only confirmed.[43]

Brisbane, the apostate and fomenter of class conflict under the name of Brutus, had clearly touched a raw nerve. A month before the "Brutus" mailings began, a Charleston confidant had informed Calhoun that even in South Carolina many masters were despondent and beginning "to think that the Institution of Slavery is doomed. That all the world is opposed to it and that we ourselves will not or cannot do any thing to avert it. . . . This feeling of despondence," he warned, "is *the only danger* of the South."[44] In the fall, after the "Brutus" scare, Governor Whitemarsh B. Seabrook recommended that the legislature give "special notice" to the "extensive dissemination of highly inflammatory essays and letters, intended to awaken jealousy in the minds of our citizens." He suggested that such an offense should be made punishable with severe and definite penalties.[45] Even later, during the 1851 secession crisis, a writer in the Charleston *Courier* asked how, even if secession was successful, "the constantly undermining process of sapping the foundations of institutions among ourselves, by the circulation of incendiary papers, and the more active exertions of traitors [will] be arrested?"[46] Indeed, the aftershocks of Brisbane and "Brutus" continued to be felt throughout the remainder of the antebellum period.[47]

The state had not seen the last of this determined abolitionist to which it had given birth. After moving to Arena, Wisconsin, in 1853, Brisbane continued his crusade against slavery, played a role in the formation of the Republican party, and served as clerk of the Wisconsin senate. In 1862 his old friend Salmon P. Chase appointed him tax commissioner for the Sea Islands in his native Beaufort District, which had been captured by a Union fleet in the previous November. It was a fitting climax to Brisbane's war against slavery that he participated in the famous "Port Royal Experiment." His odyssey completed, Brisbane spent most of the next twelve years working among the former slaves in Beaufort and attempting to reconstruct the society from which he had sprung.[48]

Notes

1. See Wilbur J. Cash, *The Mind of the South* (New York, 1941); Clement Eaton, *Freedom of Thought in the Old South* (Durham, 1940); Kenneth M. Stampp, *The Peculiar Institution: Slavery in the Ante-Bellum South* (New York, 1956); Charles G. Sellers, Jr., "The Travail of Slavery," *The Southerner as American* (Chapel Hill, 1960); Ralph E. Morrow, "The Proslavery Argument Revisited," *Mississippi Valley Historical Review* 48 (June 1961): 70-94; William W. Freehling, *Prelude to Civil War: The Nullification Controversy in South Carolina, 1816-1836* (New York, 1966); Steven A. Channing, *Crisis of Fear: Secession in South Carolina* (New York, 1970); Ronald T. Takaki, *A Pro-Slavery Crusade: The Agitation to Reopen the African Slave Trade*

(New York, 1971); Robert Nicholas Olsberg, "A Government of Class and Race: William Henry Trescot and the South Carolina Chivalry, 1860-1865" (Ph.D. diss., University of South Carolina, 1972). Channing minimizes the experience of guilt but places great stress on that fear.

2. David Johnson to J. C. Calhoun, 18 October 1848, "Correspondence addressed to John C. Calhoun, 1837-1849," in *American Historical Association Report, 1929* ed. Chauncey S. Boucher and Robert P. Brooks, (Washington, 1931), p. 482. In the same year J. H. Hammond wrote a prominent Charlestonian: "Let Kentucky & Western Virginia emancipate, it is inevitible [*sic*] that they should do so before long & I would not retard the event a moment after they believe it to be their interest. The culture of Tobacco has alone kept slaves this long in those regions." J. H. Hammond to W. M. Wightman, 7 June 1848, W. M. Wightman Papers, South Carolina Historical Society, Charleston, S.C. See also Robert Duncan Bass, ed., "The Autobiography of William J. Grayson" (Ph.D. diss., University of South Carolina, 1933), p. 142.

3. W. G. Simms to J. H. Hammond, 24 November [1849], J. H. Hammond Papers, Library of Congress, Washington, D.C. . Earlier, on July 15, 1847, Simms had written Hammond that in a few years Maryland "with Virginia and the states south of her including the Carolinas & Georgia will have incorporated among themselves new interests, which will greatly change their characteristics." Hammond responded on July 23, 1847, fatalistically: "As to going with it westward, I say no. If it was abolished in South Carolina to-morrow and not in Georgia I would not cross the river. The institutions that succeed it might drive me off, but I would try them." See also Avery O. Craven, *The Coming of the Civil War*, 2d ed. rev. (Chicago, 1966), p. 246.

4. J. H. Hammond to J. C. Calhoun, 26 September 1845, J. C. Calhoun Papers, South Caroliniana Library (hereinafter cited as SC), Columbia, S.C.

5. William Henry Brisbane Journal, vol. 1, 1835-1837 *passim*, William Henry Brisbane Papers, Wisconsin Historical Society, Madison, Wis. Volume 1 (1835-1842) consists of notes and quotations copied into an 1865 diary by Brisbane. See also biographical sketch of Brisbane in the description of the collection and his "Proslavery Essay," [1834], vol. 34. I am indebted to Nicholas Olsberg for helping me to locate the Brisbane Papers. Abbott Hall Brisbane, full brother of W. H. Brisbane's adopted brother, was a leading Carolina apologist of slavery as well as a planter, railroad promoter, civil engineer, founder of the South Carolina Industrial Institute, militia brigadier-general, West Point colonel in the Seminole War, novelist, and professor of humanities at the Citadel. *South Carolina Historical Magazine* 14 (1913): 175-77; David Duncan Wallace, *The History of South Carolina*, 4 vols. (New York, 1934), 3: 20. For a series of ten proslavery letters by A. H. Brisbane, a convert to Catholicism, to Archbishop Hughes, see *Courier* (Charleston), 24 December 1850, and 25-27 November 1851.

6. Brisbane Journal, vol. 1, 13 June 1835.

7. This was the initial mass mailing of abolitionist material by the American Antislavery Society in its "moral 'suasion" campaign. See Freehling, *Prelude to Civil War*, 340-42.

8. Brisbane Journal, vol. 1, 8 July 1835.

9. Ibid., 14-17 July 1835.

10. Ibid. See also entry for 24 August 1835.

11. Ibid., 18 July 1835. See also entries for 23, 29 August 1835. By freeing his slaves and allowing them to hire their own time Brisbane in fact was violating state law.

12. Ibid., 20 July, 23 August, 14 October, 1835; 2 April, 7 November 1836; 18 January 1838; 19 December 1841.

13. Ibid., 20 July 1835.

14. Ibid.

15. Ibid., 4 June 1836.

16. Ibid., 27 January, 24 September and *passim* 1837.

17. Ibid., 18 January 1838.

18. Ibid., 24 October 1839. See also entries for 4 January 1840; 21 August, 19 December 1841. On the latter date Brisbane freed twenty-five slaves whom he had earlier sold.

19. Ibid., 4 January 1840.

20. Ibid., vols. 1 and 2, 1841-1844 *passim*.

21. Ibid., 12 October 1841.

22. Ibid., vols. 2-6, 1844-1848 *passim*. Brisbane wrote the introduction to Levi Coffin's *Reminiscences of Levi Coffin* (1876; reprint ed. New York, 1968) and is mentioned several times therein, see pp. ii-iii, 272, 294.

23. Brisbane Journal, vols. 2-6, 1845-1848 *passim*; Dwight L. Dumond, *Antislavery: The Crusade for Freedom in America* (New York, 1961), p. 286.

24. Brisbane Journal, vol. 1, 11 May 1841.

25. Ibid., vols. 1-2, 1841-1845 *passim*.

26. W. H. Brisbane, *A Speech Delivered April 30, 1844, Before the Baptist Home Mission Society on the Question of the Propriety of Recognizing Slaveholding Ministers as Proper Missionaries of the Gospel* (n.p.), pp. 2-6, quoted in H. Shelton Smith, *In His Image But. . .Racism in Southern Religion, 1780-1910* (Durham, 1972), p. 124. See also Brisbane, *A Letter to the Baptist Denomination in South Carolina* (Cincinnati, 1840) and *Speech of the Rev. W. H. Brisbane, Lately a Slaveholder in South Carolina; Delivered before the Female Anti-Slavery Society of Cincinnati, February 12, 1840* (Cincinnati, 1840).

27. Brisbane Journal, vols. 1-6, 1835-1850 *passim*.

28. Ibid., vol. 5, 4 October 1847.

29. Ibid., 28, 29 January 1848.

30. Ibid., 30 January 1848.

31. A description and the preamble and resolutions of this meeting of 8 February 1848 are reprinted in *Courier*, 29 August 1849 and *Mercury* (Charleston), 29 August 1849. Dr. T. D. Mathews, a relative of Brisbane, was one of those who denied that Brisbane was an abolitionist. He appears to have sympathized privately with Brisbane's abolitionist views. In August 1849, the committee of safety reconvened and accused Mathews of writing an unfavorable account of the "indignation meeting" that had banished Brisbane, which was published in the Cincinnati *Globe*. Mathews admitted to having written the article and to having sent it to Brisbane, but he falsely claimed that Brisbane distorted the original article. This explanation was accepted by the committee. *Courier* and *Mercury*, 29 August 1849; *Telegraph* (Columbia), 30 August 1849; Brisbane Journal, vol. 6, 1, 15 August, 6, 12 September, 1, 3, October 1849.

32. Brisbane Journal, vol. 5, 8 February 1848.

33. "A True Carolinian" [W. H. Brisbane], *To the Voters of South Carolina* [Cincinnati, 1849]; "Brutus" [W. H. Brisbane], *An Address to the Citizens of South Carolina* [Cincinnati, 1849] are discussed below. In his journal Brisbane also refers to a third pamphlet, the *Junius Letters to Calhoun*, which I have been unable to locate. In addition to these works, Brisbane wrote *Slaveholding Examined*, which was published by the American Antislavery Society, and *Amanda*, an abolitionist novel. See Brisbane Journal, vol. 6, 1 December 1848, 5 February, 6 March, 26 April, 2 September 1849.

34. Quoted in *Spartan* (Spartanburg), 24 April 1849. Given Brisbane's fundamentalist religious orientation, it is surprising that he did not make a dogmatic, emotional, moral argument against slavery in these pamphlets. Instead, he pragmatically presented a calculated appeal to self-interest.

35. "Brutus" [Brisbane], *An Address to the Citizens of S.C.*

36. Ibid. At the end of the pamphlet Brisbane backed away from its revolutionary thrust by calling upon Carolinians to draft a new state constitution, "in which the interests of the *free* laborer shall be provided for," demand that the legislature adopt it, and, if it did not, to appeal to Congress.

37. Brisbane Journal, vol. 6, 6, 23, 28 February, 11, 12 April, and May-July *passim* 1849. The *Spartan*, 26 July 1849 printed one of Brisbane's unsigned letters received by H. C. Young of Laurens, a former state senator:

Mr. Young—Sir: Study your country's good. Give freedom to your negroes and do not go to the expense of building negro houses. Let the negroes look to their own interest and build houses for themselves. They will not be so liable to be burned down. Hire them. Pay wages. . . . Yours for Carolina

TRUE PATRIOT

38. Post offices in the Pickens, Pendleton, Abbeville, Newberry, Laurens, Richland, Sumter, and Marlboro districts received large numbers of the pamphlets. *Spartan*, 2 August, 27 September 1849; *Telegraph*, 25 June, 16, 23 July, 24 August 1849; *Mercury*, 21 September 1849; *Banner* (Abbeville), 21 August 1849; Brisbane Journal, vol. 6, 28 May, 2, 5, 26 June, 5, 17, 18, 25, 30 July 1849.

39. *Spartan*, 24 April 1849.

40. *Telegraph*, 16 May, 23, 24, 30 July, 11, 14, 24, 30 August, 17 September 1849; *Banner*, 21 August 1849; *Spartan*, 24 April, 19, 23, 26 July, 28 August, 6, 13 September 1849; *Courier*, 29 August 1849; *Mercury*, 29 August 1849; printed letter from the General Committee on Safety, 11 August 1849, Williams-Chesnut-Manning Papers, SC; Daniel Wallace to Chairman of the Committee of Vigilance and Safety in Columbia, S.C., 8 November 1849 (copy), McLean Family Papers, SC.

41. In October, 1849 Barrett was released on $1,000 bail and allowed to leave the state. His ill-fated agency and the panic it provoked may be followed in *Telegraph*, 4, 18, 25 June, 23, 24, 30 July, 21, 24 August 1849; *Spartan*, 14 June, 16 July, 2, 16, 23, 30 August 1849; *Herald* (Fairfield), 2 June 1849; reprinted in *Telegraph*, 4 June 1849; *Mercury*, 24, 30 July, 6, 9, 13, 16, 23, 27 August, 21 September 1849; *Courier*, 18 June, 8, 9 October 1849; Spartanburg Court of General Sessions, 5 October 1849, microfilm, South Carolina Archives, Columbia, S.C.; Brisbane Journal, vol. 6, 21 June-October 1849.

42. *Telegraph*, 21 August 1849. See also *Spartan*, 30 August 1849. After converting to abolitionism, Vaughan abandoned slavery and his political career in South Carolina and moved to Kentucky and Ohio where he collaborated with Cassius M. Clay, served as secretary of the Free Soil Convention, and edited antislavery sheets in Louisville, Cincinnati, and Cleveland. Eric Foner, *Free Soil, Free Labor, Free Men: The Ideology of the Republican Party before the Civil War* (New York, 1970), p. 118; Asa Earl Martin, *The Anti-Slavery Movement in Kentucky Prior to 1850* (New York, 1970), pp. 118-20.

43. *Spartan*, 26, 30 August, 6 September 1849; Brisbane Journal, vol. 6, 14 August 1849.

44. H. W. Conner to J. C. Calhoun, 12 January 1849, "Correspondence to John C. Calhoun," *Annual Report of the American Historical Association for the Year 1899*, ed. J. F. Jameson (Washington, 1900), 2: 1188-90. See also Herschel V. Johnson to J. C. Calhoun, 20 July 1849, in *ibid.*, pp. 1197-99.

45. *Journal of the House of Representatives of the State of South Carolina; Being the Annual Session of 1849* (Columbia, 1849), p. 14.

46. Cincinnatus, "Is Secession a Practical Remedy. . .," *Courier*, 13 May 1851.

47. See the example letter to *Mercury*, n.d., reprinted in *Advertiser* (Edgefield), 16 November 1854; Governor J. H. Adam's message to the legislature, 24 November 1856, *Journal of the House of Representatives of the State of South Carolina; Being the Annual Session of 1856* (Columbia, 1856), pp. 35-37.

48. Brisbane Journal, vols. 11-30, 1853-1874 *passim*; Willie Lee Rose, *Rehearsal for Reconstruction: The Port Royal Experiment* (New York, 1964), pp. 196, 201-02, 276, 278, 285, 291, 294, 380, 402.

9

THE SOUTHERN MERCHANT: A PERENNIAL SOURCE OF DISCONTENT

Ronald L. F. Davis

Students of southern history have long known that southern farmers from the colonial planter to the twentieth-century sharecropper have blamed many of their personal problems as well as their region's economic problems on the southern merchant. Historians and historical economists have produced important studies on the South's system of marketing and have documented amply the farmers' feelings of antagonism toward the merchant.[1] The region's middlemen were a perennial source of discontent for southern farmers, but was this criticism and discontent a constant and unchanging theme? Were the objections raised in the colonial era the same as those voiced in the late nineteenth century? Although there is no study of the change or continuity in the farmers' attitudes toward the southern merchant, it is possible to learn something about the nature of these complaints by reviewing what is known about the South's marketing system. Such a review should enable us to recognize the boundaries of our knowledge as well as to gain some insight into this nearly universal aspect of southern history.

Thomas Jefferson noted at the end of the colonial period that "long experience has proved to us that there never was an instance of a man's getting out of debt who was once in the hands of a tobacco merchant."[2] His statement best reflects the long line of complaints that extends back to the beginning of the colonial period. Colonial farmers and planters had expressed their dissatisfaction with, hatred of, and animosity toward tobacco merchants at every level of their involvement with them. Jefferson's comment suggests that tobacco merchants were an ensnaring group perhaps by nature of their profession, although it was believed to be especially descriptive of the South's nonresident merchants from England and Scotland.[3] As outsiders, these men were envied and accused of having unfair advantages over the colonial planter because of their superior market information, their control of production credits, their versatility in business, and their ability to profit from even the poorest of economic conditions.[4] Such complaints indicate the relatively isolated and dependent condition of colonial planters.

Even in the first years of settlement southern farmers were concerned over the merchant's advantage in the colonial system of trade and wealth. Some planters felt that merchants enjoyed unfair advantages in acquiring colonial lands and shares in the Virginia Company. Others who had secured passage on merchant commissioned vessels remembered the merchant's "meanness" in provisioning the voyage to Virginia. Some planters were merchants themselves and therefore in direct competition with agents of powerful British trading firms. Those who were not merchants often felt that their English merchants enjoyed too large a part of the profits. Obviously planters and merchants did not always have the same production goals. When prices for tobacco were high, planters sought to maximize production, often in conflict with the Virginia Company's interest in crop scarcity; at other times, merchant pressure on the planter to grow tobacco as a single crop pitted the two against each other. And there was always the question of to whom the merchant was responsible. In the colonial era, unlike the antebellum period, the tobacco merchant seldom functioned simply as the planter's agent in the selling of the crop. Although the evidence is not clear, it seems that merchants served many masters—themselves in the buying and selling of tobacco on their own accounts, European houses in London and Glasgow as their agents, planters, and themselves again working as planters. The region's farming population mistrusted the merchant's shifting role.[5]

Most common were grumblings about the planter's indebtedness to his English merchants. Richard Pares has explained that much of the planter's indebtedness resulted from the merchant's customary encouragement of business. It was felt that merchants encouraged planter expenditures because of the commissions they created. The planter's indebtedness to the merchant also somewhat assured future commissions on the shipment of next year's crop. A merchant's encouragement made it difficult to avoid indebtedness, and planters often complained, as Jefferson noted, that it was nearly impossible to switch merchants once so ensnared.[6]

In the antebellum cotton period of the nineteenth century, planter dissatisfaction with the southern merchant changed in tempo and character. Merchants were still believed to be a necessary evil, especially if one was indebted to a coastal merchant or a country store, but it was not the same complaint of the colonial period. Harold Woodman has noted in his study of the cotton factor, or merchant, that southern cotton farmers seldom held their factors responsible for the conditions of trade or the state of the market. Rather, cotton farmers criticized the dependency of both farmer and merchant on northern buyers and outside sources of supply. While some planters complained that their agents failed to pass on savings in the trade, occasionally falsified sales, or needlessly tied up capital after the sale of the crop, in general both factors and country merchants were considered competent agents of the farming interests and worthy of respect. When planters and farmers criticized the region's merchants they were attacking a marketing system that they believed to be controlled by the northern centers of trade. The merchant was not seen as an essential cause of the antebellum discontent of southern farmers.[7]

After the Civil War southern agrarians once again lifted their voices in angry denunciations of the southern merchant. The region's failure to modernize, its single crop economy, its system of debt peonage and backward farming practices, its racism, its shabby materialism, its loss of honor, and its system of land monopoly were all considered intimately linked to, if not caused by, the southern merchant. Although contemporaries well understood the complexity of the problems facing them as farmers in the postbellum South, they firmly believed that an independent farming class would not reemerge until the hold of the merchant was broken. Farmers blamed the merchant for the origins of sharecropping, for the displacement of the antebellum planting class, and for the institutionalization of a system of interest charges that literally imprisoned two-thirds to three-fourths of the southern farming population. By 1880 the southern merchant served to symbolize all that was evil about southern agriculture.[8]

In comparing the three periods it seems clear that there was much continuity in the nature of the farmers' complaints about southern merchants. There were, however, some differences. In both the colonial and postbellum periods southern farmers viewed the merchant as the primary source of their discontent. In both periods it was felt that merchants should be regulated or controlled in their business and in their conduct. Local courts in both periods struggled to protect the planters from merchant claims, liens, and mortgages, and in both periods the southern merchant was viewed as an underminer of the best interests of southern society.[9] In contrast, the antebellum period, except for the typical complaints of farmers about their agents, witnessed far less conflict between farmers and merchants.

If the perceptions and attitudes of southern farmers toward merchants differed over time as the foregoing review suggests, the obvious question is why? Why did the general dissatisfaction of the colonial period become modified in tone in the antebellum period only to heighten again after the Civil War? Existing scholarship fails to address this problem in any depth. Based upon the literature at hand, however, it is possible to say that the institutions of marketing in the three periods, though similar in function, experienced profound alterations in character. These alterations undoubtedly contributed to popular attitudes and perceptions. T. H. Breen recently has explored the tobacco mentality of Virginia planters in the colonial era as a possible explanation for their decisions and attitudes. As Virginians were tobacco farmers before they were anything else, Breen suggests that most of their activities flowed from that reality.[10] The role of the merchant was a significant part of that planting culture, and as that role changed so too did popular perceptions.

The colonial era is best understood as a two-hundred-year period of evolution and maturation in the production and marketing of tobacco. In that time planters and farmers moved from a pioneer state of production in which merchants were essential to the survival of the colonists to a period of advanced maturity and the beginnings of economic decline and readjustment. Obviously merchants played different roles over this long span of colonial development. In the early period the agents of the Virginia Company, for instance, held tremendous power over the colonial farmer. They set prices, influenced patterns of settlements, established trading practices, and controlled most of the means of production.[11] In time merchants became landlords, resident planters, entrepreneurs operating on their own accounts, resident factors, receivers for British firms, and agents of Glasgow chain store establishments. While by the 1750s the once powerful merchant had become something of an agent of colonial planters in the selling of tobacco, his job was never simply that of a retainer. The actual role of the merchant often depended upon a multitude of circumstances that usually were related to the political and economic forces at work in England. Seldom did the merchant function merely as an agent of the colonial planter.[12]

In the up-country, beyond the fall lines, there emerged Scottish country stores. These offered a new breed of merchant with new loyalties and a new way of doing business. These Scottish merchants dealt with the numerous smaller farmers of the interior. They purchased cotton on the spot for shipment to their parent firms in Glasgow. They supplied cash, credits, and supplies and appear to have been little interested in becoming part of the local gentry. How they related to the tidewater merchants is unknown, but by 1750 they had captured the lion's share of the interior trade. Little more than this is known about them.[13]

With the invention of the cotton gin in the 1790s a new system of marketing soon emerged, cotton factorage. The cotton factor was the planter's agent in every sense of the term. Unlike the colonial merchant, the cotton factor seldom operated as the agent of outside interests; nor did he have one foot in planting and land speculation as his colonial counterparts had had. The typical cotton factor was an entrepreneur who made it his business to find the best buyer for the planter's crops. In doing so the factor received a standard commission on the sale. These men offered planters a full range of services from receiving crops, paying and handling transport and storage costs, holding for top prices, and seeking the best markets to providing credit and provisions. For each marketing transaction the factor charged a fee, but it was a standard charge seldom open to competition or exploitation. In Woodman's words, "the cotton factor was the planter's commercial alter ego, his personal representative in the marketplace."[14]

The country store existed as an appendage to the factorage system. In the antebellum period, the country store serviced the needs of small and intermediate cotton farmers in the same way that the factorage system serviced large planters. Store merchants provided their farm customers with supplies, purchased their cotton or took it as barter, advanced credits for making the crop, and shipped the cotton to coastal factors on consignment. Although most storekeepers obtained credit and cash advances from their factors, it would be a mistake to assume that these merchants were agents of the coastal houses. They functioned as independent businessmen selecting and securing their connections as they deemed appropriate.[15]

The antebellum country store stands in stark contrast to the colonial and postbellum store. For one thing the colonial store was relatively independent of its creditors. It seems that they were either plantation stores, servicing neighbors, or they functioned as extensions of the Glasgow merchant firms. The postbellum country merchant was never just an agent of outside suppliers or creditors, although he often acted as the chief representative of giant cotton firms, especially in the late nineteenth century. The merchant in antebellum times related somewhat differently to the surrounding community. He seldom held liens on the crops for advances made or a mortgage on the farmer's property, which would become the dominant practice of storekeepers after the Civil War. Nor did the antebellum merchants become planter-merchants to any significant extent as they did before the American Revolution and after the Civil War. Unlike country stores in the other periods under review, few antebellum country stores monopolized the trade of their customers. The antebellum merchant was not in a position to charge "usurous" interest rates for credit or prices for goods. The antebellum country stores, as agents of the farming class, operated within the planter-dominated character of the region's political economy.[16]

After the Civil War a revolution occurred in the marketing of the South's cotton. The role of the factor as a seller of the crop on consignment nearly disappeared. A more extensive network of railroads, new techniques of trade, and better means of communication moved cotton markets inland and made them immediately accessible to a system of country stores. Factors, or agents of the planters, were no longer needed to seek out the best European or northern markets. That information was now readily available to the country merchant. Warehouses and services followed the market to the country and the port cities played an increasingly smaller role in the distribution of supplies and farm produce. Merchants no longer looked to the coastal factor for credit or felt isolated from northern manufacturers or eastern wholesalers. Suppliers and buyers now came to the interior stores. Gone forever were the wagon trips and boat journeys by merchants in search of goods at reasonable wholesale prices. Cotton, already ginned and compressed for shipping, moved from interior warehouses by rail to port cities for immediate loading or use by manufacturers.[17]

The most important features of these changes were those that propelled the country merchant into a new position of power and control over the lives of southern farmers. The emancipation of the slaves threw hundreds of thousands of farmers into the retail end of the southern market overnight. Their needs were simple but had a profound effect: credit to farm, supplies to carry themselves through a year of farming, and land, tools, and mules for production. The new freedmen had no resources except their labor power, and they were determined to use that power to sever as much as possible all relations with their old masters. Planters had few resources except their lands, and these were nearly valueless unless a system of labor could be fashioned out of the chaos of the war. After much complex and often violent confrontation in which the freedmen's determination to establish himself in a situation of relatively independent farming status was a crucial feature, the southern merchant emerged as the chief means by which the planter obtained labor and the freedmen lands for farming. This was no compromise between the planter and freedmen but rather a development best characterized as a victory for southern blacks, although it proved to be a hollow one as they were soon reduced to a debt peonage similar to slavery. The key to understanding the merchant's role was the introduction of the crop lien. The lien gave the merchant legal claim to crops for advances made, while it reduced the farmer's status to that of a peculiar class of workers—neither wage laborer nor tenant. The system carried with it the single crop characteristics of the colonial period: land monopoly (the southern merchant could become a landlord because of defaults or by leasing plantations) and sharecropping.[18]

In comparison to the antebellum merchant, the country merchant in the postbellum period became a landlord. Unlike the tidewater planter/merchants of the colonial period, however, neither the postbellum merchant nor his agent were greatly involved in the daily supervision of labor. Although the merchant owned or rented lands, he seldom farmed these lands under his own direction or as their chief cultivator. Rather these merchant/landlords furnished sharecroppers and tenants under various degrees of supervision. In time the system evolved to such a point that some plantations were organized like factories, with supervisors in charge of the coordination and direction of the sharecroppers. Even here, however, the supervisor's role was that of looking after the place in a more general sense than had been the case before the war. The question of just how much the merchant/planter, or planter/merchant, was involved in the supervision of his tenants is yet unresolved. Evidence to date suggests that the landlord's involvement was far less than that of the antebellum or colonial planter. On some plantations using wage hands, the merchant/planter lived on the place and closely disciplined his workers. But landlords seldom supervised sharecroppers and cash tenants on a daily basis. Rather, the merchant/planter exercised enough control to see that the crops were made and that the equipment was properly cared for and used. Even on the most mechanized plantations of the 1940s the plantation manager showed relative restraint in the supervision of his sharecroppers and tenants.[19]

Although planter/merchants exercised far less daily supervision over blacks after the Civil War than under slavery, sharecroppers and tenants nevertheless were boxed into a system of debt peonage that left them unprotected from the racial hatred and abuse of the dominant society. This entrapment meant that the country merchant assumed from the planter/slave master the primary responsibility for the perpetuation of racial controls. It was the merchant who preserved the status quo in these matters. In a sense, the instruments of supply, tenancy, and the crop lien reinforced the region's racist political economy and society in ways unknown before the war. Merchants controlled their tenants by means of the crop lien and a series of laws and court interpretations that reduced the farmer to the status of a dependent laborer.[20] Once they held him in debt, merchants exercised a kind of land and credit monopoly over the farmer, not in the sense of binding him to a single store but in the sense of binding him to similar conditions of credit and supply regardless of the store or merchant to whom he was indebted.[21] Unlike the antebellum period, the merchant was responsible for the general direction of labor, for the provision of credits and supplies directly to the black farming community, for the distribution of lands to farmers, and for the social stability of the neighborhood.

It was this state of relative dependency on the merchant that generated the farmers' antagonism and hatred in the third quarter of the nineteenth century. It is ironic that this happened in view of the fact that freedmen at first had thought of the merchant as a means of liberation from the planters. When given the chance, freedmen had preferred to contract with merchants for provisions and frequently sought to make these men their landlords as well. In fact, the freedmens' determination to resist dependency upon the antebellum planter for supplies was an essential first step in their transition from wage laborers to sharecroppers and tenants. Planters, on the other hand, immediately saw the merchant as their chief rival for power. Although they did support crop lien laws as a necessary means of securing credit to once again begin planting, planters fought long and hard to keep their crops and lands free from claims, liens, and mortgages.[22] By 1880 few contemporaries saw much for which to thank the merchant. Landless farmers (black and white sharecroppers and tenants) saw themselves in a hopeless state of economic bondage, while the surviving planter class held the merchants in contempt, unless they had themselves survived by becoming merchants.

This brief review of the merchant's role in southern history indicates that much is yet to be learned. For one thing, the differences in the character of that role in the three periods discussed may be more apparent than real. Reading the history of the southern merchant prior to Woodman's study would lead to the conclusion that the antebellum merchant differed little from the postbellum merchant. Woodman's study shows the differences. Perhaps a similar study of the colonial marketing system would be equally revealing of the differences between that period and the period following the Civil War. It is highly probable that the shared antimerchant attitudes of these two periods mask substantial differences in the character and functions of the region's merchants and in the nature of the farmer and planter conflict. Rhetoric does take on a life of its own, and the antimerchant expressions that reached peaks in the 1680s and 1770s may have developed a cumulative and ideological momentum that was somewhat self-sustaining. By 1865, the South had a rich tradition of antimerchant rhetoric from which to draw upon when analyzing the problems of its political economy.

In reality we know very little about the colonial merchant when compared to what we know about his kin of several generations later. Who were these early merchants? How did they compare and differ in their business activities? In their politics? In their societal dealings? What about their role in the slave trade? In the rise of the plantation? The questions extend on and on. Only when such a study is undertaken may we hope to better understand the southern perceptions of the merchant as a perennial source of discontent.

Certain features of the antimerchant expressions of discontent are worth investigating. First, did the absentee character of the southern merchant throughout the region's history play a significant part in the region's antimerchant character? Second, what was the background of the farmer's notion of credit and his mistrust of speculation? Southern farmers generally mistrusted and assumed the worst of anyone giving credit or involved in speculation. Negative attitudes toward future operations in the 1880s were strikingly similar to planter dissatisfaction with the thought of merchants profiting from crop speculations in the seventeenth century. Third, farmers throughout southern history have resented the fact that merchants seemed to have earned their commissions and enjoyed profits from activity not clearly recognizable as work. These three aspects of agrarian criticism suggest that a common ideology, or view of the world, supported the antimerchant bias of southern history. Much of this bias apparently reflected a belief in the harmony and equality of individuals living and working in a society based upon ties of affection, benevolence, and moral feelings. Merchants, as middlemen between that world of harmony and independence and the modern world of contracts and paper profits, were resented as much because they were symbols of an unwholesome reality as because they were considered "mean." It would be farfetched, perhaps, to make too much of this symbolic opposition, since the indebtedness and abuse of southern farmers was sufficient basis for their concern, but it is important to understand that grappling with the problem may require a consideration of the changing nature of the South's marketing system.

Notes

1. See especially Lewis C. Gray, *History of Agriculture in the Southern United States to 1860*, 2 vols., (Gloucester, Mass.: Peter Smith, 1958) and Roger L. Ransom and Richard Sutch, *One Kind of Freedom: The Economic Consequences of Emancipation* (Cambridge, Engl.: Cambridge University Press, 1971).

2. Paul L. Ford, ed., *The Writings of Thomas Jefferson*, 10 vols. (New York: G. P. Putnam, 1892-1899), 4: 288.

3. Louis Morton, *Robert Carter of Nomini Hall: A Virginia Tobacco Planter of the Eighteenth Century* (Charlottesville: The University Press of Virginia, 1941), pp. 188-204.

4. The best single source for understanding the role of the merchant in the colonial economy remains Lewis C. Gray's monumental study of southern agriculture. Other important works include Aubrey C. Land, "Economic Base and Social Structure: The Northern Chesapeake in the Eighteenth Century," *Journal of Economic History* 25 (December 1965): 639-54; "Economic Behavior in a Planting Society: The Eighteenth Century Chesapeake," *Journal of Southern History* 33 (November 1967): 469-85; Arthur Pierce Middleton, *Tobacco Coast: A Maritime History of Chesapeake Bay in the Colonial Era* (Newport News, Virginia: The Mariners' Museum, 1953), pp. 93-214; Richard Pares, *Merchants and Planters* (Cambridge: Cambridge University Press, 1960); Jacob M. Price, *Capital and Credit in British Overseas Trade: The View from the Chesapeake, 1700-1776* (Cambridge, Mass.: Harvard University Press, 1980); Jacob M. Price, "The Rise of Glasgow in the Chesapeake Tobacco Trade, 1707-1775," *William and Mary Quarterly* 11 (April 1954): 179-99; Samuel M. Rosenblatt, "The Significance of Credit in the Tobacco Trade: A Study of John Norton & Sons, 1768-1775," *William and Mary Quarterly* 19 (July 1962): 383-99. James H. Soltow, "Scottish Traders in Virginia," *Economic History Review* 12 (1959): 83-98.

5. The best single source for understanding the continual and varied nature of these complaints is Richard Pares's *Merchants and Planters*.

6. Ibid.

7. Harold S. Woodman, *King Cotton and His Retainers: Financing & Marketing the Cotton Crop of the South, 1800-1925* (Lexington: The University of Kentucky Press, 1968).

8. See Stephen J. DeCanio, *Agriculture in the Postbellum South: The Economics of Production and Supply* (Cambridge, Mass.: MIT Press, 1974), for a recent statement of the issues.

9. See Philip Alexander Bruce's *Economic History of Virginia in the Seventeenth Century*, 2 vols. (New York: Peter Smith, 1935), 2: 331-91, Richard Pares, *Planter and Merchants*, p. 31; Harold Woodman "Post-Civil War Southern Agriculture and the Law," *Agricultural History* 53 (January 1979): 319-37.

10. T. H. Breen, "The Culture of Agriculture: From Tobacco to Wheat in Tidewater, Virginia, 1760 to 1790" (to be published by Norton and Co. in a collection of essays).

11. See Carville E. Earle, *The Evolution of a Tidewater Settlement System: All Hallow's Parish, Maryland, 1650-1783* (Chicago: The University of Chicago, 1975), pp. 62-215; and James H. Soltow, *The Economic Role of Williamsburg* (Williamsburg: Colonial Williamsburg, 1965), pp. 1-107.

12. See Edmund S. Morgan, *American Slavery and American Freedom: The Ordeal of Colonial Virginia* (New York: W. W. Norton, 1975), pp. 180-211, Jacob M. Price, *Capital and Credit*, pp. 124-39.

13. The nature of the interior trade and the rise of the Scottish merchant are probably the two most visible gaps in the scholarship on the southern merchant, notwithstanding the work of Soltow, Pares, and Price. For treatment of the Glasgow merchants, see Thomas M. Devine, *The Tobacco Lords: A Study of the Tobacco Merchants of Glasgow and Their Trading Activities* (Edinburgh, Scotland: John Donald Publishers Ltd., 1975).

14. Woodman, *King Cotton*. Woodman's study is recognized as the standard work on the subject. His efforts have rescued the cotton factor from the anti-merchant bias exhibited by most students of the subject in discussing the post-Civil War. See especially, Alfred Holt Stone: "The Cotton Factorage System of the Southern States," *American Historical Review* 20 (April 1915): 557-65.

15. Lewis Atherton, *The Southern Country Store, 1800-1860* (Baton Rouge: Louisiana State University Press, 1949). Woodman and Atherton seem to disagree on the extent to which the store served only as an appendage of the factorage system.

16. See Atherton, *The Southern Country Store* and Woodman, *King Cotton*.

17. Woodman, *King Cotton*, pp. 205-359.

18. The literature on the origins and functioning of sharecropping is now substantial; however, there is little in the way of consensus. Much of the secondary literature has been written by historical economists interested in the efficiency of the system. While some of this work is perceptive to say the least, by looking at the system only in terms of efficiency these writers have failed to provide a historical context. A selected list of the best work on this subject includes Stephen J. DeCanio, *Agriculture in the Post-bellum South: The Economics of Production and Supply* (Cambridge, Mass.: MIT Press, 1974); Robert Higgs, *Competition and Coercion: Blacks in the American Economy, 1865-1914* (New York: Cambridge University Press, 1977); Leon F. Litwack, *Been in the Storm so Long: The Aftermath of Slavery* (New York: Alfred A. Knopf, 1979); Jay R. Mandle, *The*

Roots of Black Poverty: The Southern Plantation Economy after the Civil War (Durham, N.C.: Duke University Press, 1978); Roger L. Ransom and Richard Sutch, *One Kind of Freedom: Economic Conosequences of Emancipation*; Joseph D. Reid, "Sharecropping and Agricultural Uncertainty," *Economic Development and Cultural Change* 24 (April 1976): 549-76; Joseph D. Reid, "Sharecropping as an Understandable Market Response: The Post-Bellum South," *Journal of Economic History* 33 (March 1973): 106-30; James L. Roark, *Masters Without Slaves: Southern Planters in the Civil War and Reconstruction* (New York: W. W. Norton, 1977); Jonathan M. Wiener, *Social Origins of the New South: Alabama 1860-1885* (Baton Rouge: Louisiana State University Press, 1978); Joel Williamson, *After Slavery: The Negro in South Carolina During Reconstruction, 1861-1877* (Chapel Hill: The University of North Carolina Press, 1965). Harold D. Woodman, "Sequel to Slavery: The New History Views the Post-Bellum South," *The Journal of Southern History* 43 (November 1977): 524-54; C. Vann Woodward, *Origins of the New South, 1877-1913* (Baton Rouge: Louisiana State University Press, 1951).

19. See Ronald L. F. Davis, *Good and Faithful Labor: From Slavery to Sharecropping in the Natchez District, 1850-1890* (Westport, Conn.: Greenwood Press, 1982). Martin Rubin, *Plantation Country* (Chapel Hill: The University of North Carolina Press, 1951); and T. J. Woofter, Jr., *Landlord and Tenant on the Cotton Plantation* (Washington, D.C.: U.S. Works Progress Administration, 1936).

20. Harold S. Woodman, "Post-Civil War Southern Agriculture and the Law," *Agricultural History* 53 (1979): 319-37.

21. Davis, *Good and Faithful Labor*.

22. Ibid.

10

DEDICATED SERVANT OR ERRANT PROFESSIONAL: THE SOUTHERN NEGRO PHYSICIAN BEFORE WORLD WAR II

E. H. Beardsley

Until after World War II, Negro physicians in the South and, to a lesser extent, in the North were virtual prisoners of American racism and the segregationist structures it spawned. Denied the training and income of white doctors and unable (and often unwilling) to maintain their skills once in practice, southern black physicians could not deliver the quality of medical care their Negro patients needed, nor could they do much to raise the southern black population's level of health, although a few tried. The southern way of life, then, not only stunted the growth of an entire professional group but in so doing added yet another chain to hold down the people these doctors served.

One basic problem facing Negro medical students in the early twentieth century was the availability and quality of professional education. For all practical purposes, the only schools open to them were Negro colleges, which by the 1920s had been reduced to two, the Meharry and Howard University medical schools. Until the 1930s, when an infusion of foundation money permitted a general upgrading, the quality of their programs was poor. Between 1903 and 1946, the percentage of Meharry and Howard graduates who failed their medical boards was, on the average, about six times higher than the percentage at the better white schools.[1]

Even after those two institutions began to pull abreast, an equally troublesome and still more refractory problem remained: the inability of many Negro graduates to find acceptable internships. In the 1920s the number of accredited positions available in Negro hospitals, virtually the only ones open to blacks, was around seventy per year, which was just about 60 percent of the number needed. By the 1930s the total had increased to about ninety per year, but that still left Negro graduates thirty to forty short. Those Negro physicians who failed to receive an accredited post had no choice but to give up the internship year entirely or to accept positions in small, backward facilities, often in the South, where their professional decline promptly began.[2]

Once in practice the Negro doctor felt the warping and dulling effect of professional segregation even more acutely. Although northern Negroes were not beyond the reach of this effect, southern doctors and their patients were its major victims. Here, the Negro physician's gravest handicap was his inability to practice in white hospitals, the facilities of which were strictly limited to members of local AMA affiliates. Since no county professional organization in the South admitted Negroes—and would not do so until about 1950—the doors of established hospitals were closed to the region's black doctors. Even after those facilities began admitting Negro patients in the 1930s their physicians, if Negroes, were seldom allowed to accompany them through the hospital doors. Obviously the much-heralded doctor-patient relationship was less important than maintenance of professional segregation.[3]

Exclusion from the county medical society had still other drawbacks for both the black physician and his or her patients. Since local and state health departments were nearly always under the control of white medical associations, black doctors had no regular relationship with official health agencies. As a result, those bodies never fully understood the extent and nature of Negro health problems. In addition, Negro physicians were nearly always excluded from the postgraduate courses and fellowships that health departments offered in the interest of continuing education.[4] White medical societies also promoted professional training at conventions and occasional seminars. Black professionals, however, were never invited to those sessions largely out of the fear that black attendance there might encourage blacks to push themselves into social sessions as well.[5] Relegated to second-class professional citizenship, black doctors came to be viewed with suspicion by many of their own patients who, associating good medicine with white doctors, shifted their patronage accordingly.[6]

Because of racism and professional exclusion, many able Negro physicians fled the South for the North or West. The early career of Louis T. Wright illustrates this out-migration of talent. In 1917, after training at Howard, Wright returned home to Atlanta determined to do his part to improve the health of his people. He did not stay long. His first encounter with Georgia officialdom convinced him that his future lay elsewhere. Sitting in the Fulton County Courthouse one day while waiting for a clerk to register his license, he heard a voice calling: "Louis! Louis!" Realizing that it was he who was wanted, Wright upbraided the clerk, telling him that his name was Dr. Louis T. Wright. The clerk wandered off but moments later returned, calling, "Wright! Wright!" Wright refused to reply, whereupon the official kicked his foot and challenged: "You aren't going to sell any dope are you or do any abortions?" Shocked into anger, Wright exploded: "Let me tell you something. I'll choke you right here if you open your god damn mouth again."

Once he cooled off he realized that if he remained in Atlanta for long, he would end up in prison or worse, and so at the first opportunity he left the South for what ultimately became a successful and influential career in New York City.[7] Not many Negro doctors had so dramatic a reminder of the ubiquity of southern racism, but many shared Wright's view of medical prospects in the South and, like him, left.

Of course, a considerable number stayed. In the interwar period the two Carolinas and Georgia counted some 425 to 440 Negro physicians, and while a variety of motives dictated their decision to remain in the South, a fair number probably viewed the situation as Dr. Peter Kelly of Conway, South Carolina, did. Kelly, who turned his back on another opportunity, decided to "let down my bucket right close to home" because of the great missionary work to be done.[8]

Indeed, there were Negro doctors who let down their buckets in every southern state and, despite the considerable odds they faced as black physicians, compiled a record of achievement that was as selfless as it was extraordinary. The contributions of two such physicians, Matilda A. Evans and L. W. Long of South Carolina, while no more than typical of other doctors elsewhere, illustrated the general achievement.

Evans originally had intended to become a medical missionary, but on receiving her degree in 1898 from the Woman's College of Philadelphia, she decided that her hometown of Columbia needed her more. Only the second female physician to practice in the state, she soon saw that the Negro's most pressing medical need was for hospitals. In the course of the next eighteen years she established and operated three such facilities. Although she enjoyed moral and some tangible support from area whites and sank much of her own income into the ventures, none of them survived more than a few years. Not only was money a problem, but her black colleagues resisted and even obstructed her work. One of them in fact went so far as to bring a charge of malpractice against her. But Evans endured, as did her hospitals, in one location or another until 1916, and in the process she provided care to black patients from as far away as North Carolina and Georgia. For many of them, including the Negroes of Columbia, Evans' hospitals were the only ones available.[9]

In 1916 Evans embarked on a new venture in the field of preventive medicine. Although her Negro Health Association, which aimed to put a Negro nurse in every South Carolina county, was an utter failure, Evans revealed a clear grasp of the primary health needs of her people. She felt that carrying services and education directly into Negroes' homes was the only way that any health progress would be made among the race. That such a program had to be initiated privately and received no encouragement from the state's white health establishment is a telling comment on both the outlook and performance of the South Carolina Board of Health at that time.

Not that Evans did not try to involve the white community in her venture. In fact, in appealing for broad community support she showed a keen understanding of white attitudes and how to play upon them. In *The Negro Health Journal*, the short-lived organ of her association, she emphasized repeatedly that the sick Negro not only endangered his or her white employer but the broader community as well.[10] Every year, she told readers, illness and death among black people robbed South Carolina of some $20 million that would otherwise have circulated through the white community. Supporting the Negro Health Association would help reduce those losses, of course, but whites should also pay black workers higher wages, so that they could afford the food and medical care their health required. The cost would be fully returned to the whites, Evans assured, for "no class of working people spends money as do Negroes when they have it."[11]

In 1930, after a period of concentrating on her private practice, Evans again turned her energies to community welfare. Although the hospital situation in Columbia had improved by then, the absence of clinical facilities for Negro children and expectant mothers remained a problem, and when the depression hit, Evans moved to address it. With assurances of support from black businessmen, she opened a free child and maternal clinic in the basement of a black Baptist church. Although it was begun only on a trial basis, the level of demand and the children's medical needs were so great that it became a permanent operation. By 1932 the Evans Clinic was a fixture in the life of area blacks. The Negro press regularly promoted it, and even the Richland County legislative delegation and the state board of health found a place for it in their budgets. But clearly, Evans was its mainstay. In 1935 she died, and the clinic ended with her. Fortunately, the work she began soon resumed as part of the public maternal and child health program brought into existence by the passage of the Social Security Act in that same year.[12]

About the time Evans was launching her last project, an equally productive career was unfolding in the little rural town of Union, where in 1931 L. W. Long, fresh from medical studies at Meharry, set up a hometown practice. In some ways Long faced a more barren vista than Evans had in 1900. Not only was there no hospital for blacks and no organized public health service for either race, there was only one black physician to minister to the county's 12,500 Negroes. Moreover, Union Negroes lacked the economic resources available in the larger cities like Columbia, which had an established black middle-class.[13]

In several respects Long's contributions parallel those of Evans. He established the first Negro hospital in the area and on his own undertook to provide such preventive health services as school inspections and mass immunizations, which no public agency was then offering. Ironically, that work ultimately served white children, too. Seeing that Negro pupils were receiving something that theirs were not, Union whites began to demand a health center so that they could receive similar services and reestablish their "rightful" ascendency.[14]

In addition to these programs, Long turned his energies to the problems of the Negro medical profession, which he found to be in a "state of coma" when he returned to South Carolina. The Palmetto Medical, Dental, and Pharmaceutical Association, created some thirty-five years before, still met each year but mainly for the purpose of "handshaking and cordialities."[15]

Long's determination to inject new purpose into professional affairs resulted in his initiation of an annual medical clinic in 1932. As one-day affairs that featured locally and nationally known physicians (of both races), the Union clinics offered black doctors a rare opportunity to keep abreast of new developments in medicine. The first attracted an audience of sixteen and featured Chicago's Charles Drew, who was already at work on his plasma process for preserving blood. Like his hospital, Long's clinic—the only one then available to South Carolina Negro doctors—continued without a breakdown to the 1970s.[16]

What made L. W. Long unique among his South Carolina colleagues, however, was his stance on medical segregation. Initially he, like nearly all southern Negro physicians, had gone along with professional separatism, believing that the system, undesirable as it was, was simply one of life's realities and that kicking against it would do no good and would endanger him considerably.

In 1940 Long rejected that posture. Confessing to colleagues that he now thought of himself as a "revolutionist," he began to argue that there were "many things that should be done immediately if we are to quicken and improve our Association."[17] In fact, by the time he assumed the presidency of the Palmetto Medical, Dental, and Pharmaceutical Association in 1940, Long was convinced that the Negro profession in the South was "on the brink of destruction" and that its only hope for survival lay in its integration with the white medical establishment.[18] The sort of integration Long had in mind included the admission of Negro doctors to white hospitals, the employment of black physicians by the state board of health, and the enlargement of opportunities for black medical students. Knowing that the desegregation of the state's medical college was still years away, Long was prepared to settle for a system of state scholarships that would permit Negroes to acquire training outside the region.[19]

In calling for a frontal attack on medical segregation, Long was moving much faster and further than his colleagues cared to go. But if the ideas he put forward in 1940 did not win his colleagues' backing, they at least assaulted the prevailing complacency and helped to prepare black doctors to accept such ideas when they resurfaced a decade later as part of a broad civil rights movement.[20]

If the majority of black doctors in the prewar South demurred on the issue of integration, it would be nice to report that most were at least eager to work for professional betterment and health improvement within the segregated system. Unfortunately, the record does not seem to warrant that conclusion. It is impossible to speak with certainty about the way in which the average southern Negro physician defined his role and approached his tasks, but the available evidence suggests that at best most doctors passively accepted prevailing health and medical conditions. At worst, far too many physicians were (or let themselves become) less than competent practitioners, and some consciously exploited their patients.

Even though there were Negro professional associations in most southern states by World War I, a large proportion of black doctors chose not to take advantage of the one opportunity most of them had to exchange experiences and sharpen skills. The 1914 meeting of South Carolina's association attracted only 32 doctors and dentists out of about 110 in the state. It is difficult to determine if that attendance was typical because of scanty records, but W. H. Young, the association's president in the early 1940s, still found it necessary to upbraid his colleagues for showing so little interest in the annual meetings.[21]

The same inertia gripped the associations, themselves. The Palmetto Medical, Dental, and Pharmaceutical Association was slow to offer its members the kinds of programs they needed. When surgical and medical clinics were made a regular feature in the late 1930s, the initial programs had little substance. According to a guest clinician from Howard not only were public health issues neglected but the "clinics were not organized. In the absence of facilities for x-ray . . . it was impractical to hold a worthwhile tuberculosis clinic."[22]

Disinterest and lack of opportunity combined to turn many doctors into back numbers who offered their patients less than adequate care. One black doctor in Baltimore in the early 1930s was dismayed by the "careless and unscientific manner in which some physicians . . . handle their patients." Frequently they never performed blood or Wasserman tests or advised patients to take treatment for venereal disease.[23] South Carolina's W. H. Young agreed that many doctors were not doing their best. "In the first place, some of our offices and drug stores are too filthy for a decent person to enter. In the second place many of us aren't prepared to render the services our patients need."[24] In 1932 M. O. Bousfield, a well-known corporate physician from Chicago, visited a new Negro hospital in Jacksonville, Florida, and was appalled by what he found. "The men in Jacksonville are away behind the time and by no means equal to the demands of such a hospital. It is pitiful." On the whole he found Jacksonville was a "dreary place to contemplate from the medical point of view. . . . The brothers are squabbling over the hospital—playing five up and finding fault."[25] Wrangling and infighting among southern physicians was widely observed by Negro visitors from the North and caused them much concern. New York's Peter Marshall Murray found dissension in every southern hospital he visited, and he concluded that until Negro doctors learned to cooperate, the best recourse would be to put black hospitals under control of able white physicians.[26]

To the southern doctors' credit, many did considerable charity and public health work. A 1941 survey found that nearly half the patients of rural Negro doctors were charity cases. A number of physicians contributed substantially to preventive medicine, vaccinating children and running prenatal and adult clinics nearly always for free. But in pre-World War II South Carolina, at least, it tended to be the same small group who carried that burden. Perhaps Carolina doctors were too busy with demanding private practices or perhaps they were like the many Negro physicians of Baltimore who, reportedly, refused to cooperate with free clinics on the ground that "they take bread from our mouths."[27]

Whether or not an appreciable number of southern Negro doctors actually put dollars before people and whether or not blacks were more guilty of such calculation than whites are questions that resist definitive answers. If contemporary observation can be credited, it would appear that southern black doctors as a group dealt sharply, if not harshly, with patients in matters of fees. Peter Marshall Murray told a group of South Carolina practitioners in 1932 that their patients were "not satisfied with the services rendered when contrasted with the prices demanded."[28] Negro doctors, in fact, could be just as hard on poor black people as white doctors were. It seemed to Septima Clark, health and civil rights leader in Charleston, that if you did not have money, Negro doctors soon stopped coming to your house.[29]

The financial squeezing of patients was most apparent in the South's black hospitals. When in the mid-1920s the Duke Endowment began to support Negro hospitals in the two Carolinas with capital grants and subsidies for indigent care, it was struck by the harshness with which its clients dealt with patients, usually out of necessity. "Out hospitals," said a Duke official, "often collect from patients who are not able to pay and who should not be forced to pay, but the hospital had to exist. . . . Hospitals actually take mortgages on houses, cows, pigs, and homes of poor farmers as security for hospital bills."[30]

In some cases a harsh policy was aimed at more than just survival. Certain hospitals, the endowment discovered, were practicing out-and-out fraud against not only their patients but also the fund. Two particularly shady operations, uncovered in the early 1930s, were those associated with the Waverly Fraternal Hospital and the Good Samaritan Hospital in Columbia, South Carolina. These hospitals padded their indigent rolls in order to maximize subsidies from Duke. Money not absolutely needed for patient care—and a significant number of chronically ill were admitted who needed little looking after—was then split among hospital owners, trustees, and certain doctors.[31] In addition, Duke's contacts reported, many hospital physicians "were collecting professional fees from Negroes who were treated in the hospital as free."[32] One of Duke's investigators was Bousfield, the Chicago physician. Bousfield talked to staffs of both hospitals and, even before the evidence of fraud came to light, reported that "he had never seen a place where Negroes were so exploited by their own race as they were in these hospitals."[33]

There is considerable evidence, then, to suggest that Negro doctors in South Carolina and throughout the South did less than they might have done to keep themselves up to date and to meet the health needs of their people. How, in the end, should one understand and judge that performance? Should they all have striven for progress and change as did Matilda Evans and L. W. Long? Or was that an unreasonable expectation? Paul Cornely of Howard University perhaps put the issue in its proper perspective when he said that "one must not blame the victim."[34] And victim the southern black physician surely was, for the racism that blighted his professional preparation also stalked his career as a practitioner.

The unremarkable performance of the southern black doctor, especially as it related to the health needs of the Negro people, was a function of more than social environment. As was the case for the average white physician, the Negro doctor's training conditioned him to be conservative in his approach. It taught him, for example, that treatment of individual patients was his primary goal. Grappling with broader social questions or challenging restraints on professional growth was not his role. By its very nature, professional education (for white and black doctors alike) encouraged individualism and a disregard, if not a disdain, for preventive medicine. In addition, Negro medical students, even at black colleges, were subjected to the view that the Negro race was a sick race and that its ills were grounded either in wasteful living or in some inherent physiological weakness.[35] The chances of changing circumstances such as those were slim, at best, and so the black doctor often began his practice with the kind of fatalistic attitude that killed real effort.

Finally, there was a feeling among black doctors that if they were to have the social and financial success that their training and sacrifices entitled them to enjoy, they could not antagonize the white medical establishment. Success for the Negro doctor depended on the maintenance of relationships with white physicians, which could be broken easily if they stepped outside agreed-upon roles.[36] A Negro physician who looked at his career in this way found good reason not only to accept social and professional practices that were medically counter-productive but also to bear down on those people (his Negro patients) whose patronage was crucial to his expected success.

Notes

1. W. Montegue Cobb, "Progress and Portents for the Negro in Medicine," *Crisis* 55 (1948): 115, 116, 118.
2. "Negro Doctors and Hospitals," *Opportunity* 3 (1925): 227; Peter Marshall Murray, "Presidential Address," *Journal of the National Medical Association* 24 (1932): 4 (hereinafter *Jour. NMA*).
3. L. W. Long, "Presidential Address" (April, 1941), Minutes of the Palmetto Medical, Dental, and Pharmaceutical Association (hereinafter, Minutes Palmetto Assn.), p. 2. Copies in possession of the author.
4. Paul Cornely, "Trends in Public Health Activities Among Negroes in 96 Southern Counties During the Period, 1930-1939," *American Journal of Public Health* 32 (1942): 1123.
5. The fear of social mixing remained a barrier to professional integration in some states through the 1950s; see *Jour. NMA* 49 (1957): 115, and 50 (1958): 223.
6. Paul Cornely, interview, 21 May 1979.
7. Cobb, "Louis T. Wright, 1891-1952," *Jour. NMA* 45 (1953): 135-36.
8. Peter Kelly, interview, 23 June 1978; for the number of Negro doctors see U.S., Bureau of the Census, *Negroes in the United States, 1920-32* (Washington, D.C.: Government Printing Office, 1932), p. 293.
9. *Palmetto Leader*, 22 March, 1930; Jesse T. Hill and John Evans, interview, 22 June 1977; George Bunch, To Whom It May Concern, 28 December 1906, letter in possession of Jesse T. Hill; Mariana Davis, *South Carolina's Blacks and Native Americans, 1776-1976* (Columbia, S.C.: Bicentennial Commission, 1976), pp. 157-58.
10. *The Negro Health Journal* 1 (September 1916): 4.
11. Ibid., pp. 1, 5.
12. *Palmetto Leader*, 21 June 1930; 20 September 1930; 27 September 1930; 30 January 1932; "A Brief History of the Evans Clinic" (1932), pamphlet in possession of author.
13. L. W. Long, interview, 6 July 1977.
14. Ibid.; *Union Daily Times*, 23 April 1979.
15. Long, "Presidential Address," Minutes Palmetto Assn., p. 3.
16. Minutes Palmetto Assn., 1913; Long, interview, 6 July 1977; *Union Daily Times*, 23 April 1979.
17. Long, "Presidential Address," Minutes Palmetto Assn., p. 3; Long, interview, 6 July 1977.
18. Long, "Presidential Address," Minutes Palmetto Assn., p. 6.
19. Ibid., pp. 2-4.
20. Joseph Robinson to Long, 17 March 1917, quoted in Long, "Presidential Address," Minutes Palmetto Assn., p. 7.

21. Minutes Palmetto Assn., 1914; W. H. Young, "Presidential Address" (April, 1942), Minutes Palmetto Assn., p. 7.

22. Report of Howard Payne, April 1939, Private Papers of Modjeska M. Simkins, Columbia, S.C.

23. B. M. Rhetta, et. al., "Report of the Committee on the Venereal Disease Situation," March 1932, Box 4, Peter Marshall Murray Papers, Moorland-Spingarn Research Center, Howard University, Washington, D.C.

24. Young, "Presidential Address," Minutes Palmetto Assn., p. 7.

25. M. O. Bousfield to Peter Murray, [1932] Box 4, Murray Papers.

26. Murray to Bousfield, 17 November 1932, Box 4, Murray Papers.

27. Rhetta et al., "Venereal Disease Situation," Box 4, Murray Papers.

28. *Palmetto Leader*, 7 May 1932, p. 4.

29. Septima Clark, interview, 15 December 1977.

30. Graham Davis to Michael Davis, 23 June 1930, Box 7, Graham Davis Correspondence, Duke Endowment Archives, Manuscript Department, William R. Perkins Library, Duke University, Durham, N.C.

31. W. S. Rankin to Lillian Rhodes, 10 June, 1927, Box 180, North Carolina and South Carolina Hospital and County Files, Duke Endowment Archives; Memo, Good Samaritan Hospital, 19 March 1929, ibid.; R. Beverly Herbert to Rankin, 18 June 1939, ibid; G. P. H., "Good Samaritan Hospital, Columbia," 14 October 1931, ibid.; Graham Davis, Memo, Waverly Fraternal Hospital, n.d., ibid.

32. G. F. H., Memo for Rankin, 2 July 1938, ibid.

33. G. D., Memo, Waverly Fraternal Hospital, n.d., ibid.

34. Cornely, interview, 21 May 1979.

35. Ibid.; on the erroneous teaching at Negro medical schools, see Peyton Anderson, M.D., "The Neglected One-Tenth," *Opportunity* 13 (1935): 210.

36. Cornely, interview, 21 May 1979.

III

FOLK CULTURE AND HISTORIOGRAPHY

The concluding section of this anthology emphasizes the need for new historiographical approaches to the southern enigma. Each essay in this section offers fresh insights into the southern experience.

In the first essay, Professor Charles Joyner asserts that the mystery still surrounding the South's historical experience can be solved only through an understanding of the folk culture, or traditions, of black and white southerners. Professor Joyner proposes a new methodology in studying southern folk culture. It is an approach that synthesizes social history and folk life studies, or what he calls "historical folk life." Under his new methodology, the researcher might study agricultural and agrarian history, demographic patterns, and folk architecture, cooking, costume, and arts and crafts over an extended period. Joyner reminds us that only the South has "a genuinely biracial folk culture." Hence unlike other approaches that attempt to explain the southern enigma, his approach has the advantage "of resting upon the common folk culture of both black and white southerners rather than defining the southern experience in terms of whites alone."

Professor Grady McWhiney in the following essay, "Education in the Old South: A Reexamination," finds that the cultural traditions of white southerners during the antebellum years were reflected in their attitudes toward education. Most had far less regard for formal instruction than northerners. Southern schools were "primitive" in comparison to those in the North. Student misbehavior, even violence, was commonplace and "drinking, gambling, and carousing were the rule" in southern colleges. The disdain of many white southerners for schools was the cultural legacy of their predominantly Celtic ancestors, who "were oral and aural." Therefore, McWhiney concludes, most southerners "admired more the skills of the hunter, fisher, fighter, and fiddler" than those skills taught in northern schools.

The dynamics of southern folk culture also are explored in "The Ancient Pedigree of Violent Repression: Georgia's Klan as a Folk Movement" by Charles L. Flynn, Jr. In recent decades "liberal" historians have explained the Klan almost exclusively as an instrument of racial control, while Marxist historians have interpreted the Klan with equal vigor as a tool of class repression. Flynn finds both of these explanations to be unsatisfactory, arguing that they ignore the multifaceted reasons for vigilante violence as well as the complex social dynamics that existed between blacks, yeoman whites, and the planter class. After examining these themes, Flynn's innovative essay suggests that the American Klan may better be viewed as a traditional, moralistic folk movement whose roots are traceable to similar vigilante groups in early modern Europe. As such, Klan violence "reflected racial, economic, political, marital, and sexual values that they sought to protect as an unsystematic, even self-contradictory whole . . . rather than as separable by object or motive." In more general terms, Flynn concludes that the time has come for southern historians to go beyond both liberal and Marxist ideologies, for only by doing so can historians hope to reach an adequate understanding of the complex social mechanics of southern society.

Probably no event in American history has spawned more historiographical battles than the coming of the Civil War. Various historians have emphasized the institution of slavery, the expansion of slavery, a "blundering generation of politicians," economic conflict, emotions, constitutional interpretation, and local politics as the primary cause for the war. William J. Cooper enters this battle in his essay, "The Politics of Slavery Affirmed: The South and the Secession Crises." Cooper rejects earlier interpretations as inadequate to explain the dynamics and chronology of secessions in the three regions of the South. A better explanation, he contends, is the politics of slavery, which were formed by a complex mixture of the institution of slavery, the southern political structure, and the values of southern white society. In Cooper's analysis, the politics of slavery embodied the South's vision of the "good society," while Lincoln's philosophy embodied its antithesis. After meticulously analyzing the South's widespread commitment to the concept and how it shaped events in every southern state during the winter and spring of 1860-61, Cooper concludes, "the cause of secession makes clear that no other interpretive idea so illuminates the form and substance of antebellum southern politics as does the politics of slavery."

In "The Paradoxes of Confederate Historiography," the final essay of this anthology, Professor Emory Thomas points out that historians of the region have studied both the antebellum and postbellum South exhaustively to the neglect of the wartime years. He suggests, therefore, that new insights into the old questions of southern experience and southern identity may be gained by studying the Confederate period. Indeed, Thomas concludes, people caught up in "crisis and convulsion" reveal more of themselves than they do in less turbulent times.

11

THE SOUTH AS A FOLK CULTURE: DAVID POTTER AND THE SOUTHERN ENIGMA

Charles Winston Joyner

The South is an enigma. It is easy enough to say that the central theme of its history is a common resolve, indomitably maintained, to remain a distinctive entity, a place to come to, not so much because of the courage and honor and hope and pride and compassion and pity and sacrifice that have been the glory of its past; nor because of the defeat and tragedy and guilt and poverty and blood and irony that have been the burden of its history (for everything that rises must fall); nor because of its arrogance and pride and satiety and knowledge of anguish and foreknowledge of death; and not because yesterday won't be over until tomorrow, and tomorrow began ten thousand years ago; nor even because the militant South is militant, or the lazy South is lazy, or the enduring South endures, for the past is never dead—it's not even past—although the South's peculiar institution—that is to say, its politics—has undergone a transformation: from one-party to a party-and-a-half, from democratic autocracy to autocratic democracy; and not because Johnny Reb is both patriot and traitor, who always rallies 'round the flag and who also tried to overthrow the government of the United States by force and violence (for values are sometimes uncertain when the human heart is in conflict with itself, and it is difficult to tell those Williams boys—Hank and Tennessee—apart, much less the old verities and truths of the heart), and Ted Turner acts like Rhett Butler, and Jimmy Carter like Ashley Wilkes, and Jesse Helms thinks he is John C. Calhoun; nor because of protodorian minstrel shows, cavalier romances, and bourbon whiskey (none of them all that helpful at the Bloody Angle), although other voices in other rooms and in other parts of the forest, found Coca Cola, *Gone With the Wind*, and the latter-day Ku Klux Klan in the toad's head of defeat; nor even because the people of paradox cast down their buckets into a long and quite un-American experience with poverty and were subjected to military defeat, occupation, and reconstruction (as a substitute for victory) because they entrusted their future hopes and past pride to men with valor and strength but without pity or honor (Was it any wonder Heaven saw fit to let them lose?), although the knowledge they carried to the heart in that regard was far more closely in line with the common lot of mankind than the national legends of opulence and success and innocence; and least of all because a latter-day abolitionist anoints it both a "sport, a freak, an inexplicable variant from the national norm" and a distant mirror "in which the nation can see its blemishes magnified" in a golden eye; but rather in spite of the immoderate past, in spite of the regional image of the Sahara of the Bozart, where agrarian poets in brown studies take their stand in defense of hookworm and intellectual malnutrition; an illiterate Yoknapatawpha where scrawny, sallow, sex-crazed women subsist on a diet of sowbelly and segregation; a primordial Chattahoochie where doomed, inbred hillbillies violate with seething degeneracy innocent Atlanta boaters; a faraway country where folks all outlive themselves by years and years and years, where men of substance, of flesh and bone, are infantilized into Little Black Sambos in concentration camps called plantations, subject to the sadistic whims of Simon Legree and his Aryan stormtroopers of the Invisible Empire (while Brer Fox lay low); a land of squalid opulence and doomed immortality, haunted by God, where rampant racism and bloody violence bear it away with repressive fundamentalist piety, where beefy, Bible-thumping rednecks lurk in every grease pit south of Cincinnati, not for glory, and least of all for profit, but because they labor under a curse, although the South may have been predestined by Providence to be a mudsill under national self-esteem. The historian's duty has been to write about such things. It has been his mission to help the South endure by trying to apprehend and expiate the irreconcilable mutation and change of successive overlapping generations. Southern history has been pursued, its brazen face sculpted, its deliverance promoted, its origin explored, its emergence proclaimed, its renaissance heralded, its romanticism lamented, its burden brooded over, its myth demythologized, its mystique debunked, and its epitaph pronounced. I decline to accept the end of the South—that the South will go out of history into historiography and the awful responsibility of time. I decline to accept that, or even quite relinquish yet the ancient commission of the historian: to ponder still the same old unanswerable enigma.[1]

Space does not permit an extended analysis of all the elements of the southern enigma alluded to above (and this list is by no means complete). Some of them are authentically southern; some are not. Some are authentically southern but not distinctively so. Some are statements that no sober man would make and no sane man believe. To comprehend the southern paradox is to isolate both the authentic and the distinctive elements of southern culture. It is in the historical experience of the region that C. Vann Woodward finds the South's claims to a distinctive heritage.[2] Without an understanding of the culture upon which that historical experience has operated, however, the southern enigma will remain a mystery.

In his perceptive 1961 essay, "The Southern Enigma," David M. Potter finds the essential distinctiveness of the South embodied in a folk culture. "On the face of it," he states, "it seems a matter of observation and not of theory to say that the culture of the folk survived in the South long after it succumbed to the onslaught of urban-industrial culture elsewhere." Potter finds the relation between land and people in the South "more direct and more primal" than elsewhere in the nation. "In the folk culture of the South," he believes, "it may be that the relation of people to one another imparted a distinctive texture as well as a distinctive tempo to their lives."[3]

Potter does not explore in that essay or in other writings the implication of that insight, nor does he even describe what he means by the "folk culture" of the South. He seems to have been influenced by Robert Redfield's conception of folk culture as "an organization or integration of conventional understandings" in a folk society in which behavior is "traditional, spontaneous, and uncritical" and in which "the patterns of conduct are clear and remain constant throughout the generations." Redfield's characterization of the folk society as "small, isolated, non-literate, and homogeneous," however, seems to fit truly primitive societies better than it does the South in either its old or its new incarnations.[4]

Potter was influenced also by the incisive and fertile arguments of Howard Odum, a sociologist, who claims that "the biography of the South is essentially the story of the folk." Acknowledging the significance of social stratification and social change in the South, Odum insists that "the folk society of the South is well nigh all inclusive and is reflected on many levels of time and class." But Odum also finds southern folk culture, despite class differentiation, "strangely unified in its complex fabric of many weavings." Odum marvels at "how timeless and resistless are the processes and products of folk society" despite social change.[5]

If Odum's concept of folk society is more complex and more convincing than that of Redfield, especially when it is applied to the eighteenth- and nineteenth-century South, it still remains more focused on the rural and quasi-peasant experience than one might wish. Southern distinctiveness may have been embodied in a folk culture when the South was overwhelmingly pastoral, but if folk culture exists only in rural societies, is the concept of any value in analyzing the urban-industrial culture of the twentieth-century South? Is there a folk in the city?

It is surely no derogation of the achievements of Potter, Redfield, and Odum to suggest that their concept of folk culture depends on an equation of "folk" with "rural" and "static" that is not supported by recent folkloristic scholarship. Modern folklorists do not accept such a priori limitations as Redfield's insistence on isolation, illiteracy, and homogeneity as the hallmarks of folk culture, or Odum's and Potter's dichotomy of folk *versus* urban-industrial. Folklorists have found and studied the folk in cities. They have found a dynamic mutual interaction between oral traditions and literate traditions. They have found the assimilation of cultural patterns through cultural contact to have been basic to all the folk cultures, rural and urban, past and present, they have studied. Finally they have found folk tradition to be dynamic, not static, changing slowly but inexorably.[6]

Neither Redfield, Odum, nor Potter is as specific as he should be in distinguishing between folk culture and folk society. Anthropologist Clifford Geertz views culture as the mental rules governing behavior, while society is the field of action in which behavior takes place. Culture, he claims, "denotes an historically transmitted pattern of meanings embodied in symbols, a system of inherited conceptions expressed in symbolic forms by means of which men communicate, perpetuate, and develop their knowledge about and attitudes toward life." For example, the concept of royalty is cultural, but the embodiment of that concept in monarchies and courts is social. "Culture is not a power, something to which social events, behaviors, institutions, or processes can be causally attributed," notes Geertz, "it is a context, something within which they can be intelligibly—that is, thickly—described."[7]

To penetrate the southern paradox, then, one must penetrate its context—the folk culture of the South. If culture is context rather than cause, it is clear that the relation between culture and society is not one-to-one. Culture may change at a different rate than societies. The idea of independence, for instance, may have attained cultural legitimacy for American colonists or southern secessionists before independence was a social reality. In the same way, African rulers and deities may have retained a cultural legitimacy among enslaved Africans in the New World society in which they had no social power.

Historians continue to ignore folk life, because they customarily focus their studies on change; folk life, which is regarded as static, is of little relevance to their concerns. All too frequently, however, these historians have succumbed to what Eric Hobsbawm calls "the temptation to isolate the phenomenon of overt crisis from the wider context of a society undergoing transformation." For their own part, too many folklorists concentrate on microanalysis of folklore performance in a single time frame. There is a pervasively static quality in such writings that misses the dynamic relationship between past and present that is represented by the word "tradition." Folk culture and historical change are inextricably related. As E. P. Thompson notes, both "resistance to change and assent to change arise from the whole culture."[8]

What is needed, I believe, is a synthesis of social history and folk-life studies, a synthesis that might be called "historical folk life." Such a synthesis would draw upon two scholarly traditions that developed in Europe and have begun to affect American scholarship in recent years—the folk-life studies movement pioneered by European students of *volkskunde*, or regional ethnology, and the *Annales* school of French social historians.

The folk-life approach was pioneered by folklorists in Scandinavia, Switzerland, and the British Isles. While American folklorists were preoccupied with the lore of the folk, European folk-life scholars were more interested in the folk themselves, embracing in their work the customs and material culture of the folk as well as their oral traditions. According to Don Yoder, a leading American folk-life scholar, "not only does the researcher study the verbal arts of folksong, folktale, riddle, etc.—which the folklorist has long ago made his province—but also agriculture and agrarian history, settlement patterns, dialectology or folk speech, folk architecture, folk cookery, folk costume, the folk year, arts and crafts." In practice, however, most American folk-life scholars concentrate on material culture alone and eschew analyzing what Yoder calls "this exciting totality of the verbal, spiritual, and material aspects of a culture."[9]

The *Annales* historians, so called after the journal founded by Marc Bloch and Lucien Febvre in 1929, have pioneered "a new kind of history" that is concerned with the social and cultural past of human beings previously considered "inarticulate." They have sought out new kinds of evidence in census reports, court records, deed registries, and church records; and they have asked new kinds of questions of their evidence, questions about the material basis of human existence and about the relationships of human beings to their environment in the past. Rather than wars, treaties, and monarchs, the *Annalistes* have, in a monumental series of studies, stressed the importance of geography, ecology, and demography. Emphasizing the structures of social, cultural, and technological life in a given geographic environment over long time periods ("la longue duree"), they have achieved "a history whose passage is almost imperceptible," according to Fernand Braudel,"a history in which all change is slow." Their achievement is impressive, but it has not been accomplished without loss. In some *Annaliste* scholarship change has become not just imperceptible but nonexistent (*l'histoire immobile*"), and human beings have become imperceptible. Human beings are buried under layers of *structures* that "encumber history," according to Braudel, "and thus control its flow." The individual remains anonymous, "imprisoned within a destiny in which he himself has little hand," as Braudel sees it. "All efforts against the prevailing tide of history," he adds, "are doomed to failure." In *Annales* scholarship the formerly inarticulate masses do achieve equal representation: Everyone is rendered equally inarticulate.[10]

One need not share the deterministic bias of the *Annales* "school" or the material culture bias of the folk-life "movement" to recognize in the synthesis of the two an important new approach to the history of the folk. Until recently, historians have tended to confine their studies to elite groups, eschewing the task of examining the folk culture on which, as Potter pointed out, the historical experience of the South impinged. The important new scholarship in Afro-American folk history in the South has no counterpart in studies of Euro-American southern folk.[11]

The scholar who would study the historical folk life of the South is confronted with numerous problems, not all of which can be dealt with here. One must begin with careful ethnographic description. All of the comparative and analytical work of historical folk life depends upon precise description. Merely to recognize the importance of ethnographic description, however, does not guarantee its attainment. The first problem is cultural comprehension. When dealing with folk culture, scholars too often simply have assumed that all they had to do was to present the "objective" facts about the customs and shared beliefs of the folk, which usually has meant that the scholars present the facts in terms of their own culture and priorities. This has led to such atrocious nonsense as the establishment of cultural genres by scholarly fiat. The scholar's problem is to comprehend how the folk make sense for themselves out of their culture. Indeed, the scholar would do well to remember that culture itself is actually a logical construct created in the mind of the observer, who derives the construct from the behavior of the cultural actors. The problem for the scholar of historical folk life is just how much logical constructs can convey an accurate picture of the culture. Obviously the qualifications for historical folk life are pretty hard to come by. The closer one is to the cultural group under investigation, the more difficult it is to explain it to others; the closer one is culturally to one's audience, the greater the difficulty in comprehending the subject. If the observer of southern folk culture is a southerner, it may be easier to comprehend the culture than to make it comprehensible to nonsoutherners. If, on the other hand, the scholar is from outside the region, communicating with a nonsouthern audience may be easier than comprehending the southern folk culture.[12]

The student of historical folk life has much to learn from the folklorist's emphasis on context and on the relation of parts to wholes in culture. From the earliest anthropological studies of isolated and self-contained primitive communities came the characteristic anthropological tendency toward holism. The student of southern folk culture would do well to bear in mind, however, that the relation of parts to wholes in folk culture is more complex than in primitive cultures. The South has never been a land of isolated, self-sufficient subsistence farmers, lacking contact with the centers of commerce and intellect, but rather a region that has produced staples for the world market.[13]

The syncretic relationship between folk tradition and the centers of commerce and intellect has been an important element in the development of southern folk culture; but the most significant syncretic relationship has been that between the African and British components of that culture. The central theme of southern folk history might well be described as the achievement of cultural integration. Cultural integration generally went unrecognized, partly because the South spent a great deal of energy in an effort to create a segregated society and partly because early students of the culture attributed British origins to many African elements in the culture and African origins to many British elements. As Winthrop Jordan notes in another connection, "many absurd assertions" have been advanced by scholars who tried to compare two things "about one or both of which they were ignorant."[14]

Another important reason for the failure to recognize the extent to which cultural integration was achieved lies in the tendency of folklorists and anthropologists to seek the "purest survivals" of British and African traditions. For most of this century, collectors of Afro-American folklore have concentrated their research on the areas where black communities remained most culturally isolated—the Sea Islands. Collectors of Anglo-American folklore have concentrated on remote valleys of the southern highlands, where examples of Anglo-American ballads and tales can be recovered in a nearly "pure" state. This polarized concentration represents the preoccupation of the scholars, not that of the southern folk themselves. Between the islands and the highlands, black and white southerners have been swapping songs and stories, accents and styles, for centuries. Out of this convergence of African and British traditions, so different yet so alike, emerged a new southern folklore, a folklore with both an African and a British heritage but as different from either as water is from hydrogen and oxygen.

Southern folk culture developed out of a communicative process among the various folk cultures of uprooted Africans and uprooted Britons, commencing with the arrival of the first settlers and their attempts to adjust inherited cultural meanings to one another and to a new environment. Neither African nor British traditions were unaffected by the other, and the influence was often reciprocal. Since people neither remember nor forget without reason, conscious or unconscious, one of the major influences upon the development of southern folk culture was the similarity of any given element of Old World folk culture to elements in the tradition of the other race. Elements of the culture had to be meaningful—unforgettable—or they were eventually forgotten. In a cultural sense, every white southerner has an African heritage as well as a British one, and every black southerner has a European heritage as well as an African one. In the South, and only in the South, a genuinely biracial folk culture was created. Afro-Americans in the North have been immigrants into a preexistent culture; in the South they were settlers.

David Potter was correct when he stated that the South's best claim to historical distinctiveness can be found in its folk culture, despite his failure to indicate what he meant by the term or to explore its implications or to note that its central theme has been cultural integration. Historical folk life has the advantage, which is missing in other purported explanations of the southern paradox, of resting upon the common folk culture of both black and white southerners rather than upon a definition of the southern experience in terms of whites alone. And folk culture shows signs of greater longevity than other explanations. Southerners, regardless of race, retain the essential elements of folk culture to a higher degree than others. Black and white alike, they remain, as John Shelton Reed notes, "more likely than non-Southerners to be conventionally religious, to accept the private use of force (or the potential for it), and to be anchored in their home-place."[15]

Scholars might still have something to learn, if they would, from the study of historical folk life. To understand southern folk culture in all its complexity is to understand something very fundamental—the essential character of the southern folk.

Notes

1. Literary allusions in the first paragraph include the following: William Faulkner, "Speech of Acceptance upon the Award of the Nobel Prize for Literature," widely anthologized; Ulrich B. Phillips, "The Central Theme of Southern History," *American Historical Review* 34 (1938): 30-43; William Faulkner, *Requiem for a Nun* (New York, 1951); Ellen A. Glasgow, *Barren Ground* (New York, 1925); John Hope Franklin, *The Militant South* (Cambridge, 1956); David Bertelson, *The Lazy South* (New York, 1967); John Shelton Reed, *The Enduring South* (Lexington, Mass., 1972); Faulkner, *Requiem for a Nun*; Kenneth M. Stampp, *The Peculiar Institution* (New York, 1956); Jack Bass and Walter DeVries, *The Transformation of Southern Politics* (New York, 1976); James Parton, *A Life of Andrew Jackson* (New York, 1859); Faulkner, "Speech of Acceptance"; Wilbur J. Cash, *The Mind of the South* (New York, 1939); George B. Tindall, *The Ethnic Southerners* (Baton Rouge, 1976); Truman Capote, *Other Voices, Other Rooms* (New York, 1948); Lillian Hellman, *Another Part of the Forest* (New York, 1946); Henry W. Grady's 1886 address, "The New South"; Booker T. Washington's 1895 "Atlanta Compromise" address; C. Vann Woodward, *The Burden of Southern History* (Baton Rouge, 1960); William Faulkner, *Absalom, Absalom* (New York, 1936); Allen Tate, "Ode to the Confederate Dead" (1928); Howard Zinn, *The Southern Mystique* (New York, 1964); Carson McCullers, *Reflections in a Golden Eye* (New York, 1941); H. L. Mencken's 1917 essay, "The Sahara of the Bozart"; John Crowe Ransom, "Bells for John Whiteside's Daughter" (1924); "Twelve Southerners," *I'll Take My Stand* (New

York, 1930); James Dickey, *Deliverance* (Boston, 1970); Louis D. Rubin, *The Far-away Country* (Seattle, 1963); Faulkner, *Absalom, Absalom*; Ralph Ellison, *The Invisible Man* (New York, 1952); Stanley M. Elkins, *Slavery* (Chicago, 1959); Joel Chandler Harris, *Uncle Remus: His Songs and His Sayings* (New York, 1881); James McBride Dabbs, *Haunted by God* (Richmond, 1972); Flannery O'Connor, *The Violent Bear It Away* (New York, 1960); F. N. Boney, "The Redneck," *Georgia Review* 25 (1971): 333-42; James Henry Hammond's "mudsill" speech before the United States Senate, March 4, 1858; George B. Tindall, ed., *The Pursuit of Southern History* (Baton Rouge, 1963); Lewis P. Simpson, *The Brazen Face of History* (Baton Rouge, 1980); C. Vann Woodward, *Origins of the New South* (Baton Rouge, 1951); George B. Tindall, *Emergence of the New South* (Baton Rouge, 1968); Richard H. King, *A Southern Renaissance* (New York, 1980); T. Harry Williams, *Romance and Realism in Southern Politics* (Athens, 1961); Zinn, *The Southern Mystique*; F. Garvin Davenport, Jr., *The Myth of Southern History* (Nashville, 1970); Harry Ashmore, *An Epitaph for Dixie* (New York, 1957); Robert Penn Warren, *All The King's Men* (New York, 1946); Faulkner, "Speech of Acceptance"; Faulkner, *Requiem for a Nun*.

2. Woodward, *Burden of Southern History*, ix-xi.

3. David M. Potter, "The Enigma of the South," *The Yale Review* 51 (1961): 142-46, 149-51.

4. Robert Redfield, "The Folk Society," *American Journal of Sociology* 52 (1947): 297-98. Cf. George M. Foster's critique, "What Is Folk Culture?" *American Anthropologist* 55 (1953): 159-73.

5. Howard W. Odum, *The Way of the South: Toward the Regional Balance of America* (New York, 1947), p. 64; Howard W. Odum, *Folk, Region, and Society* (Chapel Hill, 1966), pp. 219-38, 253-54. Bertram Wyatt-Brown, in his "The Ideal Typology and Ante-bellum Southern History: A Testing of a New Approach," *Societas* 5 (1975): esp. pp. 4, 8-10, 14, describes the Old South in terms much like Odum's folk society. The South, he contends, "stressing oral over literate means of expression," developed "a family-centered, particularistic, ascriptive culture" that honored "qualities related to gender, age, racial appearance, bloodlines," p. 14.

6. Richard M. Dorson, "Is There A Folk in the City?" *The Urban Experience and Folk Tradition* ed. America Paredes and Ellen J. Steckert (Austin, 1971), pp. 185-228; James Borchert, *Alley Life in Washington: Family, Community, Religion, and Folklife in the City, 1850-1970* (Urbana, Ill., 1980); Charles W. Joyner, "A Model for the Analysis of Folklore Performance in Historical Context," *Journal of American Folklore* 88 (1975): 254-65.

7. Clifford Geertz, *The Interpretation of Cultures* (New York, 1973), pp. 14, 89; Sidney Mintz and Richard Price, *An Anthropological Approach to the Afro-American Past: A Caribbean Perspective* (Philadelphia, 1976), p. 16.

8. Eric J. Hobsbawm, "From Social History to the History of Society," in *Historical Studies Today* ed. Felix Gilbert and Stephan R. Graubard (New York, 1972), p. 20; E. P. Thompson, "Time, Work-Discipline, and Industrial Capitalism," *Past and Present* 38 (1967): 80. Examples of both the richness and the limitations of the contextual school of folklore performance studies include Dan Ben-Amos, "Toward a Definition of Folklore in Context," *Journal of American Folklore* 84 (1971): 3-15; Roger D. Abrahams, "Introductory Remarks to a Rhetorical Theory of Folklore," *Journal of American Folklore* 81 (1968): 144-45; Alan

Dundes, "Texture, Text, and Context," *Southern Folklore Quarterly* 28 (1964): 251-65; and Dell Hymes, *Foundations in Sociolinguistics: An Ethnographic Approach* (Philadelphia, 1974), pp. 3-66.

9. Sigurd Erixon, "European Ethnology in Our Time," *Ethnologia Europaea* 1, no. 1 (1967): 3-11; Sigurd Erixon, "An Introduction to Folk Life Research or Nordic Ethnology," *Folkliv* 14-15 (1950-51): 5-15; Ake Hultkrantz, "The Conception of 'Folk' in Sigurd Erixon's Ethnological Theory," *Ethnologia Europaea* 2-3 (1968-69): 18-20; Ake Hultkrantz, ed., *General Ethnological Concepts*, International Dictionary of Regional European Ethnology and Folklore, vol. 1 (Copenhagen, 1960), pp. 126-44; Richard Weiss, *Volkskunde der Schweiz: Grundriss* (Erlenbach-Zurich, 1946); Herman Baltl, "Folklore Research and Legal History in the German Language Area," *Journal of the Folklore Institute* 5 (1968): 142-51; Ronald H. Buchanan, "A Decade of Folklife Study," *Ulster Folklife* 2 (165): 63-75; Ronald H. Buchanan, "Geography and Folk Life," *Folk Life* 1 (1963): 5-15; Alexander Fenton, "An Approach to Folk Life Studies," *Keystone Folklore Quarterly* 12 (1967): 5-21; Alexander Fenton, "Historical Ethnology in Scotland," *Ethnologia Europaea* 1, no. 2 (1967): 125-29; Alexander Fenton, "Material Culture as an Aid to Local Historical Studies in Scotland," *Journal of the Folklore Institute* 2 (1965): 326-39; J.W.Y. Higgs, *Folk Life Collection and Classification* (London, 1963); J. Geraint Jenkins, *Studies in Folk Life: Essays in Honour of Iorwerth C. Peate* (New York, 1969); Iorwerth C. Peate, *Tradition and Folk Life: A Welsh View* (London, 1972); Don Yoder, "The Folklife Studies Movement," *Pennsylvania Folklife* 13, no. 3 (July, 1963): 43-56; Don Yoder, ed., *American Folklife* (Austin, 1976). The quotations are from Don Yoder, "Folklife," in *Our Living Traditions* ed. Tristram P. Coffin, (New York, 1968), pp. 47-48.

10. The most important works of *Annales* scholarship in English are Marc Bloch, *Feudal Society*, trans. L. P. Manyon (Chicago, 1963); Marc Bloch, *Land and Work in Medieval Europe*, trans. J. E. Anderson (New York, 1969); Marc Bloch, *French Rural History: An Essay on its Basic Characteristics*, trans. Janet Sondheimer (Berkeley, 1970); Lucien Febvre, *A New Kind of History: From the Writings of Lucien Febvre*, trans. and ed. Peter Burke (New York, 1973); Fernand Braudel, *The Mediterranean and the Mediterranean World in the Age of Philip II*, trans. Sian Reynolds, 2 vols. (New York, 1972-1975); Fernand Braudel, *Capitalism and Material Life, 1400-1800*, trans. Miriam Kochan (New York, 1973); Fernand Braudel, *On History*, trans. Sarah Matthews (Chicago, 1980); Emmanuel Le Roy Ladurie, *Times of Feast, Times of Famine: A History of Climate Since the Year 1000*, trans. Barbara Bray (Garden City, N.Y., 1971); Emmanuel Le Roy Ladurie, *The Peasants of Languedoc*, trans. John Day (Urbana, Ill., 1974); Emmanuel Le Roy Ladurie, *Montaillou: The Promised Land of Error*, trans. Barbara Bray (New York, 1978); Emmanuel Le Roy Ladurie, *The Territory of the Historian*, trans. Ben and Sian Reynolds (Chicago, 1979); Emmanuel Le Roi Ladurie, *Carnival in Romans*, trans. Mary Feeney (New York, 1979). Braudel called for study of the *longue durée* in "Debats et combats," *Annales, E. S. C.* 13 (1958): 725-53. The quotations are from Braudel's *The Mediterranean and the Mediterranean World*, pp. 20 and 1244, and his *Capitalism and Material Life*, p. 442.

11. John Blassingame, The Slave Community: Plantation Life in the Antebellum South (New York, 1972); Eugene D. Genovese, *Roll, Jordan, Roll: The World the Slaves Made* (New York, 1974); Herbert S. Gutman, *The Black Family in*

Slavery and Freedom (New York, 1976); Charles W. Joyner, *Slave Folklife: Culture Change in a South Carolina Slave Community* (Urbana, Ill., forthcoming); Lawrence W. Levine, *Black Culture and Black Consciousness: Afro-American Folk Thought from Slavery to Freedom* (New York, 1977); Gerald W. Mullin, *Flight and Rebellion: Slave Resistance in Eighteenth-Century Virginia* (New York, 1978); George P. Rawick, *From Sundown to Sunup: The Making of the Black Community* (Greenwich, Conn., 1972); Peter H. Wood, *Black Majority: Negroes in South Carolina from 1670 through the Stono Rebellion* (New York, 1974).

12. Herbert Halpert, "American Regional Folklore," in "Folklore Research in North America," *Journal of American Folklore* 60 (1974): 355-56; Herbert Halpert, "The Functional Approach," in "Conference on the Character and State of Studies in Folklore," *Journal of American Folklore* 54 (1946): 510-12; Richard M. Dorson, "Standards of Collecting and Publishing American Folktales," in "The Folktale: A Symposium," *Journal of American Folklore* 80 (1957): 54; Kenneth S. Goldstein, *A Guide for Fieldworkers in Folklore* (Hatboro, Pa., 1964), p. 7; Ward H. Goodenough, *Description and Comparison in Cultural Anthropology* (Chicago, 1970), p. 110; Stephen Tyler, *Cognitive Anthropology* (New York, 1969), p. 6; Alfred Kroeber and Clyde Kluckhohn, *Culture: A Critical Review of Concepts and Definitions* (Cambridge, Mass., 1952), p. 182; William P. McEwen, *The Problem of Social-Scientific Knowledge* (Totowa, N.J., 1963), pp. 34-35; Benjamin N. Colby, "Ethnographic Semantics: A Preliminary Survey," *Current Anthropology* 7 (1966): 3-32.

13. Cf. Robert Redfield, *Peasant Society and Culture* (Chicago, 1956), p. 5; Foster, "What Is Folk Culture?" p. 164.

14. Charles W. Joyner, "Southern Folklore as a Key to Southern Identity," *Southern Humanities Review* 1 (1967): 211-22; Charles W. Joyner, *Folk Song in South Carolina* (Columbia, 1971); Winthrop D. Jordan, *White Over Black: American Attitudes toward the Negro, 1550-1812* (Chapel Hill, 1958), p. 605.

15. Reed, *The Enduring South*, p. 83.

12

EDUCATION IN THE OLD SOUTH: A REEXAMINATION

Grady McWhiney

"I have always been cheated most by men who could write," explained a southerner who owned forty slaves and considerable property but could neither read nor write; his nine grown sons were also illiterate. "Send my sons to school to learn to read and write? Not I," he informed a visitor. "It would make just such devils of them as you Yankees are!"

To prove his point the southerner told how a Connecticut drummer had sold him a clock for ten dollars that was "warranted to last ninety-nine years." When a forty-dollar clock arrived instead of what the old man had ordered, he refused to pay for it and was sued. In court the judge insisted that the written order called for a forty-dollar clock; furthermore, the paper that supposedly guaranteed the clock for ninety-nine years only warranted it to *last* ninety-nine years, not to keep time. "Now," asked the old man, "do you suppose I am fool enough, since that, to believe there is any benefit in learning to write?"[1]

Most southerners, whether or not they considered literacy compatible with honesty, had far less regard for formal education than the average northerner. As early as 1753 the governor of South Carolina observed that the people of the up-country "abound in Children, but none of them bestow the least Education on them, they take so much care in raising a litter of Piggs, their Children are equally naked and full as Nasty."[2] On the eve of the American Revolution, Reverend Charles Woodmason described backcountry Carolinians as ignorant and impudent:

Very few can read—fewer write. . . . Few or no Books are to be found in this vast Country . . . Nor do they delight in Historical Books or in having them read to them, as do our Vulgar in England for these People despise Knowledge, and instead of honouring a Learned Person, or any one of Wit or Knowledge be it in the Arts, Sciences, or Languages, they despise and Ill treat them—And this Spirit prevails even among the Principals of this Province.[3]

Formal education enjoyed scarcely more respect at the end of the antebellum period than it had in colonial times. Some scholars have argued that the whites of the Old South received relatively more schooling than is often acknowledged, and it is true that by 1861 there were more children in school in the South than at any previous time, but most of those schools were privately and inadequately supported.[4] Rarely did they provide quality or effective instruction. Georgia, for example, had a state university as well as academies in each county, but some of these were as poorly conducted as the elementary schools over which the state exercised no control. A school could be started by anyone inspired to teach and able to find an empty building and paying pupils. One such instructor, a deserter from the British navy, established military discipline and whipped accordingly, but he did not last long. In his unheated school, he placed students in a circle and made them dance around the room to keep warm or set the boys to wrestling so that their blood would circulate faster. He was replaced by a "wandering, drunken Irishman," who "knocked, kicked, cuffed, and whipped at a great rate." The Irishman, in turn, was followed by two other drunks who frequently dismissed classes in order to go on binges.[5]

Most southern schools were primitive compared to those in the North. "A majority of our farmers' daughters," boasted a Yankee, "can walk from their dwellings to schools of a quality such as at the South can be maintained not twice in five hundred square miles."[6] Another northerner stated, "The standard of education in [southern] academies has always been far below that of the common schools in the New England States. . . . I visited several academies, and in none of them were reading, writing, and arithmetic so thoroughly taught as they are in the common schools of Maine and New Hampshire."[7] A northern lady who made several trips through the South between 1853 and 1859 observed: "Education is not extended to the masses here as at the North."[8]

Foreigners agreed, as one of them expressed it, that in "the northern States, education in the common acceptation of the term, may be considered as universal."[9] They especially praised the New England school system. "The Public institutions of Boston are admirably conducted," announced one Englishman.[10]

Even southerners who visited the North admitted "that there is no other region inhabited by the Anglo-Saxon race. . .where national education has been carried so far."[11] Northerners even educated their women and not just in English literature and the polite arts but in Latin and mathematics as well, because these subjects reputedly developed their "mental strength and acuteness." A southerner observed: "The Yankees are too shrewd, and too habitually observant of practical utility, not to perceive this truth, and act accordingly."[12]

A statistical difference between northern and southern education even became apparent in the 1850 federal census, which indicated that more than 20 percent of the South's native whites could neither read nor write, compared to only 0.42 percent of New England's.[13] A Maine physician who had traveled in the South contended that there were many more illiterate southerners than the census indicated. He found not only the "non-slaveholders . . . ignorant and degraded, but . . . the slaveholders in the planting districts . . . quite as destitute of learning as the poor whites," and he reported that a friend once "called on 21 families of slaveholders, and found only two—a man and his wife—who could read."[14] Another visitor to the South in the 1850s could not find a single bookstore in Austin, Texas, and only one in Nashville.[15] Southerners, reported still another tourist, had no respect for knowledge or for academics.[16]

Despite the efforts of such idealists as Thomas Jefferson and Archibald D. Murphey, the only southern states to adopt systems of free public education prior to the Civil War were Kentucky and North Carolina.[17] In South Carolina German-born Christopher G. Memminger tried unsuccessfully to secure statewide public schools similar to those in Charleston.[18] Although school laws in Louisiana looked impressive, they were rarely enforced; one teacher's certificate bore the marks, rather than the signatures, of twelve parish school directors. Late in the antebellum period the state school superintendent recommended to the Louisiana legislature a law requiring at least two of the state's three directors of common schools be able to read and write.[19] Classes even in North Carolina, which boasted the most educationally advanced common school system in the Old South, met only four months a year.[20]

There was much opposition to North Carolina's public school system, which had developed slowly and imperfectly. In 1800 a newspaper reported that nine-tenths of the state's population was illiterate. Twenty-nine years later Tryam McFarland explained that his senate committee had reported unfavorably on a "bill for the education of poor children" because "the vast expenditure required" for such a program would necessitate additional taxes, which the people would resist; moroeover, the "equal contribution of all for the benefit of some [would] be equally irreconcilable with strict justice and the sentiments of the Community at large." It seems unlikely that the North Carolina legislature would have adopted a public school system if Congress had not voted in 1836 to distribute the United States Treasury's surplus revenue among the states. North Carolina's share—$1,433,757.39—became in effect the public school fund, but the 1839 school act was more form than fact since it required neither the erection of schoolhouses nor the support of the schools by county taxation. There was no way to punish counties for deciding, as the Cumberland County Court did in 1855, that "the school tax is for the present dispensed with." Edgecombe County did not levy its first school tax until 1855, and in many counties the amount of the school tax levied varied considerably from year to year. Teachers of any kind were difficult to find, and county courts frequently appointed "one of the most illiterate . . . citizens" chairman of the board of superintendents. Because of many problems and defects in the system, A. W. Brandon, chairman of the Rowan County Supervisors, exclaimed in 1854: "I do not think the Public Schools will ever prosper and work well."[21]

There were, of course, well-educated people in the Old South. Some of them could match knowledge and pens with the best of northern scholars. Frank L. Owsley has pointed out that "if college attendance is any test of an educated people, the South had more educated men and women in proportion to population than the North, or any other part of the world." In 1860 1 out of every 247 whites in the South was attending college, compared to only 1 out of every 703 in the North.[22] What Owsley failed to reveal, however, was how poor some of the colleges were and how little was learned by some of the students. The records of student life at many southern colleges reveal drinking, gambling, and carousing as the rule rather than the exception.[23]

A few southerners read and collected books, but usually they were considered eccentrics by their neighbors. In colonial Virginia two of the most prominent book collectors were William Byrd II, who besides reading Greek, Latin, and Hebrew had a library of more than 3,600 volumes when he died in 1744, and Robert "King" Carter, who owned some 1,500 volumes by 1774.[24] The South Carolina novelist, William Gilmore Simms, had amassed a library of 10,700 volumes when Yankee troops burned it in 1864.[25] Hugh Davis, an Alabama planter, had a collection of 631 books at the time of his death in 1862.[26]

The library of John D. Ashmore of Anderson District, South Carolina, as itemized by its owner in 1856, reveals what kinds of books at least one educated southern planter collected. Ashmore owned 1,475 titles— 320 on literature, 171 on philosophy or politics, 66 on travel, history, or biography, 56 on religion, 24 on military affairs, and 838 reference works or unclassified items. He listed among his holdings such titles as *Shakespeare* (two volumes), *The Christian Library* (six volumes), *McCauley's Miscellanies* (two volumes), *Elements of Moral Philosophy*, *Works of Calhoun*, *Scott's Works*, *Napoleon and His Marshals* (two volumes), *Washington and His Generals* (two volumes), *Scott's Campaign in Mexico*, *Militia Tactics*, *Jefferson's Writings*, *Helper's Impending Crisis*, *Helper's Impending Crisis Dissected*, *Lincoln & Douglas Debates*, *Patent Office Reports*, *Compendium of the Seventh Census*, *Penal Codes in Europe*, *Course of Latin Studies*, *Columbian Orator*, *Accounts of Irish Heirs*, *Religious Instructions for Negroes*, *Brittons & Saxons*, *High Life in New York*, *Dickens' Works*, *Scott's Poetry*, *Burns' Poetical Works*, *Family Preacher*, *The Victims of Gaming*, *Mothers of the Bible*, *The Young Mother's Guide*, *The Young Bride*, *Conversational Philosophy*, *Geog-*

raphy of the Heavens, Murray's English Grammar, Dictionary of Congress, Niles Register, biographies of Henry Clay, John C. Calhoun, Zachary Taylor, Daniel Webster, and Alexander H. Stephens, and more than 700 public documents on agriculture.[27]

Ashmore was a literate and ambitious planter but still enough of a southerner to reveal how much he hated the materialism he practiced. On December 20, 1853, he wrote in his farm journal: "My provision crop this year is abundantly sufficient I think for the next years support . . . provided it is used with care and economy—Damn such a word."[28]

The better educated southerners—usually the well-off and the ambitious—were often sufficiently "Yankeefied" to want their children educated by northerners. These individuals either brought in tutors from the North or sent their sons and daughters to northern schools. A woman whose father had migrated to Georgia from the North recalled: "There were no public schools in those days [the 1840s], and good private schools were few and far between, so when my father's four oldest children, who were girls, were old enough to begin their education, he went on to East Hampton in Massachusetts and brought back a teacher, and built a little school-house in the grove where she took a limited number of scholars." When his boys were old enough to start school, he went back to Massachusetts for a male tutor.[29] A visitor to Natchez observed: "The principal persons of wealth send their children for instruction . . . to the New England states—a distance of three thousand miles. There is an academy here, but it is neglected."[30]

Various reasons were given for sending children to the North, but most of them were designed to protect young southerners from their traditions and culture. "*Our* boys & girls at home are too apt to take things carelessly all the time . . . without ever feeling themselves called upon for any great excitement to ambition, energy or reflection," stated a South Carolinian.[31] A Louisianian believed there were too many corrupting influences in the South: "The more you see of our society, especially our young men, the more you will be impressed with the importance of a change in our system of education if we expect the next generation to be anything more than a mere aggregation of loafers charged with the duty of squandering their fathers' legacies and disgracing their names."[32] Frederick Law Olmsted claimed that many planters sent their sons to northern schools to prevent them from having sexual relations with slaves. One planter told him that there was "no possibility" of children "being brought up in decency at home."[33]

Although there was no guarantee that southerners who were exposed to a northern education would become "Yankeefied," people who feared that their children would learn alien ways and ideals in the North had good reason to be concerned.[34] Northern teachers often tried to blot out as much of a student's southernism as possible. One young man explained to his father how the "solemn class smoke" at Yale University was supposed to bury "all sectional and personal animosities and unite us as brothers."[35] For this to work, however, all had to accept the Yankee version of truth.

Frequently southerners brought back from northern colleges what R. H. Garnett, a Virginian, called "their second-hand history and shallow philosophy." At home these brainwashed youngsters, according to Garnett,

joined the place-hunting politicians in an outcry against Southern indolence, and its fancied cause, Southern slavery; they pointed us to Northern opulence and the growth of Northern cities, not as what they really are, . . . but as examples of their superior enterprise and industry until at last we began to believe, what was so often dinned into our ears, that slavery was the moral, social and political evil they pretended.[36]

Antisouthern teaching was so persistent in northern institutions that a traveler in the late antebellum period noted that South Carolinians no longer sent their children to colleges outside the South because the "students returning from the North so often came home 'tainted with Abolitionism.' "[37] In 1855 C. K. Marshall, a Mississippian, concluded that it was impossible "for southerners to be safely educated at the north. They cannot come back with proper feelings towards their families and their people."[38]

Marshall was right. Northern schooling did not always destroy the traditional values of southerners, but it did often enough to be dangerous. Of the approximately 350 southerners who graduated from West Point and were in the military service at the outbreak of the Civil War, only 168 of them joined the Confederate army. Their West Point education, although far less "Yankee" in content than that at most northern schools, and the service that followed from it, kept 162 southerners in the Union army and willing to fight against their own kin.[39]

Southerners awoke relatively late to the dangers of northern schooling. Not until the 1850s did James De Bow announce: "It is time to call home our youth from north of Mason and Dixon's line. Subject them no more to the poison of Yale and Amherst, and . . . Harvard."[40] Why, asked another man, should southerners continue to lavish "their wealth . . . upon [Yankee] institutions and faculties who esteem it a condescension to teach Southern pupils, and spurn their parents and guardians as graceless barbarians?"[41]

Most southerners resented what a group of Georgians called the hypocritical northern "Reverend professors and Clergymen" who used the lectern and the pulpit to denounce the people of the South.[42] Such antisouthernism was widespread. Henry Adams of Massachusetts characterized his Harvard classmate, William H. F. ("Rooney") Lee, the son of Robert E. Lee, in his autobiography as

simple beyond analysis; so simple that even the simple New England student could not realize him. No one knew enough to know how ignorant he was; how childlike; how helpless before the relative complexity of a school. As an animal, the Southerner seemed to have every advantage, but even as an animal he steadily lost ground.

Adams concluded that "the Southerner had no mind; he had temperament. He was not a scholar; he had no intellectual training; he could not analyze an idea, and he could not even conceive of admitting two; but in life one could get along very well without ideas, if one had only the social instinct."[43]

While never completely successful in their efforts to keep southern students at home, the advocates of "a southern education for Southrons" continued to denounce Yankee institutions. De Bow wrote:

Better would it be for us that our sons remained in honest ignorance and at the plough-handle than that their plastic minds be imbued with doctrines subversive to their country's peace and honor, and at war with the very fundamental principles upon which the whole super-structure of the society they find at home is based.

De Bow was delighted in 1860 by what he called the "exodus of Southern students recently from Colleges of the North."[44] Edmund Ruffin of Virginia, who assailed Yankee "hostility & malignity," was ecstatic when he learned that "267 of the southern medical students at the two colleges in Philadelphia, have, by agreement left those institutions."[45]

Many southerners not only agreed with De Bow that it would be better for their children to remain "in honest ignorance" than to become "imbued with doctrines subversive" to southern society but also objected when certain subjects were neglected or emphasized at northern schools. One man denounced the instruction at Harvard because he heard twenty-six of the graduating class speak at commencement and all "their speeches were poorly written and worse spoken." In the opinion of this southerner any school that failed to teach oratory was worthless. Another southerner claimed that to get on with the Yale faculty, a "diminutive and low-minded set," one must be "a dull plodding mathematician." He insisted that the "best passport to Yale College is a New England appearance and a knowledge of mathematicks."[46] As most southerners loved oratory and disliked mathematics, Yale and Harvard were good places to avoid.

Southerners also frequently objected to the importation of Yankees to teach in the South. Parson William G. Brownlow of Tennessee castigated

Memphis school officials for bringing "a gang of low-flung nutmeg dealers" from Connecticut to instruct southern children. Humorist Joseph G. Baldwin of Alabama pictured Miss Charity Woodey, "a new importation from Yankeedom," as "one of the 'strong-minded women of New England' who exchange all the tenderness of the feminine for an impotent attempt to gain the efficiency of the masculine nature." Such women, he noted, in "trying to *double-sex* themselves, *unsex* themselves, losing all that is lovable in woman and getting most of what is odious in man. . . . She had come out as a missionary light to the children of the South, who dwell in the darkness of Heatheness," and was quick "in delivering her enlightened sentiments upon the subject of matters and things about her."[47] After barricading the door to the room of an unpopular Yankee professor, students at the University of Alabama "put a blower on top of the chimney to smoke him out. When, red-eyed and shaking, he found that he could not open his door he raised a window to get aid and the boys threw rocks at him."[48]

But the dislike of Yankee professors was only an excuse for misbehavior, which was common among southern students. A general lack of self-discipline coupled with a high sense of honor and a propensity for violence hampered their scholarly pursuits. "There is not that substantial family discipline maintained, and the salutary home influence in the South, that are every where seen in New England," observed one Yankee:

The child of the slaveholder is taught to resist every insult, every aggression upon his rights, with physical force, and, if need be, with a fatal weapon. He is instructed to regard a "coward" as the meanest, most odious character in the world, and he shuns no danger to avoid such an opprobrious epithet. Thus the son is often first sent to the pistol gallery, before he is taught to read.[49]

Two northerners once watched five Georgia boys throwing knives at a tree. When two of the boys, George and John, quarreled, George threw a rock at John, who avoided it by jumping behind a tree. "John, you mean coward," roared George, "dodge behind a tree, eh! You mean dog! I'll have nothing more to say to you." The other boys joined George in denouncing John as a "mean coward" who was afraid of a little rock. "We'll never play with you again," they exclaimed as they left John standing disgraced behind the tree. As one of the northerners noted:

Let that scene be repeated the next day, and Johnny would not dodge the stone. He would not endure another frown of public opinion like that, and thus lose the confidence and companionship of all his little comrades. He will "stand his ground" the next time—and then, as he advances in years, he will take the knife, and, at last, the bullet preferring *death* to the name and disgrace of a *coward*.[50]

Schooling often clashed with the values and unrestrained habits of young southerners. When a female teacher scolded a boy of eight, he "drew his knife, and defied her to punish him." She managed by a ruse to disarm him, but his brother, age ten, pulled a pistol from his jacket and forced her to dismiss school for the day. When she informed their father of what they had done and told him that they would be spanked upon their return to school, he replied: "I can beat my boys enough at home, madam."[51] A graduate of Bowdoin College, teaching in Tennessee, complained that twice in one term when he had tried to "punish boys belonging to his academy, they had drawn pistols upon him, and he was unable to inflict the punishment." In Pontotoc, Mississippi, a young man who objected to his younger brother being punished killed the principal of the male academy with a bowie knife.[52]

One man refused to let his undisciplined son attend school because he was afraid the boy would kill his classmates and the teacher. It was necessary to keep the lad away from school, said one of his brothers, "unless there's some way of getting the devil out of him." Another brother announced: "He'll get shot before he's eighteen. He *drawed* his knife twice on me already; and unless we keep him at home, young as he is, a rope or a rifle will soon be the finishing of him."[53]

Southern youths frequently continued their violent ways in college. On numerous occasions southerners assaulted their classmates or professors. After whiskey was discovered in his room at the University of Alabama, George Lister "assaulted a professor with a deadly weapon." A few years later Thomas Jefferson Gordon was expelled from the same institution for attacking a professor.[54] One South Carolinian admitted that he was dismissed from West Point for two offenses: "One for having used a dagger too freely in a *personal* contest; and the other for having made an *unprovoked* attempt to shoot a man, who had let fall some unguarded words, hostile to my feelings."[55] A Mississippian also was expelled from the academy for wounding another cadet in a duel. After the Mississippian left West Point, a classmate wrote to him: "Perry has nearly recovered (I believe), he *Limps* considerably yet from the wound he received in his *seat of honor*. You will receive in a few days a letter signed by the whole corps save seven or eight *Damned Yankees* . . . commending your conduct &c."[56] More than once students at South Carolina College threatened professors and fired weapons at them. The president of the school complained that "the windows under my bedroom have been repeatedly shattered at various hours of the night and guns fired under my window." At the University of Virginia one professor was horsewhipped and another was murdered by students. The president of Oakland College in Mississippi was stabbed to death by a drunken student.[57]

Southerners were not just violent and undisciplined students; they

displayed a contempt for formal education that went beyond mere row-
diness. A foreigner who visited South Carolina College found the students "very disorderly, frequently disturbing congregations on . . .
Sunday, because the [president of the college] is too idle to preach, and
thereby keep them together. Saw several of these learned young gentlemen stretched on a table, with their learned legs carelessly hanging out
of their chamber windows, which seemed nearly all broken. Want of
discipline is here too palpable, but there is no lack of whiskey."[58] A
schoolmistress admitted that her pupils dispersed in the spring because
they were "disinclined for study as soon as the weather became oppressive."[59] A schoolmaster in backcountry Georgia found his forty-five
pupils—"fifteen grown young men, five of them married, five grown
young ladies, and boys and girls of all sizes and ages"—unteachable:

These children had been born and raised to the age I found them among the
cows and drunken cowdrivers on the outer borders of the State, and they were
positively the coarsest specimens of the human family I had ever seen. . . . In
the course of the first day they had half a dozen fights in the house; talking and
laughing went on incessantly. . . . Those married and grown up young men
participated in the devilment and seemed to enjoy it hugely.[60]

Witnesses repeatedly told of the difficulties of teaching southern children. A visitor at a Georgia academy noted that while "the teacher was
demonstrating a sum on the board, two lads had a misunderstanding,
and one of them knocked the other down. The noise attracted the attention of the teacher, who looked around before the boy had time to
get up; but he took no notice of it. The recitations in reading and arithmetic—writing was inadmissible for want of writing desks—were far
inferior to those in the common schools of New England." A teacher
from New Hampshire told a fellow Yankee that he could not confine
southern boys long enough without interruption to teach them anything.
Pointing to a bright ten-year-old, he said, "There is a boy that has been
here the most of a whole term,—but he has not learned all his letters.
His father will permit no restraint upon him when he wishes for any
amusement,—such as gaming and fishing,—and it is useless for me to
try to teach him to read."[61]
Southerners generally cared little for reading. They were oral and
aural, just as their Celtic ancestors had been. The southern woman
described by a traveler as "sitting with a pipe in her mouth, doing no
work and reading no books" would doubtless have agreed with the
southern man who, when asked by a Yankee if he liked to read, replied:
"No, it's damn tiresome."[62] It has often been said, only partly in jest,
that more southerners wrote books than read them. "You know," a
North Carolinian informed a visitor, "we people . . . do not like books

so well, but we like to remember and memorize many things that we do love." A Virginian told the Yankee tourist Jared Sparks that "there will be no such thing as book-making in Virginia for a century to come. People here prefer talking to reading, as Mr. Houston said of those in Tennessee."[63] Another Yankee, who was surprised "to find the houses of slaveholders so generally destitute of books," believed "there were more books, and more of men of liberal education . . . in the State of Maine, with her half a million inhabitants, than in all the slave States!"[64]

The aversion to reading even extended to reading music. Most southerners learned to sing and to play musical instruments by ear. A New Englander who visited a southern "singing school" wondered "how music could be taught, where so many of the people could not read." He discovered that the teacher used no books; sixty pupils were "taught by rote," and they sang well. "Remarkably well," admitted the visitor who "was indeed surprised to hear them sing so well." When he asked why no books were used, the teacher replied, "in a tone of decided prejudice against *book* knowledge: 'We don't believe in this blind note-singing here.' " In contrast to the practice in the North, singing in southern churches was often done without hymn books.[65] In fact, most southern musicians did not read music. Even in the late twentieth century the best southern country and bluegrass instrumentalists played and composed by ear. "I always just play by ear what I hear," explained Jesse McReynolds, the mandolinist who developed the complex "cross-picking" style. "Back in them [early] days," recalled bluegrass fiddler Kenny Baker, "all a man had to do was just play it one time and I could remember it."[66]

Because so many southerners deprecated formal education, outsiders usually considered them benighted. An Englishwoman who taught school in the South thought southerners "easy contented beings; unsullied by contact with the world, simpleminded and guileless more than any other people under the sun; and if not over-much given to intellectual pursuits, they win esteem by more lovable qualities."[67] Less charitable observers called them empty-headed and superstitious. "In no part of the Union," said a New Yorker, "will you find so many current superstitions as among Southerners."[68] These superstitions, critics noted, included belief that a cock crowing at midnight signaled the death before dawn of the one who heard it; that it was bad luck to break a mirror, to let a black cat cross one's path, or to wear a garment wrong side out, and that it sometimes rained fish and frogs.[69]

Frederick L. Olmsted found many southerners to be remarkably ignorant by his standards. Of some Tennesseeans, he reported: "Their notions of geography were amusing. . . . They thought Virginia lay to the southward, and was a cotton-growing state. . . . New York, they thought, lay west of Georgia, and between them and Texas."

About some things, however, southerners displayed understanding and wisdom. They knew, for example, that the North was where the "Yankees came from—'the people that used to come peddling.' "[70] An untutored Virginia lady shrewdly observed: "I reckon all cities are pretty much alike."[71] A Tar Heel, when told that New York City contained some 700,000 people, offered a perceptive comment on city life: "I suppose there's some people been living there all their lives that don't know each other, and never spoke to one another once yet in their lives, ain't there?" he asked. Assured that such was the case, he remarked: " 'Tain't so here, people's more friendly, this country."[72] And when Olmsted informed another North Carolinian, who had his geography somewhat confused, that Charleston was not near New York, the man replied with a shrug: "Ain't it? well, it was Charleston . . . or New York, or some place out there."[73]

These rustic southerners repeatedly made it clear that they could do without instruction; they were by no means dissatisfied with their condition. Indeed, many of them had all they wanted. Olmsted stayed overnight with some relatively well-off North Carolinians whom he described as "good-natured, intelligent people, but very ignorant. . . . The man told me that he had over a thousand acres of rich tillable land, besides a large extent of mountain range," reported Olmsted. "I did not see a single book in the house, nor do I think that any of the family could read." When Olmsted took out a map to explain his route, the man "said he 'wasn't scollar'd enough' to understand it, and I could not induce him to look at it." Yet the man lived comfortably and was thoroughly content in his ignorance. "He reckoned he's got enough to make him a living for the rest of his life," Olmsted noted, "and he didn't know any use a man had for more'n that." A determined Yankee book drummer once told a southerner that "a set of books on scientific agriculture" would teach him to "farm twice as good as you do." To which the southerner replied, "Hell, son, I don't farm half as good as I know how now."[74]

Even their critics admitted that not all southerners were stupid. The Yankee prison physician who attended Jefferson Davis during his incarceration after the war was impressed by Davis' "large, varied, and practical education; the geology, botany, and all products of his section appearing to have in turn claimed his attention. Not the superficial study of a pedant, but the practical acquaintance of a man who has turned every day's fishing, shooting, riding, or pic-nicking, to scientific account."[75] A New Hampshire schoolmistress who taught in the South was even more emphatic about the native intelligence of southerners. "As a general thing, pupils at the South are not as far advanced in intellectual attainments at the ages of ten and twelve as the same class of students in the North," stated Emily P. Burke, "but as far as my experience goes, when they are brought under good intellectual development more rapid, than has been the case with children of the same age I ever had the care of at the North."[76] A traveler admitted that many ordinary southerners "are ignorant, so far as book-learning is concerned, but they are well supplied with common sense."[77] "They have a high estimation of their own qualities & look on book learning as all superfluous," observed another northerner; "many of them are stupid & ignorant & on the contrary you find some who are sharp witted & very intelligent."[78]

What many observers found so strange and so difficult to understand was the ordinary southerner's notion of what was worth learning, which clashed with the standard Yankee curriculum. The skills of the scribbler, reader, and figurer—so necessary to trade and industry—were of small concern to the average southerner; he admired more the skills of the hunter, fisher, fighter, and fiddler. These and other leisurely activities were considered by him to be natural and worthwhile, fun to learn and to practice, and consistent with honesty and honor.

A visitor at an Alabama school noted that "the pupils are, mostly, as rude as the house—real young hunters, who handle the long rifle with more ease and dexterity than the goosequill, and who are incomparably more at home in 'twisting a rabbit,' or 'treeing a possum,' than in conjugating a verb." He concluded that the "long rifle is familiar to every hand; skill in the use of it is the highest accomplishment which a southern gentleman glories in; even the children acquire an astonishing expertness in handling this deadly weapon at a very early age."[79]

An upper-class southerner recalled how her father tried but failed to make a scholar of her brother, "who was more interested in his hunting and traps than in his studies." One day when the boy came home late for dinner he gave his usual explanation that he had been in the woods looking at his traps. "Did you catch anything?" asked his father. To the reply of "no, sir," the father, who had covertly placed a book in the trap, asked, "Why, wasn't your trap down?" The boy admitted that it was, but there was nothing in it "but a Davies' Arithmetic." The boy, explained his sister, "was a very matter-of-fact youth and took it as quietly as though it was the most natural thing in the world to catch a Davies' Arithmetic in a trap in the woods." The boy continued to hunt.[80]

The attitude toward education of the unsophisticated southerner was the same as that of his Celtic forebears whom English observers consistently described not merely as unschooled but uninterested in being schooled. "At the English Conquest," wrote Thomas Crofton Croker in the early nineteenth century, "Ireland was unquestionably in a state of profound ignorance; . . . and 'to the present day,' says Sir Richard Cox, 'very few of the Irish aim at any more than a little Latin, which every cow-boy pretends to, and a smattering of logic, which very few of them know the use of.' "[81] In the early eighteenth century M. Martin noted that the Scots of the Highlands and Western Isles "do for the most part labour under the want of knowledge of letters, and other useful arts and sciences."[82] The Celts, like their southern descendants, disdained reading and writing, were superstitious, loved music, dancing, stories, and oratory. They played the fiddle and other instruments by ear.[83] An authority on the Scots observed: " 'When God made time He made plenty of it' is a favourite saying of these people who are gay, witty, amusing. . . . They are naturally poetic, musical and . . . impractical."[84] Martin pointed out that the Scots of the Western Isles "neither sell nor buy, but only barter for such little things as they want; they covet no wealth."[85]

Men who were reluctant to become part of an industrial society understandably rejected the arts and sciences needed to maintain such a society. Neither rustic southerners nor their Celtic ancestors repudiated education, but rather they favored skills that would sustain, not help to destroy, their preferred life-style. Somehow they seemed to understand, just as American Indians often understood, that Yankee or English education was as dangerous to them and to their culture as Yankee or English bullets. "Tell our Great Father at Washington," some Indian leaders informed a government agent, "that we are very sorry we cannot receive teachers among us; for reading and writing . . . is very bad for Indians. Some of the Creeks and Cherokees learnt to read and write, and they are the greatest rascals among all Indians."[86]

What outsiders taught under the guise of enlightenment and independence was subservience to alien ways and values. Many southerners saw formal education as an insidious way to acculturate and enslave them. Learning to read and to write would not free them; it would put them more at the mercy of the Yankee. They could remain free only by perfecting the skills that reinforced their own life-style. In an argument against the establishment of a public school system in North Carolina, one man stated that it was unnecessary as well as undesirable "that *everybody* should be able to read and cipher. If one is to keep a store or a school, or to be a lawyer or physician, such branches may, *perhaps*, be taught him; though I do not look upon them as by any means indispensable; but if he is to be a plain farmer, or a mechanic, they are of no manner of use, rather a determent."[87]

Two things must be remembered about education in the Old South. First, only a small minority of antebellum southerners could both read and write and did so frequently. As exceptions to the prevailing social pattern, they were more Yankeefied in their outlook and actions than their neighbors or kinsmen, who, even if they could read and write, rarely took up pen or paper.

Aleksendr I. Solzhenitsyn, the traditionalist and Nobel laureate, has pointed out that writers who leave the Soviet Union and attempt to write for an international audience often can no longer produce true Russian literature. Because it is so difficult, perhaps impossible, to translate the richness of the Russian language, the works of émigré writers usually fail to present the real "Russian consciousness." An excellent example is Vladimir Nabokov. "To reach Western readers," observed Solzhenitsyn, "Nabokov was obliged to use his brilliant knowledge of English. This meant breaking with the past. He was born anew, with a new soul, but he lost his Russian roots."[88]

Something similar happened to many of the southerners who were exposed to Yankee education. Often they adopted nonsouthern views and ways that weakened or destroyed their native values and traditions. Historians too rarely have recognized the significance of this acculturation process. As willing captives of their own educational biases, they frequently have assumed that the better educated southerners—those who habitually wrote letters or kept diaries—represented the views and experiences of the majority. These historians have based their works mainly upon such sources, but the records kept by literate and Yankee-fied southerners reflect less the doings and beliefs of the majority than the acts and thoughts of a small though admittedly influential minority. Used for generalizations about the whole of southern society, these documents distort more than they clarify because they represent what Solzhenitsyn defined as "works not very deeply rooted in the consciousness or the experience of the people."

Most Southerners simply embraced their cultural traditions when they spent their time hunting rather than reading, fishing rather than writing. To them hunting and fishing were as natural and as pleasant as loafing; reading and writing were as unnatural and as unpleasant as studying. The average southerner learned only what he needed to learn and sometimes not even that. Generally he learned only that which was enjoyable, for pleasure meant more to him than profit. His knowledge might be considered useful, but that was not essential.

The most admired skills were those that allowed one to live in accord with his environment yet dominate it. Most southerners learned to be reasonably satisfied with their place in this world and with what they might expect in the next. They were unburdened by a work ethic and unhurried by driving ambition. They were like the Scots who, one writer said, were "better versed in the book of nature than many that have greater opportunities of improvement."[89]

The goal of the average southerner—the end of all his attainments—was to be fixed comfortably enough to fully enjoy his leisure. "To give their sons a liberal education is a paramount idea with the planters," observed a visitor to the South, "but when you come to talk about acquiring a profession and practicing it, that is altogether a different affair. With many persons the impression seems to be that the only elegant way in which to pass through life, is to have a plantation and do nothing at all."[90]

Notes

1. Charles G. Parsons, *Inside View of Slavery: or, a Tour Among the Planters* (Cleveland: Jewett, Proctor, and Worthington, 1855), pp. 180-85.
2. Governor James Glen quoted in Mary Katherine Davis, "The Feather Bed Aristocracy: Abbeville District in the 1790s," *South Carolina Historical Magazine* 80 (April 1979): 146. My thanks to Dr. Warner O. Moore for this reference.
3. Charles Woodmason, *The Carolina Backcountry on the Eve of the Revolution: The Journal and Other Writings of Charles Woodmason, Anglican Itinerant*, ed. Richard J. Hooker (Chapel Hill: University of North Carolina Press, 1953), pp. 52-53.
4. Frank L. Owsley, *Plain Folk of the Old South* (Baton Rouge: Louisiana State University Press, 1949), pp. 145-49; Avery O. Craven, *The Growth of Southern Nationalism, 1848-1861* (Baton Rouge: Louisiana State University Press, 1953), pp. 167, 271-73. .
5. Ellis Merton Coulter, *Old Petersburg and the Broad River Valley of Georgia: Their Rise and Decline* (Athens: University of Georgia Press, 1965), pp. 27-28.
6. Frederick Law Olmsted, *The Cotton Kingdom: A Traveller's Observations on Cotton and Slavery in the American Slave States*, ed. Arthur M. Schlesinger (New York: Alfred A. Knopf, 1953), p. 560.
7. Parsons, *Inside View*, p. 178.
8. Lillian Foster, *Way-side Glimpses, North and South* (New York: Rudd & Carleton, 1860), p. 108. See also Charles Fenno Hoffman, *A Winter in the West*, 2 vols. (New York: Harper & Brothers, 1835), 2: 192.
9. Joseph Sturge, *A Visit to the United States in 1841* (Boston: Dexter S. King, 1842), p. 171. See also Michel Chevalier, *Society, Manners and Politics in the United States: Being a Series of Letters on North America*, trans. Thomas Gamaliel Bradford (Boston: Weeks, Jordan, and Company, 1839), p. 334.
10. George William Frederick Howard, Seventh Earl of Carlisle, *Travels in America* (New York: G. P. Putnam, 1851), p. 13. See also Adam Hodgson, *Letters from North America. . .*, 2 vols. (London: Hurst, Robinson & Co., 1824), 2: 3.
11. J. C. Myers, *Sketches on a Tour Through the Northern and Eastern States, the Canadas and Nova Scotia* (Harrisonburg, Va.: J. H. Wartmann and Brothers, 1849), p. 364.
12. Anon., "Letters from New England—4," *Southern Literary Messenger* 1 (February 1835): 274-75.
13. U.S., Bureau of Census, *Compendium of the Seventh Census: 1850* (Washington: Government Printing Office, 1851), p. 153.
14. Parsons, *Inside View*, pp. 177-178.
15. Frederick Law Olmsted, *A Journey Through Texas: or, A Saddle-Trip on the Southwestern Frontier. . .*(1857; reprint ed., New York: Burt Franklin, 1969), pp. 111, 36.
16. Joseph Holt Ingraham, *The South-West; By a Yankee. . .*, 2 vols. (New York: Harper & Brothers, 1835), 1: 233-34.

17. Clement Eaton, *A History of the Old South: The Emergence of a Reluctant Nation*, 3d ed. (New York: Macmillan Publishing Co., 1975), pp. 436-38.

18. John Hope Franklin, *A Southern Odyssey: Travelers in the Antebellum North* (Baton Rouge: Louisiana State University Press, 1976), p. 56.

19. Olmsted, *Journey Through Texas*, pp. 52-53.

20. Eaton, *History of the Old South*, p. 439.

21. Guion Griffis Johnson, "Public Schools," in *The Southern Common People: Studies in Nineteenth-Century Social History*, ed., Edward Magdol and Jon L. Wakelyn (Westport, Conn.: Greenwood Press, 1980), pp. 55-73.

22. Owsley, *Plain Folk*, pp. 147-48.

23. James B. Sellers, *History of the University of Alabama, 1818-1902* (Montgomery: University of Alabama Press, 1953), pp. 197-257. See also E. Merton Coulter, *College Life in the Old South* (New York: Macmillan Company, 1928); Philip A. Bruce, *History of the University of Virginia, 1819-1919*, 5 vols. (New York: Macmillan Company, 1922); D. W. Hollis, *The University of South Carolina*, 2 vols. (Columbia: University of South Carolina Press, 1951-56); and James F. Hopkins, *The University of Kentucky: Origins and Early Years* (Lexington: University Press of Kentucky, 1951).

24. Louis B. Wright, *The Cultural Life of the American Colonies, 1607-1763* (New York: Harper & Brothers, 1957), p. 145; Louis Morton, *Robert Carter of Nomini Hall: A Virginia Tobacco Planter of the Eighteenth Century* (Charlottesville: University Press of Virginia, 1964), p. 214.

25. Clement Eaton, *The Mind of the Old South*, rev. ed. (Baton Rouge: Louisiana State University Press, 1967), p. 262.

26. Weymouth T. Jordan, *Hugh Davis and His Alabama Plantation* (Montgomery: University of Alabama Press, 1948), p. 18.

27. Schedule of Books Owned, May 1856, John D. Ashmore Papers, Southern Historical Collection, University of North Carolina, Chapel Hill, N.C.

28. John D. Ashmore Farm Journal, 20 December 1853, Ashmore Papers.

29. Marion Alexander Boggs, ed., *The Alexander Letters, 1787-1900* (Athens: University of Georgia Press, 1980), p. 122.

30. Thomas Ashe, *Travels in America. . .*, 3 vols. (London: Richard Phillips, 1808), 1: 317.

31. Charles Manigault quoted in Michael P. Johnson, "Planters and Patriarchy: Charleston, 1800-1860," *Journal of Southern History* 46 (February 1980): 65.

32. Braxton Bragg to G. Mason Graham, 27 June 1860, David F. Boyd Family Papers, Walter L. Fleming Collection, Louisiana State University, Baton Rouge, La.

33. Olmsted, *Cotton Kingdom*, p. 240.

34. Franklin, *Southern Odyssey*, p. 71.

35. Boggs, ed., *Alexander Letters*, p. 152.

36. R. H. Garnett, "Education in Virginia," *De Bow's Review* 10 (April 1851): 476.

37. James Silk Buckingham, *The Slave States of America*, 2 vols. (London: Fisher, Son & Co., 1842), 1: 54.

38. C. K. Marshall, "Home Education at the South," *De Bow's Review* 18 (March 1855): 430-31.

39. Ellsworth Eliot, Jr. *West Point in the Confederacy* (New York: G. A. Baker

& Co., 1941), p. xv; E. B. Long with Barbara Long, *The Civil War Day By Day: An Almanac, 1861-1865* (Garden City, N.Y.: Doubleday & Company, 1971), p. 709.

40. "Editorial, Book Notice," *De Bow's Review* 21 (October 1856): 440-41.

41. "Southern Education and School Books," *De Bow's Review* 22 (March 1857): 312.

42. "Social System and Institutions of the South," *De Bow's Review* 21 (November 1856): 552.

43. Henry Adams, *The Education of Henry Adams: An Autobiography* (Boston: Little, Brown, 1918), pp. 56-59.

44. *De Bow's Review* 10 (March 1851): 362; 28 (February 1860): 243.

45. William K. Scarborough, ed., *The Diary of Edmund Ruffin: Volume I, Toward Independence, October, 1856-April, 1861*, 2 vols. to date (Baton Rouge: Louisiana State University Press, 1972), 1: 377, 384. See also John S. Ezell, "A Southern Education for Southrons," *Journal of Southern History* 17 (August 1951): 303-327.

46. Hugh Blair Grigsby quoted in Fitzgerald Flourney, "Hugh Blair Grigsby at Yale," *Virginia Magazine of History and Biography* 22 (April 1954): 166-90; A. F. Rightor to Andrew McCollam, July 25, 1851, Andrew McCollam Papers, Southern Historical Collection, University of North Carolina, Chapel Hill, N.C.

47. Brownlow quoted in Bell I. Wiley, "The Spurned Schoolteachers from Yankeedom," *American History Illustrated* 14, no. 10 (February 1980): 15; Joseph G. Baldwin, *The Flush Times of Alabama and Mississippi: A Series of Sketches* (1853; reprint ed., New York: Sagamore Press, 1957), pp. 212-13.

48. Sellers, *History of the University of Alabama*, p. 210.

49. Parsons, Inside View, p. 179.

50. Ibid., pp. 179-80.

51. Ibid., pp. 180-81.

52. Ibid., pp. 181-82.

53. Hoffman, *Winter in the West*, 2: 192.

54. Sellers, *History of the University of Alabama*, pp. 209-10.

55. Amey Robinson Childs, *Planters and Businessmen: The Guignard Family of South Carolina, 1795-1830* (Columbia: University of South Carolina Press, 1957), p. 67.

56. Ripley A. Arnold to St. John R. Liddell, 21 March 1835, Moses, St. John R. Liddell and Family Papers, Louisiana State University, Baton Rouge, La.

57. Sellers, *History of the University of Alabama*, pp. 224-25.

58. William Faux, *Memorable Days in America: Being a Journal of a Tour to the United States. . .* (London: W. Simpkin and R. Marshall, 1828), p. 53.

59. Catherine C. Hopley, *Life in the South from the Commencement of the War: Being a Social History. . .from the Spring of 1860 to August 1862*, 2 vols. (1863; reprint ed., New York: Da Capo Press, 1974), 1: 110.

60. Gideon Lincecum, "Autobiography of Gideon Lincecum," *Publications of the Mississippi Historical Society* 8 (1904): 459.

61. Parsons, *Inside View*, pp. 182-83.

62. Sir Charles Lyell, *A Second Visit to the United States of North America*, 2 vols. (New York: Harper and Brothers, 1849), 2: 73; Olmsted, *Cotton Kingdom*, p. 301.

63. B. A. Botkin, ed., *A Treasury of Southern Folklore. . .* (1949; reprint ed., New York: Crown Publishers, 1980), p. 306; Jared Sparks, "Journal of a Southern

Tour of 1826," in *The Life and Writings of Jared Sparks, Comprising Selections from His Journals and Correspondence*, ed. Herbert Baxter Adams, 2 vols., (Boston: Houghton, Mifflin and Co., 1893), 1: 417.

64. Parsons, *Inside View*, p. 182.

65. Ibid., pp. 186-87.

66, McReynolds quoted on the album cover of *The Jim & Jesse Story*, CMH 9022; Baker quoted on the album cover of *Kenny Baker: Portrait of a Bluegrass Fiddler*, Country Records 719.

67. Hopley, *Life in the South*, 1: 90.

68. Hoffman, *Winter in the West*, 2: 291.

69. Frederick Hall, *Letters from the East and from the West* (Washington: F. Taylor and W. M. Morrison, 1840), pp. 338-39; Johann David Schopf, *Travels in the Confederation [1783-1784]*, trans. and ed. Alfred J. Morrison, 2 vols. (1911; reprint ed., New York: Bergman Publishers, 1968), 2: 135.

70. Frederick Law Olmsted, *A Journey in the Back Country* (1860; reprint ed., New York: Schocken Books, 1970), 240.

71. Hopley, *Life in the South*, 1: 91.

72. Olmsted, *Journey in the Back Country*, pp. 250-51.

73. Ibid., p. 249.

74. Ibid., pp. 258-59; Jonathan Daniels, *A Southerner Discovers the South* (New York: Macmillan Company, 1938), pp. 163-64.

75. John J. Craven, *Prison Life of Jefferson Davis. . .* (New York: Carleton, 1866), pp. 95-96.

76. Emily P. Burke, *Reminiscences of Georgia* (Oberlin, Ohio: J. M. Fitch, 1850), pp. 195-204.

77. Charles Lanman, *Adventures in the Wilds of the United States and British American Provinces*, 2 vols. (Philadelphia: J. W. Moore, 1856), 1: 500.

78. Henry Benjamin Whipple, *Bishop Whipple's Southern Diary, 1843-1844*, ed. Lester B. Shippee (Minneapolis: University of Minnesota Press, 1937), p. 77.

79. Philip Henry Gosse, *Letters from Alabama. . .* (London: Morgan and Chase, 1859), pp. 44, 140.

80. Boggs, ed., *Alexander Letters*, pp. 127-28.

81. Thomas Crofton Croker, *Researches in the South of Ireland. . .* (1824; reprint ed., New York: Barnes and Noble, 1969), p. 325.

82. M. Martin, "A Description of the Western Islands of Scotland," *A General Collection of the Best and Most Interesting Voyages and Travels in All Parts of the World* ed. John Pinkerton, 10 vols. (London: Longman, Hurst, Rees, and Orme, 1809), 3: 573.

83. Alwyn Rees and Brinley Rees, *Celtic Heritage: Ancient Tradition in Ireland and Wales* (London: Thames and Hudson, 1961), pp. 83-84, 89-90; Croker, *Researches*, pp. 78-79, 232, 234-35; Martin, "Description of the Western Islands," pp. 579, 611-614, 638; Moray McLaren, *Understanding the Scots: A Guide for South Britons and Other Foreigners* (New York: Bell Publishing Co., 1972); Michael Davie, ed., *The Diaries of Evelyn Waugh* (Boston: Little, Brown, 1976), p. 201; Thomas Keightley, *The Fairy Mythology* (London: G. Bell, 1878), p. 419.

84. McLaren, *Understanding the Scots*, p. 36.

85. Martin, "Description of the Western Islands," p. 581.

86. Washington Irving, *Wolfert's Roost and Other Papers*, rev. ed. (New York: G. P. Putnam and Son, 1865), pp. 332-33.

87. Johnson, "Public Schools," p. 57.

88. Hilton Kramer, "A Talk with Solzhenitsyn," *New York Times Book Review* 85, no. 9 (May 11, 1980): 3, 30-32.

89. Martin, "Description of the Western Islands," p. 573.

90. Lanman, *Adventures*, 2: 175.

13

THE ANCIENT PEDIGREE OF VIOLENT REPRESSION: GEORGIA'S KLAN AS A FOLK MOVEMENT

Charles L. Flynn, Jr.

Historians have treated the Ku Klux Klan violence of Reconstruction in ways emblematic of their interpretations of southern history as a whole. "Redeemer" historians have described the Klan as the salvation of good government and virtue. Since the 1950s "liberal" historians have lamented Klan violence as still more evidence of a pervasive and brutal regional racism, an unjustified effort to save the South from imaginary "black rule."[1] At present increasingly *de rigueur* class conscious historians concentrate upon Klan coercion of black workers. Klan activity, they say, was used to maintain planter control of land and labor.[2]

While the works of "redeemer" historians are dismissed now as hopelessly disfigured by the racism of their age, the problems that arise with works by so-called liberal and class-conscious historians are less easily defined. In the 1970s, the liberal school began to fade because it reduced the complexity of southern history to a division between white and black. Racism was the major issue of the 1950s and 1960s and, therefore, it seemed, also of the past. Liberals failed to give credence to the substantial evidence of class conflict among whites. Perhaps they simply failed to recognize it. For this reason they were unable to recognize the apparent paradox of yeomen efforts in the Klan to uphold a social order in which they, as well as blacks, were abused. Because the social mechanics that governed relations among whites remained unexplored, the liberal exposition of southern history seemed increasingly facile and incomplete.

Advocates of the class interpretation of southern history have a curiously similar problem. They see racism, racial injustice, and nearly everything else as a function of economic self-interest, and almost always the economic self-interest of an oppressive planter class. In this effort to reduce the complexity of southern history to a division between exploiter capitalists and exploited everybody else, the yeoman white, his racism, and (again illustratively) his participation in the Klan have no convenient place. Yeomen had no evident economic stake in the plantation system or the racist order upon which it depended. While class conscious historians have described conflict among whites and while they have analyzed the division between white landowner and black worker in terms of class, they have not been able to explain the connection between yeomen and the racist order. As Eugene Genovese has acknowledged, a complex of largely unaddressed issues still surrounds the role of white yeomen in southern society.[3]

Two examples well illustrate the class conscious treatment of yeomen and the Klan. In a 1974 article on South Carolina, J.C.A. Stagg dismisses racism as an insufficient explanation for Klan violence. The Klan was most active, he claims, in those areas in which planter control was most immediately threatened, that is, where gang labor was giving way to share and rental arrangements. Unfortunately, although Stagg uses several "examples" of a correlation between Klan violence during Reconstruction and land tenure some ten years later, he establishes no overall pattern, and since Klan activity across the South was common in the hill and mountain counties where plantations were rare, Stagg's explanation is hardly sufficient.[4]

Jonathan Wiener, like Stagg, draws a close connection between planter interests and Klan violence, but he finesses the issue of yeomen more explicitly. In his work on Alabama, Wiener defines the vigilantism of the yeomen-dominated up-country and the planter-dominated black belt as of different genres, as though patterns of Klan violence differed substantially in the two regions.[5] Why this distinction is valid remains a mystery, for it serves only as a dismissal—an ostensible justification for excluding yeomen from discussion.

A study of Ku Klux Klan violence in Georgia and its connection to the yeoman culture there confirms the inadequacy of a simple class interpretation of the Klan and, by implication, of southern history in general. In Georgia, the largest incidence of Klan violence occurred in a cluster of about seventeen Upper Piedmont and black belt counties running east and southeast from Atlanta to the South Carolina border. A second center of Klan activity included eight Upper Piedmont and mountain counties along the northern and western boundaries of the state.[6] Nothing in the emergence of sharecropping and renting distinguishes these counties from those others that were relatively free of Klan violence.[7] It is remarkable, however, that the yeoman-dominated Upper Piedmont and mountain counties were disproportionately represented and that these counties with only two exceptions were never controlled by local Republicans. Even some of the black belt counties were consistently controlled by Democrats.[8] It seems, therefore, that explanations associating Klan violence with planter interests alone or with the rise of sharecropping and renting, traditional explanations based on the desire to redeem government from Republican control, and even explanations relating politics and the control of black labor cannot explain adequately the situation in Georgia or probably across the South. To explain the broad support Klan brutality received among white southerners, including both planters and yeomen, remains a challenge. For such an explanation one should turn again to the statements of contemporary white southerners, the statements cited approvingly by "redeemer" historians and disapprovingly by liberal historians.

White southerners explained the Klan in amorphous, moralistic terms. "There is a kind of vague notion with a great many people," testified C. D. Forsyth of Floyd County, Georgia, "and it is an honest conviction with them, that they are in danger from the colored population. . . . As a general thing," he continued, "when a person . . . attempts to justify the operations of the Klan, they do it upon the theory, that it is necessary to keep the colored people down, to keep them in subordination, and in my opinion . . . that is the ground of the whole of it."[9] As Allen Trelease has shown, shrill justifications of Klan violence reflecting those vague notions described by Forsyth were repeated endlessly in Georgia and across the South and appeared even in the Klan's own declaration of purpose.[10] These statements went far beyond claims of racial superiority and far beyond racial justifications for economic relations. The justifications offered for Klan violence show that whites defined values of caste and defined them with a literally moral authority. Class and caste are not the same thing. Caste is a rigid, culturally defined system that is unsatisfying to the class conscious school, which seeks an economic base for group behavior.

As part of a European and American vigilante tradition, Klansmen were involved in a customary folk movement that upheld values they believed had moral authority. Although the political violence that most attracted the attention of congressional Republicans largely disappeared after Redemption, the more general, though less intense, pattern of vigilante justice at the hands of disguised bands (the appearance of which long antedated the Civil War) remained common. After Reconstruction, these groups continued to be called Ku Klux, instead of the earlier name of Regulators, or White Caps, after their unusual headgear.[11] The interchangeable names show that these groups were understood to be synonymous with those of Reconstruction. Their violence reflected the racial, economic, political, marital, and sexual values they sought to protect as an unsystematic, even self-contradictory, whole (like those of almost any group) rather than as separable by object or motive.

Well into the twentieth century, gangs of disguised men in Georgia threatened, beat, whipped, and killed serious and sometimes not-so-serious white and black offenders. Examples are numerous. In one county, a gang drove out "the very worst negro strumpets." White strumpets were driven from another. A man who had beaten his wife was dragged to the woods and whipped, while another man, who had married a "notorious town 'scamp' " only a few days after his previous wife died, was similarly punished.[12] Such attacks were not confined to Georgia or to the South; they were common in the Midwest, chronic on the frontier, and appeared even in New England.[13]

Although at first the supposition may seem far-fetched, this illegal "justice" is related to the "noisy masked demonstrations used to" punish wrong doers in medieval and early modern Europe. The historian E. P. Thompson was the first, to my knowledge, to make this connection.[14] In France these demonstrations were called *charivaris*; in England, "rough music." *Charivaris* often were associated with seasonal or religious festivals in which a community simultaneously mocked and affirmed its values. Lords of Misrule dispensed justice in the inverted world of the carnival, but real offenders, whether wife beaters, shrews, submissive husbands, the sexually incontinent betrothed, or others who offended sexual or marital values, were punished by the crowd.[15] These offenses included many of those that Ku Klux Klan or White Caps before, during, and after Reconstruction found punishable.

As part of the obscure symbolism of the festivals, men who punished offenders with beatings often dressed as women and wore paper masks or blackened faces. Beyond the ordinary benefits of disguise, Natalie Zemon Davis has found reasons for men to dress as women in the normative sex roles of the period: men drew upon the "sexual power and energy of unruly woman and her license . . . to tell the truth about unjust rule."[16]

The relation of dress, morality, and *charivari* to the moral content of Ku Klux Klan or White Cap violence is not the digression it may seem at first. *Charivari* continued to persist in attenuated form in the South and in sections of the Middle West well into the twentieth century. Even its name survived in the mutilated form of "shivaree."[17] It is more than coincidence that blacks sometimes described Ku Klux Klan disguises as dresses.[18] Certainly it is more than coincidence that "at the turn of the century" in Terrell County, Georgia, "masked men dressed in women's clothing took an accused arsonist from the custody of the sheriff and disappeared into the cypress swamps. A few days later the black man returned home [having been] severely beaten with a buggy trace."[19]

One may wonder why the Ku Klux Klan or White Caps adopted full-length gowns to go along with their hoods or masks, for gowns were not well-suited to horse-borne troops. Some claimed the disguise made them look ghostly and helped to frighten superstitious blacks, but no freedman believed Klansmen were ghosts, and because robed vigilantes rode beside others who only blackened their faces or wore paper masks, the ghostly explanation seems incomplete.[20] It is possible that the long, impractical gowns were a stylized anachronism, a symbol of fraternal, festival justice sapped of its former cultural significance. It is even possible that not all the symbolism had been lost for under the chivalric code of white southerners women remained the repository of moral values.[21]

Like the violence of the Ku Klux Klan or White Caps, *charivari*-related violence was not limited to enforcing sexual or marital values. In England, Ireland, and Scotland, bands of men dressed as women for vigilante activities that had economic objectives.[22] During the mid-nineteenth century, French peasants in the foothills of the Pyrenees adopted the traditional feminine disguise associated with the cause of morality for a long, violent battle to preserve their customary right to pasture stock and gather wood in the forests owned by local seigneurs and bourgeois.[23] This *"Guerre des Demoiselles"* was significantly similar to Ku Klux or White Cap efforts to protect moonshine from the impositions of federal tax officials in mountainous, isolated sections of late nineteenth-century Georgia—a later-day version of the whiskey rebellion.[24]

In fact, after Reconstruction, even without considering moonshine-related violence, the defense of economic "rights" or economic "justice" was the only cause equal to racial norms and sexual purity in the moral violence of vigilante bands.[25] There was no clear distinction between property right and moral right. There was no clear distinction between offenses against persons and offenses against property. The same vigilante bands that punished sexual or marital offenders during and after Reconstruction punished thieves, arsonists, swindlers, and "insubordinate" workers.[26] Some things were simply right and others simply wrong. The pattern of violence seen so intensely during Reconstruction was still in evidence in parts of the South during the twentieth century.[27]

This broad tradition of vigilantism demonstrates why Ku Kluxism was a culturally available alternative for white southerners, planters as well as yeomen. Indeed, this tradition alone can explain why the Klan and similar organizations appeared over much of the South in a consistent pattern of behavior even though the organizations were basically local rather than regionally coordinated.[28]

This tradition also provides a context in which to interpret the elements of violence that different groups of historians have singled out for attention. Political activity by black and white Republicans, theft, arson, "insolence" from blacks, "insubordination" on the part of a worker, teaching a school for freedmen, the protection of moonshine, cohabitation or fornication of black males with white females, and the violation of marital or sexual standards among whites were occasions for whippings or even murder at the hands of bands composed of planters and yeomen in the black belt and in the hills.[29] Whether one concentrates upon the intense outburst of political violence during Reconstruction, as liberals have, or one singles out the abuse of workers, as class conscious historians have, the violence of Ku Klux bands must be considered as part of an unsystematic whole.

As a whole, the pattern of Klan violence reveals that whites—planters and yeomen—found many things threatening and their sense of moral standards intensified, predictably, at the caste barrier. It should hardly be surprising that the "vague notion" that the caste barrier had been violated was compellingly symbolized for many whites in the politics of Reconstruction. Liberals concentrated upon Reconstruction politics for precisely the same reason. All whites did have a relationship—however unfriendly—with their government. It disgusted many, probably even most, whites that prominent men were disfranchised while blacks, who were supposed by whites to be beyond the caste barrier, who were not even thought of as part of southern society, received the vote. It angered many, perhaps most, white southerners that outsiders were turning their society upside down. And whatever differences they had among themselves, many or most, as "redeemer" historians have proudly noted, could join the Klan to protect the premises of the caste system with which they defined their country.

But while Ku Klux Klan violence reflects a fair degree of unanimity among whites over the inviolability of the culturally defined caste line, this does not mean that the liberal argument is adequate after all. The liberal formulation of southern history is still analytically insufficient to explain the yeoman's role in southern society and Klan violence in particular. The caste barrier was something more than racism shared with incredible vehemence. It defined not only conflict between whites and blacks but also the terms of conflict among whites.

There was one single object of Ku Klux and White Cap violence that planters and white yeomen differed over vociferously. During and after Reconstruction, yeoman bands constantly ran black sharecroppers and renters off their lands. These attacks persisted across the South through the beginning of the twentieth century, particularly during times of economic crisis, and this violence was a sign of the yeoman's fierce autonomy. Both during and after Reconstruction planters loudly condemned this sort of violence as disruptive to labor, in other words, to their profits. "The best elements of the community" condemned these actions, summarized one newspaper, "but they were powerless to prevent it."[30]

This instance of class differences between yeomen and planters may have been minor. While it certainly was not fought to the last man, it still reflects a more fundamental pattern of class conflict that dated from colonial times. The claims of Eugene Genovese and others aside, yeomen were not especially deferential to planter interests or unresentful of planter hegemony, but they did fight, as in the Klan, to maintain the caste line. Planters, wrapped in the genteel doctrines of paternalism, were equally dedicated to the caste system, but planters qualified the rigor with which they believed the caste system should be maintained when their own profits were at stake.

Historians have sometimes mistakenly described this difference as evidence of a more severe racism among the poor than among the well-to-do.[31] In fact, this difference is the obverse side of class conflict among whites, who differed little in their racist assumptions. Whether in the days of Jacksonian democracy or the days of Ben Tillman, when yeomen fought abusive planters they did so in terms of what Pierre van den Berghe and George Fredrickson have called *herrenvolk* democracy.[32] The ideology of white southerners validated caste oppression but did not legitimize class oppression among whites. Yeoman resistance to planter oppression was justified and often galvanized by claims of white equality above the caste line. This was true when poor-to-middling whites fought for the franchise, reapportionment of state legislatures, internal improvements, just systems of taxation, public education, *and* legal segregation. Notions of white equality were inextricably tied to notions of black subordination. One might claim that while racially defined subordinate labor was the basis of planter power, it was also the basis of class awareness among poor-to-middling whites. When blacks seemed upwardly mobile, when freedmen, for example, first became sharecroppers and renters, they not only threatened the yeoman's need to feel superior to someone else, but their upward mobility was by social definition a threat to the yeoman's claim to justice and equality among whites.

Only through studying this psychological nexus between the system of class divisions among whites and the caste division between whites and blacks can historians understand the social mechanics of southern society. Only then, for example, will the racism of southern Progressive reform demagogues and their appeal to poor-and-middling whites become explicable rather than paradoxical. Only then will it be possible to explain the yeoman dedication to the Klan. To understand the role of yeomen in southern society, to understand their apparently deferential yet actually independent role exemplified in the Klan, requires an appreciation of the complexities of a social structure that lie beyond the ideologies, whether class conscious or liberal, preferred by many twentieth-century historians.

Notes

1. Allen W. Trelease gives the most thorough and sophisticated rendition of this interpretation in *White Terror: The Ku Klux Klan Conspiracy and Southern Reconstruction* (New York, 1971). More typical is Herbert Shapiro's "The Ku Klux

Klan during Reconstruction: The South Carolina Episode," *Journal of Negro History* 49 (January 1964): 34-55.

2. See J.C.A. Stagg, "The Problem of Klan Violence: the South Carolina Up-Country, 1868-1871," *Journal of American Studies* 8 (December 1974): 303-18; Jonathan Wiener, *Social Origins of the New South: Alabama, 1860-1885* (Baton Rouge, 1978), pp. 61-68; Vernon Burton, "Race and Reconstruction: Edgefield County, South Carolina," *Journal of Social History* 12 (Fall 1978): 31-56.

3. Eugene D. Genovese, "Yeomen Farmers in a Slaveholders' Democracy," *Agricultural History* 49 (April 1975): 331-42.

4. Stagg in "The Problem of Klan Violence," bases his examples on the census figures from 1880. While he begins his article discounting yeoman racism as an explanation for Klan violence, he reverts to that explanation in the closing passages of his article.

5. Generalizing from the single difference that black sharecroppers and renters were run off their land in the Upper Piedmont but not in the black belt, Wiener fails to acknowledge parallels between the two regions. See *Social Origins of the New South*, p. 61. This difference will be discussed later.

6. Trelease, *White Terror*, p. 318; C. Mildred Thompson, "Reconstruction in Georgia: Economic, Social, Political, 1865-1872," [Columbia University] *Studies in History, Economics and Public Law* 44,, no. 1 (1915): 376, 361-63.

7. U.S., Census Office, *Report of the Production of Agriculture as returned at the Tenth Census, 1880* (Washington, D.C., 1883), Table 5, pp. 40-45.

8. Thompson, "Reconstruction in Georgia," pp. 362, 375.

9. Testimony of C. D. Forsyth, Floyd Co., Ga., July 10, 1871, *Testimony taken by the Joint Committee to Inquire into the Condition of Affairs in the Late Insurrectionary States: The Ku Klux Klan Conspiracy*, U.S. Congress, House of Representatives Report 22, 42d Cong., 2d sess., 1871-1872, Georgia Volume 1, p. 23. Georgia volumes 1 and 2 are volumes 6 and 7 of the committee's report.

10. Trelease, *White Terror*, pp. 16-22 and throughout. See also Richard C. Beckett, "Some Effects of Military Reconstruction in Monroe County, Mississippi," *Publications of the Mississippi Historical Society* 8 (1904): 177-86; Anne Cooper Burton, *The Ku Klux Klan* (Los Angeles, 1916), pp. 5, 9-10; Testimony of Thomas Allen (Colored), Jasper Co., Ga., 26 October 1871, U.S. Congress, *The Ku Klux Klan Conspiracy*, Georgia vol. 2, p. 608; Testimony of E. H. Chambers, Gwinett Co., Ga., 26 October 1871, ibid., p. 604.

11. Examples: "We learn there is in a certain section of the county a band of men, well organized, who style themselves kuklux. . . ." *Emanuel Itemizer* quoted in the *Atlantic Constitution*, 10 October 1883; "There are several vigilance committees, or what were known after the war times, as the Ku Klux Klans, in operation about here." *Gainesville Eagle* quoted the *Atlanta Constitution*, 27 July 1883. Even a case in which blacks gathered to whip a white man who habitually beat his wife and then left her to take "up with a negro woman, living with her as his wife" was reported under the headline "Colored Ku-Klux." *The Dawson Weekly Journal* (Georgia), 30 September 1880. On antebellum practice see testimony of John Christy, Athens, Ga., 24 July 1871, U.S. Congress, *The Ku Klux Klan Conspiracy*, Georgia vol. 1, p. 240.

12. *Atlanta Constitution*, 1 June 1883; "Those White Cap Cases," unascribed clippings, n.d., Scrapbook 3, p. 71, William Jonathan Northen Personal Papers,

Georgia State Archives, Atlanta, Ga.; *The Americus Times-Recorder* (Georgia), 12 October 1894; *Dawson News* 1 April 1891, cited in Albert Colby Smith, "Violence in Georgia's Black Belt: A Study of Crime in Baldwin and Terrell Counties, 1866-1899" (M.A. thesis, University of Georgia, 1974), p. 65.

13. On White Capping in Ohio and Indiana, see *Weekly Recorder* (Americus, Ga.), 23 November 1888; comments on the Middle West in Edward P. Thompson, " 'Rough Music' Le Charivari Anglais," *Annales: Economies; Societés: Civilisation* 27 (Mars-Avril 1972): 286-87 and 287 n. 8. On Bald Knobbers in Missouri see Robert Maxwell Brown, "Historical Patterns of Violence in America," in *Violence in America: Historical and Comparative Perspectives. A Report to the National Commission on the Causes of Violence and its Prevention*, ed. Hugh D. Graham and Ted R. Gurr (Washington, D.C. 1969), pp. 50-51.

14. Thompson, " 'Rough Music,' " pp. 286-87 and 287 n. 8. The definition of *charivari* appears in Natalie Zemon Davis, "The Reasons of Misrule," *Society and Culture in Early Modern France: Eight Essays by Natalie Zemon Davis* (Stanford, 1975), p. 97.

15. Davis, *Society and Culture*, p. 100. E. P. Thompson also lists occasions for *charivari* in " 'Rough Music,' " p. 294.

16. Davis, *Society and Culture*, pp. 149-50, 100, and throughout.

17. Thompson, " 'Rough Music', " pp. 286-87 and 287 n. 8, 307-308.

18. H. Grady McWhiney and Francis B. Simkins, "The Ghostly Legend of the Ku Klux Klan," *Negro History Bulletin* 14 (February 1951): 112.

19. Smith, "Violence in Georgia," p. 66.

20. Testimony of Charles Smith (Colored) of Walton County, Georgia, 26 October 1871, in U.S. Congress, *The Ku Klux Klan Conspiracy*, Georgia vol. 1, p. 599; and throughout; McWhiney and Simkins, "The Ghostly Legend," throughout.

21. Allen Trelease suggests that Klan regalia may have derived from such other fraternal organizations as college fraternities, the Masons, or Odd Fellows, which were especially popular in the nineteenth century. *White Terror*, pp. 4-5. This explanation pushes the origin of the feminine disguise back one step but does not explain why the Odd Fellows, for example, dressed like Odd Fellows.

22. Davis, *Society and Culture*, pp. 148-49.

23. John Merriman, "The Demoiselles of the Ariège, 1829-1831," in *1830 in France*, ed. John Merriman (New York, 1975).

24. See Trelease, *White Terror*, p. 331; Thompson, "Reconstruction in Georgia," p. 364; William F. Holmes, "Moonshining and Collective Violence: Georgia, 1889-1895," *Journal of American History* 67 (December 1980): 589-611.

25. Holmes, "Moonshining and Collective Violence," Tables 4, 5, p. 602.

26. Where violence occurred against one type of "offense," other "offenses" were also punished. See U.S. Congress, *The Ku Klux Klan Conspiracy*, Georgia vols. 1 and 2 throughout. . Brown, "Historical Patterns," pp. 50-54. See also *Atlanta Constitution*, 27 May 1883, and the Gainesville *Eagle* quoted in ibid., 29 July 1883.

27. This has been the standard observation about the "second" Ku Klux Klan.

28. Localism is shown by the existence of numerous similar organizations with different names across the South (Kentucky, Mississippi, Alabama, Texas,

Tennessee, Louisiana, and Florida) and by the lack of synchronized activity even within a single state. Trelease, *White Terror*, pp. xlv-xlvi, 51, 226.

29. On theft: testimony of C. H. Chambers, Gwinett Co., Ga., 26 October 1871, U.S. Congress, *The Ku Klux Klan Conspiracy*, Georgia vol. 2, p. 602; Testimony of Nedon L. Argier, Atlanta, Ga., 14 July 1871, ibid., 1: 172. Disciplining workers: H.D.F. Young, Agent, Bureau Refugees, Freedmen, and Abandoned Lands, to Captain M. Frank Gallagher, A.A.A. General, Atlanta, in U.S., Congress, House of Representatives, [Report on] *Conditions in Georgia*, Misc. Doc. 52, 40th Cong., 3d sess., 1868-1869, p. 60; Report of Andrew B. Clarke, Agent &c, for the counties of Lee, Terrell, and Calhoun, in letter O. O. Howard to Frank Gallagher, 14 November 1868, *Conditions in Georgia*, p. 120; Report of Assistant Acting Surgeon, Clarke Raushenbury, Agent for Worth, Dougherty, Mitchell and Baker Counties, ibid., pp. 120-22. Adultery, cohabitation, fornication: Testimony of Maria Carter (Colored), Haralson Co., Ga., 21 October 1871, U.S. Congress, *The Ku Klux Klan Conspiracy*, Georgia vol. 1 pp. 413-14; Testimony of Charles Wallace Howard, Atlanta and Bartow Cos., 31 October 1871, ibid., 2: 839; Testimony of Linton Stephens, Hancock Co., Ga., 3 November 1871, ibid., 2: 983. Education: J. W. Alvord to General O. O. Howard, 20 January 1871, in *Letters From the South Relating to the Condition of Freedmen addressed to Major General O. O. Howard Commissioner Bureau R., F., and A. L. by H. W. Alvord, Gen. Sup't Education, Bureau R., F.,, and A. L.* (Washington, D.C., 1870), p. 22; Testimony of Charles Smith (Colored), Walton Co., Ga., 26 October 1871, U.S. Congress, *The Ku Klux Klan Conspiracy*, Georgia vol. 2, p. 599. Politics: Trelease, *White Terror*, throughout.

30. On running off share hands and renters, see Thompson, "Reconstruction in Georgia," p. 364; Trelease, *White Terror*, p. 242. Similar reports cited elsewhere in Stagg, "The Problem of Klan Violence," Burton, "Race and Reconstruction," and Wiener, *Social Origins of the New South*, p. 62. Later events: William F. Holmes, "Whitecapping: Agrarian Violence in Mississippi, 1902-1906," *Journal of Southern History* 35 (May 1969): 165-85; "Negroes Stampeded; They Were Run Away from Their Texas Homes. . .Whitecaps Caused the Exodus. The Action is Deplored by the Best Elements of the Community but They were Powerless to Prevent It," *The Americus Times-Recorder*, 9 August 1895. On planter complaints see Trelease, *White Terror*, p. 326; Testimony of G. B. Burnett, Chattooga and Floyd Cos., Ga., 2 November 1871, U.S. Congress, *The Ku Klux Klan Conspiracy*, Georgia vol. 2, p. 950; Testimony of F. M. Holliday, Jackson Co., Ga., October 23, 1871, ibid., 1: 460-61.

31. Stagg, "The Problem of Klan Violence," pp. 305-306.

32. Pierre van den Berghe, *Race and Racism: A Comparative Perspective* (New York, 1967), pp. 17-18; George M. Fredrickson, *The Black Image in the White Mind: The Debate on Afro-American Character and Destiny, 1817-1914* (New York, 1972).

14

THE POLITICS OF SLAVERY AFFIRMED: THE SOUTH AND THE SECESSION CRISIS

William J. Cooper, Jr.

Secession, the separation of the American Union in 1860 to 1861, remains one of the most vexing questions that confronts American historians. Like other major historical events, the secession was characterized by a multiplicity of causal forces and clouded events that make assessment and judgment extremely difficult, even perilous. But the secession crisis compounds that interpretive difficulty because a satisfactory interpretation of secession must explain not just one phenomenon but rather three phenomena. In the crisis that shattered the Union, the fifteen slave States reacted in three distinct ways: the seven states of the lower South, from South Carolina to Texas, seceded in the winter of 1860–1861, after the election of the Republican, Abraham Lincoln; the four states of the upper South, from Virginia across to Arkansas, joined the secession movement only after the bombardment of Fort Sumter and the onset of war in April 1861; the four border slave states, Delaware westward to Missouri, never seceded.

An endless variety of interpretations, beginning in 1861, have attempted to explain why the Union broke apart when it did. In fact an imaginative scholar could write a book on the historiography of secession, alone.[1] For the purposes of this essay, it is essential to notice briefly the major arguments that historians have employed to explain secession.

The first is slavery. Surely slavery as a cause is both obvious and critical. In the crisis of the Union, the states basically divided along slavery lines, those with the institution and those without it; moreover neither secession nor the resulting civil war is at all imaginable without the institution of slavery. The existence of slavery alone, however, does not explain secession. Two serious disabilities hobble it. If slavery stands as the cause of secession, why didn't the fifteen slave states secede in unison? Simply invoking slavery does not clarify why Georgia or Alabama or Louisiana went out with the initial group, but Virginia, which had more slaves than any other state, rejected secession before Fort Sumter. With the institution of slavery used in this causal fashion, no connection is made to the political process, and secession was a political act. Politicians planned, organized, and presented their positions to the voters who chose many of those politicians as delegates to the conventions that considered secession. Any satisfactory explanation of secession must be connected to the political process.

Those same two shortcomings bedevil three other major interpretations of secession—those emphasizing the constitutional viewpoint, emotion, and economics. Southerners did speak a great deal about the Constitution and its subversion by the Republicans, but such speech cannot be translated into an explanation for the particular course of secession. Although southerners certainly became excited or emotional over the existence of the Republican party, not to say its victory in 1860, it is impossible to prove that Floridians or Texans feared Republicans more than North Carolinians or Arkansasans. In the sense that slavery was in part an economic system, economics certainly contributed immensely to secession, but scholars who make economics the paramount cause of secession by insisting that the South faced an economic Armageddon by 1860 because of the slave-labor system confront three unbridgeable chasms: first, the fact of three different secession policies and the politicalness of secession; second, the overwhelming evidence that southerners perceived no economic crisis in the late 1850s;[2] and third, the indisputable truth that a number of those most closely tied to slavery, the large planters, opposed immediate secession.

The most recent major interpretation of secession, that its course depended upon local political patterns, especially the viability of opposition parties, does have its virtues.[3] Cognizant of three different slave-state responses to the crisis of the Union, it offers a seemingly plausible explanation for them, namely the potence or impotence of such local party divisions. Moreover, the emphasis on local political patterns clearly binds secession to the political process. Even with these strengths this apparent solution has two fatal flaws. First, and most obvious, it divorces secession from slavery, which is folly. Second, it employs state and local political patterns to explain a desperate crisis on the national level. Whether or not an opposition party could elect legislators in Georgia or in Virginia had precious little to do with the southern reaction to Republicanism or the triumph of Republicanism.

Because none of these leading interpretations provides a complete or a totally satisfactory explanation of the secession crisis, it is necessary to develop another one using parts of these arguments where they are appropriate.

Secession was a supremely political act prompted by the values most cherished by southern white society and fashioned within the southern political arena. The politics of slavery offer the best possibility for illuminating this quintessentially southern phenomenon. I will give here only a brief definition of the workings of the politics of slavery. The term "politics of slavery" designates "the world created by the interaction of the four major forces in antebellum southern politics: the institution of slavery, southern parties and politicians, the southern political structure, and the values of southern white society."[4] The result of intermixing these four forces placed a political premium on the vigorous, unceasing commitment of southerners to protect southern interests. Neither politicians nor political groups could escape the need for constant, public affirmation of southern loyalty. As public men they understood that such rhetoric charted the way toward political victory, while silence led to defeat. Moreover, as southerners they realized that the rhetoric of affirmation involved more than mere incantation. It simultaneously plumbed and revealed the core of southern values. Turning to the task at hand, it is necessary to look again at the secession crisis from the perspective provided by the politics of slavery.

In his inaugural address as provisional president of the Confederate States of America, Jefferson Davis equated the southerners of 1860–1861 to their grandfathers and the fledgling southern nation to the old Union. "The Constitution framed by our fathers," he assured his audience, "is that of the Confederate States." That same Constitution formed the bedrock for southern independence. Equally important to Davis was the fathers' "exposition" of the Constitution, which gave southerners "a light which reveals its true meaning." No dimension of that truth, no purpose of the Constitution had more importance than preserving the blessings of liberty. But, mourned Davis, southerners no longer enjoyed a secure liberty because the Constitution "had been perverted from the purposes for which it was ordained." Refusing to acquiesce meekly in that perversion, southerners, according to Davis, "labored to preserve the government of our fathers in its spirit." As Davis saw it, by continuing that great work southerners would vindicate secession and secure liberty.[5]

This dirge for the Constitution and for liberty did not originate in the mind of Jefferson Davis. Quite to the contrary, such lamentations had pervaded the South throughout 1860, especially during the fateful winter of 1860–1861. In midsummer the Charleston *Mercury* admitted, "The Union of the Constitution, we presume nearly all men in the South, desire to be perpetuated." As far as the *Mercury* was concerned, however, that Union no longer existed because "usurpation and encroachment" by the North had "virtually destroyed" it. In the aftermath of Lincoln's election the New Orleans *Daily Crescent* announced, "the spirit of the Constitution, the only valuable part of it, has been utterly violated and destroyed."[6] Thus, in his inaugural Davis merely added what might be termed the closing paragraph to the eulogy that numerous southerners had pronounced over the bier of the Constitution.

Preparing themselves to meet what they perceived as a mortal threat to their most precious possession, liberty, southerners called on the memory of their grandfathers. "Let us follow the example of our ancestors and prove ourselves worthy sons of worthy sires," cried a Georgian before his legislature. Chorusing the refrain "Resistance to . . . tyranny . . . is the cherished birth-right of every citizen," southerners saw themselves emulating the heroic stance of their forebears in 1775–1776. Using the famous Boston Tea Party as a symbol of the revolutionary struggle for liberty, the Richmond *Enquirer* placed the South squarely in that tradition when it noted that furious resistance to the tax on tea "created an independent people and built up a nation." The *Enquirer* went on to claim that the South of 1860 had to protect itself against the tyrannous designs of the new oppressors. In this vision the new engine of oppression, the reconstituted perfidious England, was the new central Union created from the subversion of the Consitution by those who wanted to master the South.[7] Of course, to master meant to shackle liberty.

In its political definition liberty had always meant control of one's own affairs and institutions, of one's destiny. Southerners believed absolutely in this formulation of liberty, just as many northerners did. This commitment added nothing new to the political firmament in 1860, for total devotion to liberty had been a central feature of southern political culture since the colonial era. It had been massively reaffirmed during the Revolution and iterated frequently thereafter. For southerners, the Revolution and the Constitution along with southern-dominated or influenced political parties had insured the shaping of their own destiny. Of course, for the white South that destiny was inextricably caught up with black slavery and had been so on a conscious level since the Revolution. For white southerners the institution of black bondage provided a constant reminder of precisely what the loss of liberty entailed—dependence and utter degradation.

The contest of 1860 was traumatic for southerners because the rise and triumph of the Republican party first threatened, then palpably jeopardized the local control that denoted liberty. The emergence and the success of the Republican party obliterated the traditional arrangements that southerners believed secured their liberty. The Republican party was the first major party without a significant southern component. No southerners (except a few in the border states) ran for office as Republicans, and none helped to formulate party policy. Moreover, with their appeal aimed solely at the North, the Republicans planned a strategy for victory that did not need the South at all. The party had concerned southerners from its birth and frightened them from its first national campaign in 1856. From the southern viewpoint the Republican party loomed like a giant tidal wave ready to crush their finely crafted political world. The devastation wreaked upon that world would leave their liberty shattered. In fact a Republican victory mocked the essence of liberty—local control. Accordingly, southern eyes saw in a Republican victory a mortal threat to their cherished liberty. As a conservative editor in Nashville, Tennessee, pointedly concluded, "The universal Southern mind is in antagonism to the Republican party and its candidates."[8]

For southerners the Republican threat to their liberty was made even more unbearable because the Republicans simultaneously insulted them. The insult so clearly felt by southerners was derived from both the rhetoric and the politics of the Republican party. The combined Republican attack on the South and on slavery cast southerners in an un-American light. Although there has been debate among historians over the centrality of antislaveryism in the Republican party, southerners themselves agreed with such historians as Eric Foner who give it cardinal importance. This Republican assault on the South and its major social institution made white southerners pariahs in their own land because in the Republican lexicon, slavery and those involved with it violated the American creed. But, as David Potter has forcibly reminded us, southerners proudly identified themselves as Americans. They wore their American heritage as a badge of honor. The Revolution, the Constitution, Washington, Jackson they honored as American glories and heroes. Knowingly and with malice aforethought Republicans besmirched the escutcheon of southern Americanism. Southerners felt this to be an unforgivable slander. With their good name thus slandered southerners believed their liberty already was endangered, for in the South good name and integrity of reputation were the personal hallmarks of free and honorable men. In the words of a moderate congressman, living under a Republican administration "would degrade & disgrace the South beyond all measure."[9]

When the Republicans won the election of 1860, few southerners believed their liberty was still absolutely secure. Believing their liberty endangered or even destroyed by oppressive Republicans, southerners saw themselves left only with slavery. By definition the absence of liberty meant the presence of slavery, which southerners equated with degradation, the very opposite of honor. In this gloomy vision the white South would become enslaved to the tyrannical Republicans. Such an outlook explains why so many southerners framed the overriding issue of 1860–1861 in terms of submission. Submission was a primary characteristic of degraded slaves but spurned by honorable men in full possession of their liberty. Mary Jones, the wife of the well-known minister-planter Charles C. Jones, could see no reason for civil war even after Lincoln's election, but she told her son, "even that, *if it must come*, would be preferable to submission to Black Republicanism, involving as it would all that is horrible, degrading, and ruinous." Emphatically rejecting submission, Alabama Congressman David Clopton informed a close friend that he could face the hazards of war because he would "rather die a freeman than live a slave to Black Republicanism." To stress his conviction Clopton added, "I would be an equal, or a corpse."[10] The sentiment expressed so forcefully by Mary Jones and by David Clopton was felt by millions of their fellow southerners.

In 1860 the Democratic party ruled over southern politics. Half a decade earlier the Democrats had finally vanquished their rivals, the Whigs, after a long battle fought under the banner of the politics of slavery. That Democratic triumph in the mid-1850s was complete; the defeated Whig party disintegrated and disappeared.

The political destruction of the southern Whigs did not mean, however, that every southerner joined the dominant Democrats. Thousands of anti-Democrats fought their old foe in a variety of political formations with the different names such as the Opposition party. Even though the anti-Democrats never made a national connection to reach for national power, they faithfully adhered to the politics of slavery. In the political furor that developed in 1857 and 1858 over Kansas and the Lecompton constitution the Opposition press accused the Democrats of disloyalty to the South and of failing to guard southern interests. Addressing the proposed congressional compromise on Lecompton, which had the blessing of most Democrats, the Montgomery *Advertiser* in late March of 1858 condemned politicians who "could stoop to the miserable acts of the compromiser. How harshly does the word grate upon the Southern ear. With what unctuous sweetness does it roll from the lips of aspirants for federal position."[11] With such editorial and rhetorical cannonades anti-Democrats accused their opponents of selling out southern rights and honor and beseeched southern voters to turn to them for political salvation.

In 1860 when the anti-Democrats banded together in the Constitutional Union party, they remained devotees of the politics of slavery. As John Mering has shown conclusively, Constitutional Unionists practiced the politics of slavery with a vengeance.[12] Their appeal to southerners in the canvass of 1860 was couched in strident language: the Democrats would betray the South; only the Constitutional Unionists could be trusted to preserve the two-sided southern holy of holies— slavery and liberty.

Although anti-Democratic parties existed and flourished locally and although the Constitutional Union party made a vigorous effort in 1860, no group, apart from the Democrats, possessed major political influence at the end of the 1850s or during the cataclysm of 1860 to 1861. That position of political notableness went to the so-called Fire-Eaters, or secessionists or radicals. A new and potent force in southern politics, the Fire-Eaters had sprouted during the crisis of 1850. With the widespread acceptance of the great compromise in that year they became dormant during most of the decade, only to blossom at its end. These Fire-Eaters added a new dimension to southern politics. While Democrats and Opposition men struggled with each other over who could better protect the South in the Union, the Fire-Eaters aimed to destroy the Union. They pictured the Union as a dagger poised to plunge into the southern heart.

The presence and influence of the Fire-Eaters were connected with the pervasiveness and strength of slavery. Although no census of Fire-Eaters exists, and probably none is possible, they flourished only in those states that had a substantial percentage of slaves in their populations. The three states in which the Fire-Eaters were most prominent included South Carolina, the most densely slave of all with 57 percent, Mississippi, second only to South Carolina with 55 percent, and Alabama with 45 percent of its population slave.[13] Fire-Eaters operated on a smaller but still influential scale in Florida, Georgia, Texas, and Virginia. They were scarce elsewhere, even in Louisiana where slaves numbered 47 percent of the population.

While we know too little about these Fire-Eaters, we do know that they were not simply the large slaveowners. In fact, much of their local leadership seems to have come from relatively young town dwellers in the midst of plantation counties. Undoubtedly the intimate southern relationship between the posssession of slaves and the passion for liberty helps to explain the citadels of Fire-Eating. Because of that unique intimacy white southerners living in the center of black slavery would be extraordinarily sensitive about their liberty. Their immersion in the sea of slavery would prompt them to cry out constantly about the precariousness of liberty. When these whites perceived the destruction of slavery at hand, the possibilities assumed terrifying proportions because, according to the southern calculus, that destruction would necessarily include the extermination of liberty. In 1860 the Fire-Eaters evinced no doubt that the future of slavery was at stake; in the trumpet blast of their leading newspaper, the Charleston *Mercury*: "The issue before the country is the extinction of slavery."[14] This general hypothesis, however, does not lead directly to an understanding of the psychology that propelled individual southerners, even those living in slave-dominated areas, into political radicalism. We need to know a great deal more about the Fire-Eaters, and the lack of a notable book about them forms one of the most glaring gaps in the historiography of the antebellum South.[15]

Fire-Eaters fervently believed that the South faced a simple but momentous choice "between secession and submission to abolition domination." According to the Fire-Eaters, southerners often failed to recognize the starkness of their alternatives because political parties and party politicians clouded the issue. Fire-Eaters poured out some of their harshest rhetoric on what they denominated the venality of party and party loyalists. "The truth is," asserted the Charleston *Mercury*, that party activities "are, more or less, fraudulent in their incipiency and practices." In the view of the *Mercury*, parties certainly did not serve the southern people who "have very little to do with them."[16]

To overcome the party-inculcated torpor that made southerners lethargic to their danger, Fire-Eaters took as their mission what they called the life-and-death southern predicament. In the midst of the presidential contest of 1860, Edmund Ruffin of Virginia sent to the governor of each slave state a pike he had obtained from John Brown's cache of weapons. On each pike Ruffin affixed the label: "SAMPLE OF THE FAVORS DESIGNED FOR US BY OUR NORTHERN BRETHREN."[17] While such dramatic acts did not make up the bulk of Fire-Eater activity, still speakers and editors, especially in the lower South, constantly thundered the Fire-Eater gospel: only secession can save southern slavery and southern liberty. Expounding their text, Fire-Eaters denounced southerners who opposed them as infidels and traitors who would stand idly by while the South was manacled and dragged to social and political perdition.

Through their public onslaught, the Fire-Eaters were responsible for the promulgation of two important ideas. Their solution to all southern problems was secession, and they continually and forcefully preached its necessity. Although others had spoken about secession, its possibility and its legality, the Fire-Eaters gave form, emphasis, and attractiveness to the concept. By 1860 few southerners denied the legitimacy of secession, though many disputed its efficacy. Turning to the obverse of secession, the Fire-Eaters constantly warned southerners that the Union held great danger for them. Because of the Fire-Eaters' rhetorical blitz, many southerners began to balance the protection afforded by the union with its potential for harm. Beset by the Fire-Eaters, the southern Democrats had to defend their claim that it was their influence in the Union that always insured a balance tilted toward safety, not danger.

As Mills Thornton has noted, because the Fire-Eaters advocated drastic and unprecedented action, their success depended largely on outside events.[18] Most southerners believed themselves to be patriotic Americans; they believed in America. They had no eagerness to destroy what their grandfathers had helped to create, their fathers had helped to nurture, and they had helped to guide. Secession required a great leap into the political unknown. As a result most southerners were unlikely to heed the call of the Fire-Eaters, unless outside events gave it gleaming salience. Thus John Brown's raid, the breakup of the Democratic party, and especially Abraham Lincoln's election were bountiful gifts to Fire-Eaters from the gods of politics.

Lincoln's election provided the essential catalyst that enabled the Fire-Eaters to precipitate the political reaction they craved. The Republican victory undermined the southern Democrat's pledge that they and their party guaranteed the liberty and safety of the South in the Union. Southern Democrats certainly shared the general southern view that the electoral triumph of Lincoln and the Republicans signified the culmination of more than a decade of increasingly shrill antisouthern rhetoric, attitudes, and politics. Southerners of almost every political persuasion shared the outlook of the moderate New Orleans editor who described Lincoln's win as "incontrovertible proof of a diseased and dangerous public opinion all over the North, and a certain forerunner of further and more atrocious aggression." To the conservative Daniel R. Hundley, who had adamantly opposed the Fire-Eaters, Lincoln's victory had destroyed the old fraternal America. Hundley could plot only one course for the South: "You must strike now and strike as freemen only strike, whose liberties are endangered." Practically every southerner looked upon a future Republican administration with combined apprehension and anger, or in Don Fehrenbacher's perceptive description, rage.[19] The political unknown of the Fire-Eaters' secession was matched by another political unknown, Republicans in power.

Reaction to the election created in the lower South, the stronghold of the Fire-Eaters, a volatile mixture that could explode given a spark from sectional radicals. Governors called legislatures into session, and legislatures called for prompt elections to conventions that would meet in December 1860 and January 1861 to consider appropriate action. Nothing foreordained the decisions of these conventions. Ultimately they decided for secession, a decision greatly influenced by the tactics of the Fire-Eaters, who understood the opportunity Lincoln's election had given them and hurried to apply the inexorable pressure that would ignite the explosion of secession.

For the Fire-Eaters, timing was critical. If they could accomplish secession in any one state, then the basic question would be cast differently and to their advantage. After even one state went out, other states would not decide simply to secede or to remain in the Union, but would be drawn into the more complex question of joining or opposing a sister state. Recognizing the importance of immediate action and realizing that back in 1850 to 1851 the quest for unity entailed delay and ultimately defeat, the secessionists moved into the one state they controlled absolutely. On December 20, 1860, the South Carolina convention voted unanimously to sunder all ties to the old Union. At the actual secession of the state Fire-Eaters everywhere rejoiced. Before the Alabama convention Andrew P. Calhoun, son of John C., thrilled at the event: "At this point the accumulated aggressions of a third of a century fell like shackles at her feet, and free, disenthralled, regenerated, she stood before her devoted people like the genius of liberty, beckoning them on to the performance of their duty."[20]

Everyone, secessionists and their opponents alike, understood the critical need of momentum for the secessionist cause. Joseph E. Brown, the prosecession governor of Georgia, believed that the secession of South Carolina was a prerequisite for rapid action in his state. South Carolina out, he wrote, "will cause a thrill to pass through the great popular heart of Georgia" and line her up behind South Carolina. On the other side of the political fence Congressman Zebulon Vance of North Carolina acknowledged the political acumen of the secessionists, who were "acting wisely for their ends" when they "scorn every suggestion of compromise and rush everything with ruinous and indecent haste."[21]

No one felt Fire-Eater pressure more sharply than the Democratic leaders in the lower South. This pressure illustrates the politics of slavery in bold relief. A glimpse at the reaction of two very different men from two very different states dramatizes the political interaction between the regulars and the Fire-Eaters.

United States Senator Jefferson Davis lived in a state in which the Fire-Eaters enjoyed considerable political leverage. Although Davis had been associated with advanced southern positions in the 1850s, he was not of the Fire-Eater breed, who camped on his left in Mississippi politics. In fact, after Lincoln's election he counseled a leading South Carolina Fire-Eater against any drastic move. But the intense activity of secessionists in his own state along with the secession of South Carolina caused him to make it clear that he did not oppose separate state action. From his Senate seat he advised the governor of Mississippi on arms purchases and other matters. At the same time he indicated his willingness to support an acceptable congressional compromise.[22] The Fire-Eaters had placed Davis in the classic quandary of the politics of slavery. As a southerner he felt and expressed outrage at the Republican victory like innumerable other southerners, but he was unsure about secession. But when the secessionists forced his hand, he joined them because refusal would have undermined his power base in Mississippi. If Mississippi were to go out, Davis had no intention of losing influence or authority in his own state. Because he wanted to retain his power and because he could not present a sure plan to preserve southern liberty, Jefferson Davis responded to the Fire-Eater challenge by acting with them. He had no viable ideological or political alternative.

John Slidell, United States senator from Louisiana, also responded to the politics of slavery, but in a slightly different configuration. The Fire-Eaters had less strength in Louisiana than in any other state of the lower South so Slidell, unlike Davis, did not have to worry about an influential force operating on his sectional left. Moreover, Slidell largely controlled the Democratic party apparatus in Louisiana. In addition, as a quintessential political realist and pragmatist, Slidell had never been closely associated with southern extremism, or, for that matter, with any other ideological stance. He did not advocate secession. Just before the election of 1860 he answered a Louisiana supporter, "I agree with you fully as to the necessity of avoiding any precipitate action in Louisiana." As far as Slidell was concerned his state was "not prepared to take the initiative in any measure of resistance in the event of Lincoln's election," and he was not ready "to counsel such a course." Shortly after the election, however, he announced to President James Buchanan, his close friend, "I see no probability of preserving the Union, nor do I consider it desirable to do so if we could." "Louisiana," he made clear, "will act with her sister States of the South."[23]

Slidell then became a major force in convincing Louisiana to adopt secession. He became convinced that South Carolina and other states would secede and create a southern government. Louisiana, therefore, would have to side with or against her neighbors. If Alabama, Mississippi, and Texas went out, Louisiana might be isolated with her Mississippi lifeline cut. To Slidell the choice he and his state had to make really required no choice. Louisiana would have to stand with her own kind. Accepting that eventuality as a fact, Slidell wanted Louisiana to secede promptly so that both he and his state could participate in the making of a southern government. He wanted neither Louisiana nor John Slidell left behind by events.

The relationship among the Fire-Eaters, the process of secession, Davis, and Slidell raises the question of popular support for secession and the unity behind secession. Secession was a public issue; no closed-door conspiracy broke up the Union. In every state speeches, editorials, and campaigns engaged the voting South. Initially the Fire-Eaters led the crusade, for Lincoln's election gave them multitudes of followers; then, the traditional leaders like Davis and Slidell quickly took charge. In South Carolina, Florida, Mississippi, and Texas a substantial to overwhelming majority favored immediate secession, and the outcome was never in serious doubt. In the other three states of the lower South—Georgia, Alabama, and Louisiana—the contest was considerably closer because of the strength of those who called themselves cooperationists rather than immediatists. Both the popular vote for delegates to the conventions and the early convention votes themselves revealed substantial public backing for the cooperationist position. But too great a distinction can be drawn between immediatists and cooperationists. Immediatists obviously were for immediate secession while cooperationists preferred a cooperative effort. They did not, however, oppose secession. Thus the debate in campaign and convention focused on tactics, and while tactical differences can be significant, in this instance they did not separate two adamantly opposed groups. Not all cooperationists belonged to the same camp; for some, cooperation meant a southern convention, for others, a joint statement by more than one state, for still others, simply the secession of another state. Almost every cooperationist in every state quickly and sincerely signed the ordinance of secession before the convention adjourned. These cooperationists warned in the language of one of their major newspapers, "it may prove a fatal, an unretrievably fatal error," should their stance "be misconstrued into *submission,* or a delay designed eventually to lead to submission."[24]

In the midst of the furor dominating the winter of 1860-1861 cooperationists could have said nothing else. They agreed that the South had to guard her liberty, which had been jeopardized by the Republican victory, and in order to oppose fundamentally the immediatists they had to offer a believable alternative to secession. They had none, at least none that more than a few could agree upon. The most striking characteristic of the cooperationists in the crisis was confusion. In contrast to the purposefulness of the immediatists, the cooperationists could not decide whether or not to campaign and could not agree upon a political goal to articulate before the voters. While it cannot be proved absolutely, it is almost as if in the depths of their being they thought the immediatists correct.

When delegates from the states of the lower South congregated in Montgomery, Alabama, in February 1861 to create the Confederate States of America, the initial phase of secession had run its course. Seven states from South Carolina to Texas now pledged their allegiance to a new nation. Even so, the bright hopes of the Fire-Eaters had not been realized; fifteen slave states did not stand as a phalanx, stalwartly opposing the oppressive Republican party. In fact not even one-half of the slave states had heeded the siren call of secession. Yet these eight states that did not cannot be considered as a unit; they must be divided into two parts: the upper South, four clearly slave states and the border, where the actual involvement with slavery in economic, social, and political terms was often tenuous.

The upper South, stretching more than one-thousand miles, from Virginia westward to Arkansas, did not secede upon Lincoln's election, not even upon his inauguration on March 4, 1861. The paucity everywhere and the absence in many places of the Fire-Eaters made the political pressure for immediate secession considerably less intense. In Virginia, the one state where the Fire-Eaters did have a noticeable voice, their influence was offset by the countervailing force of the strongly antisecessionist transmontane region, most of which became West Virginia during the war. While the shortage of Fire-Eaters and their unending insistence on direct action did give regular politicians more operating room, the extra room did not signify that the upper South looked upon the rise of the Republican party and the election of Lincoln as normal political occurrences. The rhetoric in the upper South matched that in their more southerly neighbors. The Constitutional Unionists were strong in all of these states, but like southern Democrats, they too attacked Republicans and supported southern liberty. This rhetoric, however, did not propel the upper South into rapid secession because the political equation lacked the crucial multiplier, the Fire-Eaters. Leaders in the upper South asserted that southern liberty, although challenged, would remain unvanquished until the nefarious Lincoln moved directly against it by either prohibiting slavery in the territories or interfering with interstate slave trade or some other equally heinous act.

Despite tangible differences with the lower South, the upper South could not escape the snares of the politics of slavery. Just as the quick secession of South Carolina and the rapid pace of elections and conventions powerfully affected the course of the lower South, the fact of seven secessions and the formation of the Confederate States of America greatly affected the upper South. At this juncture states and a combination of states replaced political parties and groups as the motivating forces behind the politics of slavery. Those politics fundamentally influenced the course of the upper South, even though a majority of voters in these states probably opposed secession. While such opposition had spawned a political realignment that enabled antisecession Democrats and Opposition men to join together in a new Union party that blocked secession in conjunction with the lower South, as a recent, careful historian of this Union movement has concluded, "the apparently commanding position won by the Union party in the Upper South in early 1861 was illusory." Although the Unionists had become a stronger political force than the secessionists, they "well knew that they were in hostage to circumstances beyond their control."[25] They would have to respond to the baton of the lower South.

With the lower South on an independent tack, the critical question facing the upper South changed slightly but fundamentally. The question no longer was just whether or not to secede but whether or not to aid southern brothers. Theoretically this question could stand forever without an answer, but in reality an answer was required. If in any way the new Confederacy and the old Union came into confrontation, then the upper South would come face to face with its ultimate decision. Its hand would be forced, and the antisecessionists in the upper South did not relish this prospect at all. "We entertain towards South Carolina the most bitter resentment," railed a vigorously antisecessionist Virginia newspaper. The Charlottesville *Review* accused South Carolina (read, the lower South) of "precipitately throw[ing] down the bulwark of the Union . . . with the full knowledge—aye, the intention—to hold Virginia and the border states between her and the Storm, and to carry out her caprices . . . while relying on them."[26]

Confrontation between the Union and either a seceded state or the Confederacy, no matter the cause or fault, meant the choice for the upper South between slavery and liberty. In the vocabulary of southern politics, coercion by the federal government entailed enslavement for the coerced states and the destruction of liberty for their citizens. The Charlottesville *Review* spoke bluntly, ". . . an issue has been made. The subjection of South Carolina or any seceding state, in consequence of their determination not to submit to the policy of the Republicans is a blow at the entire South—subjection to all. We are, thenceforth, humiliated. We are conquered. We could not hold up our heads in that Union any more."[27] Thus, when the guns roared at Fort Sumter and President Lincoln called for troops to suppress rebellion, Virginia, North Carolina, Tennessee, and Arkansas said no. As they saw it, rejecting that call meant rejecting slavery and embracing liberty. Thus, the politics of slavery underlay this second secession just as surely as they did the first.

In the remaining four slave states, the border states, a different situation prevailed. A small slave population made three of these states slave states primarily in a technical and legal sense. They were certainly not slave states in a political sense. Only Kentucky, where slaves accounted for 20 percent of the population, can be counted as a slave state. Slaves comprised only 13 percent of the population in Maryland, 10 percent in Missouri, and less than 2 percent in Delaware. In addition, the number of slaveowners among the free inhabitants was small—just a fraction over 2 percent in both Maryland and Missouri and no more than one-half of 1 percent in Delaware. Moreover, in all three states the percentage of slaves as well as slaveowners had declined markedly during the 1850s. As recent scholarship makes clear, these states were moving away from the slave South economically, socially, and politically.[28] Unionist sentiment flourished, while Fire-Eaters were rare. This different direction made secession extremely unlikely. In fact, reinforced by the tactics of an antisecessionist governor in Maryland and by the military and political moves of the federal government, it was impossible.

Kentucky requires individual attention. Kentucky had a substantially larger percentage of slaves than any other border state; her 20 percent approached the percentages of Tennessee and Arkansas. And the percentage of slaveowners in Kentucky actually exceeded that in Arkansas. Yet, Tennessee and Arkansas seceded while Kentucky did not. Geography and political tradition help explain its behavior. As in the other border states, the northern frontier of Kentucky marked the boundary between slavery and freedom. This proximity to the free states had two important consequences. First, like the rest of the border, but unlike the upper South, Kentucky was home to a powerful, unconditional Unionist sentiment. Second, conscious of their physical border location many Kentuckians wanted to avoid taking sides because they envisioned their homeland becoming a major battleground.

The political heritage of Kentucky further buttressed this desire to steer clear of overt partisanship. Even after Fort Sumter, Kentucky declared neutrality in any conflict between the United States and the Confederate States. Thinking of themselves as conciliators and aware that their great statesman Henry Clay had gained fame as a compromiser of earlier sectional crises, Kentuckians strove to provide a historical encore to Clay's performance. Attempting to emulate Clay, United States Senator John J. Crittenden led the major effort to avert secession and conflict through sectional compromise. Despite an untiring struggle, Crittenden failed, and his failure presaged the failure of his state's hopes for neutrality. Onrushing events engulfed compromise-minded Kentuckians. Within months both Confederate and Union armies entered the state. Union military superiority settled the fate of Kentucky.

'Secession marked still another triumph of the politics of slavery. Once again southern political leaders in quest of a political goal employed the powerful rhetoric of southern safety cemented to the particular southern view of liberty and forced their issue. Filling the arena of southern politics, this rhetoric expressed exactly the hopes and fears of southern voters, captured the public mind, and supplied the driving force behind southern political action. Used to clarify the complication of three secession policies, the politics of slavery elucidates a crucial event in both southern and American history. But even more important, the course of secession makes it clear that no other interpretive idea so illuminates the form and substance of antebellum southern politics as the politics of slavery.

Notes

1. Two articles discuss portions of the problem: William J. Donnelly, "Conspiracy or Popular Movement: The Historiography of Southern Support for Secession," *North Carolina Historical Review* 42 (January 1965): 70-84 and Ralph A. Wooster, "The Secession of the Lower South; An Examination of Changing Interpretations," *Civil War History* 7 (June 1961): 117-27.
2. William J. Cooper, Jr., "The Cotton Crisis in the Antebellum South: Another Look," *Agricultural History* 49 (April 1975): 381-91.
3. Michael F. Holt, *The Political Crisis of the 1850s* (New York: John Wiley & Sons, 1978), chap. 8.
4. William J. Cooper, Jr., *The South and The Politics of Slavery, 1828-1856* (Baton Rouge: Louisiana State University Press, 1978), p. xi.
5. James D. Richardson, comp., *Messages and Papers of the Confederacy*, 2 vols. (Nashville: United States Publishing Company, 1906), 1: 32-36.
6. *Mercury*, 25 July 1860; *Daily Crescent*, 15 November 1860, quoted in Dwight Lowell Dumond, ed., *Southern Editorials on Secession* (Gloucester, Mass.: Peter Smith 1964), p. 240.
7. Michael P. Johnson, *Toward a Patriarchal Republic: The Secession of Georgia*

(Baton Rouge: Louisiana State University Press, 1977), p. 30; *Enquirer*, 10 July 1860.

8. *Daily Nashville Patriot*, 19 September 1860, quoted in Dumond, *Southern Editorials*, p. 167.

9. Eric Foner, *Free Soil, Free Labor, Free Men: The Ideology of the Republican Party Before the Civil War* (New York: Oxford University Press, 1970); David M. Potter, *The South and the Sectional Conflict* (Baton Rouge: Louisiana State University Press, 1968), pp.34-83 and *The Impending Crisis, 1848-1861* (New York: Harper & Row Publishers, 1976), pp. 471-75; J. D. Ashmore to Benjamin Perry, 13 May 1860, Benjamin Perry Papers, Alabama Department of Archives and History, Montgomery, Alabama.

10. Mary Jones to C. C. Jones, Jr., 15 November 1860, in *Children of Pride: A True Story of Georgia and the Civil War*, ed. Robert Manson Myers (New Haven: Yale University Press, 1972), pp. 627-28; Clopton to Clay, 13 December 1860, C. C. Clay Papers, William R. Perkins Library, Duke University, Durham, N.C.

11. J. Mills Thornton III, *Politics and Power in a Slave Society: Alabama, 1800-1860* (Baton Rouge: Louisiana State University Press 1978), p. 361. On this general point see also William S. Hitchcock, "The Limits of Southern Unionism: Virginia Conservatives and the Gubernatorial Election of 1859," *Journal of Southern History* 47 (February 1981): 57-72.

12. Although Professor Mering did not use the term "politics of slavery," he definitely described those politics: "The Constitutional Union Campaign of 1860: An Example of the Paranoid Style," *Mid-America* 60 (April-July 1978): 95-106 and "The Slave-State Constitutional Unionists and the Politics of Consensus," *Journal of Southern History* 43 (August 1977): 395-410. See also Hitchcock, "The Limits of Southern Unionism."

13. These and all other slave-related figures refer to 1860 and are taken from the census of that year.

14. *Mercury*, 3 November 1860.

15. An exception to my lament is J. Mills Thornton's superb study of Alabama, which contains the best analysis of the Fire-Eaters we have, although for only one state. See Thornton, *Politics and Power*, esp. pp. 232-66.

16. William Kauffman Scarborough, ed., *The Diary of Edmund Ruffin*, 2 vols. (Baton Rouge: Louisiana State University Press, 1972-), 1: 473; *Mercury*, 10 July 1860.

17. Scarborough, *Ruffin Diary*, 1: 442-43.

18. Thornton, *Politics and Power*, p. 266.

19. *Bee*, 5 December 1860; Daniel R. Hundley, *Social Relations in Our Southern States*, ed. William J. Cooper, Jr. (Baton Rouge: Louisiana State University Press, 1979), p. xxi; Don E. Fehrenbacher, *The South and Three Sectional Crises* (Baton Rouge: Louisiana State University Press, 1980), chaps. 2 and 3 *passim* and especially p. 31.

20. Thornton, *Politics and Power*, p. 452.

21. Brown to Howell Cobb, 15 December 1860, Howell Cobb Papers, Ilah Dunlap Little Memorial Library, University of Georgia, Athens, Ga. Vance to William Dickson, 11 December 1860, in *The Papers of Zebulon Baird Vance: Volume One, 1843-1862*, ed. Frontis W. Johnston (Raleigh: State Department of Archives and History, 1963), p. 71.

22. Davis to R. B. Rhett, Jr., 10 November 1860 and to J. J. Pettus, 26, 31 December 1860, 4 January 1861, in *Jefferson Davis, Constitutionalist: His Letters, Papers and Speeches,* ed. Dunbar Rowland, 10 vols. (Jackson: Mississippi Department of Archives and History, 1923), 4: 541-43, 559-61, 564-65; David M. Potter, *Lincoln and His Party in the Secession Crisis* (New Haven: Yale University Press, 1962), pp. 171, 205.

23. Slidell to Edward G. W. Butler, 1 November 1860, Edward G. W. Butler Papers, Perkins Library, Duke University, Durham, N.C. Slidell to Buchanan, 13 November 1860, James Buchanan Papers, Historical Society of Pennsylvania, Philadelphia.

24. *Daily Chronicle and Sentinel,* 22 December 1860, quoted in Dumond, *Southern Editorials,* pp. 361-63.

25. Daniel W. Crofts, "The Union Party of 1861 and the Secession Crisis," *Perspectives in American History* II (1977-1978): 327-76. Quote at p. 328.

26. *Review,* 4 January 1861, quoted in Dumond, *Southern Editorials,* p. 389.

27. Ibid. See also *Review,* 25 January 1861, ibid., p. 415.

28. For example, see William J. Evitts, *A Matter of Allegiances: Maryland, 1850-1861* (Baltimore: The Johns Hopkins University Press, 1974).

15

THE PARADOXES OF CONFEDERATE HISTORIOGRAPHY

Emory M. Thomas

More than a quarter of a century ago, C. Vann Woodward established himself as the foremost interpreter of the southern historical experience with a paper entitled "The Irony of Southern History." In his essay, Woodward argued that the most significant and enduring source of distinctive southern identity was southern history. A unique southern past more than anything else, Woodward contended, made Southerners a peculiar people. In contrast to the American past, supposedly characterized by victory, prosperity, progress, and righteousness, the South had known defeat, poverty, frustration, and guilt.

The irony of this circumstance was that the southern experience, not the national norm, shared the experience of the rest of the world's peoples. While other Americans seemed convinced that "history is something unpleasant that happens to other people," southerners could afford no such illusions. Thus, Woodward concluded, the "burden" of southern history and southern historians was the need to balance the American success myth with an historical perspective that was more realistic and more universal.[1]

In the years since the presentation of "The Irony of Southern History," a host of southern historians and intellectuals have taken up Woodward's "burden" and offered an historical literature and wisdom that is, for the most part, characterized by variations on Woodward's themes of irony and burden.[2] Woodward himself has elaborated upon these themes and earned distinction as the "dean of Southern historians." Indeed Woodward's observations about experience as the source of southern distinctiveness and his analysis of the un-American nature of that experience seem as valid and brilliant today as they did in the early 1950s. In his J. Franklin Jamerson Lecture, which was published as a prestigious bicentennial essay in the *American Historical Review* in 1977, Woodward was still describing American historical writing as "a success story" and "a morality tale." He was still reminding us that "the South as loser sustained historic encounters with defeat, failure, poverty, and guilt that embarrassed its later efforts to embrace the national myth of invincibility, success, opulence, and innocence."³ While his words retain the ring of truth, times have changed considerably since 1953 when Woodward first revealed the truth of the South's ironic historical experience.

In recent decades that simple faith in American victory, prosperity, progress, and righteousness has claimed fewer and fewer believers. Americans have endured the assassinations of John Kennedy, Robert Kennedy, Martin Luther King, and others. The affluent society has conducted a war on poverty and lost; poverty then counterattacked, and thus far the economy seems to be losing. The nation has warred against racism, only to see racism open new fronts. Americans have sacrificed blood, treasure, and prestige to fight a war in Vietnam and seen their sacrifices come to naught. A people confident of their righteousness have had to confront My Lai. A people who professed to believe in law and order have had to come to terms with Kent State and Watergate. Americans who could not pronounce "ecology" in 1953 now realize, "We have met the enemy and he is us." A nation accustomed to wealth and power has had to endure simultaneous inflation and recession and to accommodate third world nations, unknown in 1953, just to slow the pace of the energy crisis. A country whose name is "United" has discovered glaring gaps between sexes, generations, and more. Suffice it to say that a people who not long ago aspired to Camelot have discovered that present reality is not of the Round Table. Americans now seem more threatened by a corporate failure of nerve than by a belief in national omnipotence.⁴

Since 1953, the South's relation to the rest of the country seems to have changed radically. A region that was once symbolized by "red suspenders" has emerged as the Sun Belt. As George B. Tindall has observed, "When Jimmy Carter emerged from obscurity to claim the White House, it was all of a sudden time to rediscover the South once again, and the craze for things Southern began to proliferate like five-string banjos in Nashville."⁵ Beyond such "Southern fried chic," Tindall points out, "new mythmakers profess to see on the Southern horizon an extended 'Sun Belt' reaching from coast to coast, its economy battening on agribusiness, defense, technology, oil, real estate, tourism and leisure. The migratory Americans. . .have begun to follow the sun in search of profits, jobs, retirement havens and general jollification." While Tindall offers some less sanguine economic facts to challenge this new illusion of prosperity and power in the South, he concedes "like Moses we seem to have reached the mountain from which we can see the Promised Land. Maybe this time we shall cross over and enter in. The question is: What then?"⁶

One further indication of the South's new status is Walker Percy's tongue-in-cheek answer to Tindall's question:

So now we'll see. I have no idea whether in the year 2000 we—and by we I mean us of the Southeast, the old Confederacy—will simply have become a quaint corner of the teeming Southern Rim, some hundred million souls with its population center and spiritual heartland somewhere between Dallas and L.A.; whether our best writers will be doing soap opera in Atlanta, our best composers country-and-western in Nashville, our best film directors making sequels to *Walking Tall* and *Smokey and the Bandit*; whether our supreme architectural achievement will be the Superdome, our supreme cultural achievement will be the year Alabama ranked number one, the Falcons won the Superbowl, and Bobby Jones III made it a grand slam at Augusta.[7]

Such speculations about the South, juxtaposed with the new mood of American angst, indicate that there is renewed irony in "The Irony of Southern history."

The time has come to ask new questions of the southern past and in so doing to expand upon the old answers to older questions about southern experience and identity. Perhaps one fruitful way to do so would be to reexamine that portion of the southern past that Woodward all but ignored—the Confederate period. For some time, southern historians have come in two varieties—scholars of the New South (like Woodward) whose works on the period since 1865 reflect assumptions about the Old South and specialists on the Old South whose works on the region before 1860 reflect assumptions about the New South. Amid the historians of the antebellum era and the postbellum period have been too few serious scholars of the wartime South. To be sure, a firm but thin rank has claimed for the Confederacy an importance that surpasses cavalry charges, but too often the Confederacy has signified no more than military defeat—defeat that destroyed the life of the Old South or defeat that conditioned life in the New South.

Certainly the 4 frantic years that compose the Confederate period seem insignificant when compared with the 254 years between Jamestown and Fort Sumter or the 116 years since Appomattox. Yet those years marked the only time in which southerners have been an independent people in full charge of their corporate destiny. Just as individuals often most reveal themselves in times of crisis and convulsion, so a people may reveal itself in the midst of a desperate war for national survival. What, then, can an understanding of the Confederate South offer Sun Belt southerners, native and naturalized?

I believe it can offer many things, but since there is neither time nor space to complete that answer, I propose to offer some more questions— questions that I hope will illustrate the intellectual viability of Confederate studies in the Sun Belt South.

Certainly the most superficial consideration of the Confederate experience would seem to reinforce Woodward's emphasis upon southerners as a "peculiar people," conditioned by a distinctive past. Whatever else it was, the Confederacy represented an attempt by southerners to divorce themselves from other Americans and their commitment to sacrifice blood and treasure to achieve self-determination as a people. This circumstance, however, is not as simple as it seems. As the latest in a long and often distinguished line of historians who reject the "peculiar" aspects of southern identity in favor of "the southerner as American," Kenneth M. Stampp has recently contended, "I think there is reason to believe that many Southerners—how many I cannot say, but enough to affect the outcome of the war—who outwardly appeared to support the Confederate cause had inward doubts about its validity, and that, in all probability, some, perhaps unconsciously, welcomed its defeat."[8] Thus the first question must involve the degree of distinctiveness the Confederate South exhibited from the American mainstream. The southern government spent in excess of $2 billion; more than 250,000 men died. An entire generation was devastated, and we still must ask if southerners really wanted to be Confederates.[9] The question involves the nature and extent of southern deviation from the American norm, past and present. It is this inquiry that has preoccupied many scholars and to which the Confederate experience seems most germane.[10]

During the past several decades, southern historiography has searched for a central theme in southern history. It has found a lazy South, a romantic South, and a state-rights South. Southerners collectively have been labeled paranoid, over-defensive "extremists." The southern experience has turned on the question of race and "unchanging white supremacy." The South was the home of frontier dirt farmers made good; the South is and was really its "plain folk." Southerners have been the schizophrenic product of an attempt to reconcile liberty and slavery, democracy and Jim Crow. The South is the product of "extreme conservatism"; it is the result of authoritarian hauteur, militancy, and violence. The South's summum bonum has been the "ideal of an agrarian society." Aristocracy, real or imagined, is the distinctive southern characteristic; the Old South was essentially a democracy. The Old South was a neoseigniorial, prebourgeois civilization that depended upon the slave plantation and the planter class. The true South can be found in its literature; no, in its history, perhaps in its mythology. "Let us begin with the weather."[11] These numerous "Souths" have little in common, save for their absence of interest in the Confederate experience. Surely the search for the essential South should begin with a study of the Confederate epoch.

In recent years Americans have read and heard much about the so-called counterculture, professed and practiced by people whose values and life styles seem at odds with those of the nation. In ways healthy and otherwise and for reasons of necessity and perversity, the South has been an American counterculture for some time. Compared to the Confederate States of America, Woodstock and Willie Nelson seem all but inconsequential expressions of counterculture.[12]

Today the strivings of the so-called "fourth world," peoples within established nations who act out a desire for independence or greater autonomy, are familiar to us. The activities of Quebec separatists, Spanish Basques, and Irish nationalists are good examples. Is it possible to consider the Confederate South as a "fourth world?" Was Jefferson Davis the southern René Levesque? How did it happen that American southerners had one large war and then abandoned their dream of independence, while the Irish have fought small wars and skirmishes for centuries?[13]

Karl Marx interpreted the Civil War as a struggle over slavery, and he favored the North as liberator of an oppressed laboring class. Modern Marxists, however, tend to view the war as a triumph of industrial capitalism over the last remnants of a landed, neofeudal aristocracy. Is it possible to be informed by Marxist analysis and yet say with Marx, "Je ne suis pas une Marxiste?" Marx nix?[14]

Underdeveloped combatants in recent military history have adopted guerrilla tactics in order to compensate for their lack of numbers or weapons. Why did the Confederates eschew full-scale partisan warfare and persist in conventional tactics and strategy? How would William T. Sherman have fared against a Confederate Viet Cong?[15]

It seems strange that Italy and Germany were undergoing unification at the same time that Americans faced disunion. Were Confederate southerners anticipating the idea of "self-determination of peoples" that preoccupied the Western world at the time of World War I? Is it an accident that a southern-born president of the United States was a champion of this concept? Is it possible the Civil War was for the South a unification experience in disguise?

The last people in this country to conduct a violent revolution were southern Confederates. How does the Confederacy compare with other revolutionary experiences? Who was the southern Tom Paine or Sam Adams or Lenin or Mao or Robespierre? When was the thermidor in the South? Why were Confederates foundering fathers instead of founding fathers?[16]

The two great ethnic minorities in the United States, Woodward has suggested, are southern Americans and Afro-Americans. It would seem, then, that the crucible of these ethnic experiences was the Confederate era. Southern whites had to confront the reality of emancipation imposed from without, and in desperation, after protracted debate, the Confederacy enacted its own form of limited emancipation by accepting blacks as soldiers. Black southerners had to cope with the transition from slavery to freedom during the war as well as after it. Nevertheless, the standard studies of the master-slave experience stop at 1860, and until Leon Litwack's *Been in the Storm So Long*, accounts of black southerners as freedmen usually began in 1865.[17]

Traditionally, when nations, even would-be nations, lose wars as completely as the Confederates did, the defeated people repudiate the wartime leadership that produced the debacle. Ex-Confederate southerners did not. On the contrary, southerners embraced the "Lost Cause" and to this day enshrine its memory. Charles Reagan Wilson has attempted to define this response in terms of civil religion, and Herman Hattaway is at work on the role of the United Sons of Confederate Veterans. Perhaps some historian should research and interpret the United Daughters of the Confederacy.[18]

The recent campaign for a constitutional convention to consider an amendment requiring a balanced budget has inspired considerable comment. Amid the clamor only one assumption has appeared consistent and universal; the convention process has never been used before. In a strict sense this is true, but what about the convention which framed the constitution of the Confederate States? The last and only time the United States Consitic utionation underwent scrutiny and alteration by convention occurred in 1861 in Montgomery, Alabama. Is there anything to be learned from this experience? Certainly the product of the Montgomery convention offers little comfort to budget balancers; in four years the Confederacy accumulated a national debt of over 700 millions of nineteenth-century dollars and sustained an inflation rate of about 6,000 percent.

Many more questions remain unasked and thus unanswered. What was the impact of the Confederate experience upon southern women? Precisely how great was the contribution of domestic manufacturing to the southern war effort? Did the Confederate experience generate an urban consciousness among traditionally agrarian southerners? What does the Confederate experience reveal about change, accelerated change, and resistance to change in matters social, economic, and political?

When scholars have addressed these and even more questions about the Confederate South, they still may have to confront the question asked in one of my classes at the University of Georgia. Having endured two or three weeks of my attempts at establishing the intellectual viability of the Civil War era, one student had had enough. He demanded to know, "What does all this have to do with killing Yankees?"

Notes

1. C. Vann Woodward, "The Irony of Southern History," *Journal of Southern History* 19 (1953): 3–19. This essay, which was Woodward's presidential address

to the Southern Historical Association, has been reprinted numerous times, most notably in the editions of Woodward's *Burden of Southern History* (Baton Rouge, 1960, 1968).

2. It has been argued that Woodward's brilliance has been a mixed blessing for southern historians who have been so dazzled by the "master's" assumptions and agenda that they have been blind to alternatives.

3. C. Vann Woodward, "The Aging of America," *American Historical Review* 82(1977): 583-94.

4. Woodward deals with some of these ills (Vietnam and Watergate) in "The Aging of America" and concludes that the American people have displayed an unhealthy propensity for rejecting or ignoring unpleasant reality. "They desperately wanted to believe, and they were prepared to go to almost any lengths to shore up the faith—innocence by 'stonewalling,' if it came to that" (p. 594).

5. George B. Tindall, "The Sun Belt Snow Job," in *The American South*, University of Georgia Alumni Seminar 1979 (Athens, Ga., 1979), pp. 3–4.

6. Ibid., p. 8.

7. Walker Percy, "Random Thoughts on Southern Literature, Southern Politics, and the American Future," *Georgia Review* 32 (1978): 510.

8. Kenneth M. Stampp, "The Southern Road to Appomattox," in *The Imperiled Union: Essays on the Background of the Civil War*, ed. Kenneth M. Stampp (New York, 1980), pp. 246–47.

9. The figures are from E. B. Long, *The Civil War Day by Day: An Almanac, 1861–1865* (Garden City, N.Y., 1971), pp. 711, 727.

10. One recent inquiry is Paul D. Escott's *After Secession: Jefferson Davis and the Failure of Confederate Nationalism* (Baton Rouge, 1978).

11. For these and more interpretations, see Frank E. Vandiver, ed., *The Idea of the South* (Chicago, 1964); Monroe L. Billington, *The South: A Central Theme* (New York, 1969); and David Potter, *The South and the Sectional Conflict* (Baton Rouge, 1968).

12. See Sheldon Hackney, "The South as a Counterculture," *The American Scholar* 42(1973): 283–93.

13. See Raimondo Luraghi's *The Rise and Fall of the Plantation South* (New York, 1978), which attempts to interpret the Confederate experience within a broad context.

14. See Eugene D. Genovese, *The World the Slaveholders Made: Two Essays in Interpretation* (New York, 1969), especially pp. 118–244.

15. The best introduction to this issue is a brief discussion in William L. Barney, *Flawed Victory: A New Perspective on the Civil War* (New York, 1975), pp. 18-19.

16. See Emory M. Thomas, *The Confederacy as a Revolutionary Experience* (Englewood Cliffs, N.J., 1971).

17. Leon F. Litwack, *Been in the Storm So Long: The Aftermath of Slavery* (New York, 1979). There are other exceptions, too. Both James L. Roark's *Masters Without Slaves: Southern Planters in the Civil War and Reconstruction* (New York, 1977) and Robert F. Durden's *The Gray and the Black: The Confederate Debate on Emancipation* (Baton Rouge, 1972) deal with white attitudes. Eugene D. Genovese in *Roll, Jordan, Roll: The World the Slaves Made* (New York, 1974) does integrate the antebellum and bellum slave experiences, but as Clarence L. Mohr contends

in "Southern Blacks in the Civil War: A Century of Historiography," *Journal of Negro History* 49 (1974): 177–95, much remains to be done.

18. See Charles Reagan Wilson, *Baptized in Blood: The Religion of the Lost Cause, 1865–1920* (Athens, Ga., 1980).

SUGGESTIONS FOR FURTHER READING

Introduction

The quantity of southern historical literature is large, rich in its diversity, and growing rapidly. In this brief bibliographical essay, it is the editors' goal to call the reader's attention to only a few of the most important works that are relevant to the essays in this anthology. For the uninitiated, a good starting point for the study of southern history is Idus A. Newby's *The South: A History* (New York, 1978). Perhaps the best one-volume survey of southern history, Newby's book emphasizes the centrality of race but still synthesizes other interpretations. Another standard text is Francis B. Simkins and Charles P. Roland, *A History of the South*, 4th ed. (New York, 1972). Narrower but useful accounts of the Old and New South respectively are Clement Eaton, *A History of the Old South*, 3d ed. (New York, 1975); Thomas D. Clark, *The Emerging South*, 2d ed. (New York, 1968); Monroe L. Billington, *The Political South in the Twentieth Century* (New York, 1975); and John S. Ezell, *The South Since 1865*, 2d ed. (Norman, Okla., 1975). The single best reference work on the South is David C. Roller and Robert W. Twyman, eds., *The Encyclopedia of Southern History* (Baton Rouge, 1979); and the best multivolume history is Wendell Holmes Stephenson and E. Merton Coulter, eds., *A History of the South*, 10 vols. (Baton Rouge, 1951–). Several of the individual volumes of this distinguished series are cited in subsequent portions of this bibliographical essay.

Aside from these and other narrative histories, many volumes are devoted almost exclusively to interpretation. The reader should begin with Wilbur J. Cash's landmark study, *The Mind of the South* (New York, 1941), and the various works of C. Vann Woodward, including *The Burden of Southern History* (Baton Rouge, 1968) and *American Counterpoint* (Boston, 1971). Other works in this genre are George B. Tindall, *The Ethnic Southerners* (Baton Rouge, 1976) and *The Persistent Tradition in New South Politics* (Baton Rouge, 1975); Michael O'Brien, *The Idea of the American South* (Baltimore, 1979); Carl Degler, *Place Over Time: The Continuity of Southern Distinctiveness* (Baton Rouge, 1977); Jack Temple Kirby, *Media-Made Dixie: The South in the Regional Imagination* (Baton Rouge, 1978); Edward D. C. Campbell, *The Celluloid South* (Knoxville, 1980); and Walter J. Fraser,

Jr., and Winfred B. Moore, Jr., eds., *From the Old South to the New* (Westport, 1981). Also valuable are such older works as Monroe L. Billington, *The South: A Central Theme* (New York, 1969); Dewey W. Grantham, ed., *The South and the Sectional Image* (New York, 1968); Frank E. Vandiver, ed., *The Idea of the South* (Chicago, 1964); T. Harry Williams, *Romance and Realism in Southern Politics* (Athens, 1961); and Charles G. Sellers, ed., *The Southerner as American* (Chapel Hill, 1960). For more detailed treatments of many of the themes raised in these books, see the following sections of this essay.

Race

The best surveys of Afro-American history continue to be John Hope Franklin's narrative treatment, *From Slavery to Freedom*, 5th ed. (New York, 1979) and August Meier and Elliott Rudwick's interpretive volume, *From Plantation to Ghetto*, 3d ed. (New York, 1976). Promising to take a prominent place with these standard accounts is Mary F. Berry and John Blassingame's *Long Memory: The Black Experience in America* (New York, 1982).

As general background to the Reconstruction period, one may wish to consult the classic traditional view of the period in William A. Dunning's *Reconstruction, Political and Economic* (New York, 1907). The standard revisionist views of Reconstruction are W.E.B. Du Bois, *Black Reconstruction in America* (New York, 1935); John Hope Franklin, *Reconstruction After the Civil War* (Chicago, 1962); Kenneth Stampp, *The Era of Reconstruction* (New York, 1965); and Robert Cruden, *The Negro in Reconstruction* (Englewood Cliffs, N.J., 1969). Helping to synthesize much of the new research that has occurred since the .publication of those volumes is James McPherson's *Ordeal by Fire: The Civil War and Reconstruction* (New York, 1982).

There are many excellent volumes available to explore the race relations of the late nineteenth century in greater depth. Among these are August Meier, *Negro Thought in America* (Ann Arbor, 1963); Rayford W. Logan, *The Negro in American Life and Thought* (New York, 1954); Lawrence J. Friedman, *The White Savage* (Englewood Cliffs, N.J., 1970); and two especially stimulating volumes by George Fredrickson, *The Black Image in the White Mind* (New York, 1971) and *White Supremacy* (New York, 1981). Still in a class by itself and indispensable to anyone grappling with the issues of the postwar South is C. Vann Woodward's masterpiece, *The Origins of the New South* (Baton Rouge, 1951).

In recent years, some of the most exciting research in Afro-American history has begun the vital task of presenting the black experience from the black perspective. Leon Litwack's article in this volume is one example of that trend as is his lengthier, prize-winning account, *Been in the Storm So Long: The Aftermath of Slavery* (New York, 1979). Other important books that elucidate the resourceful black reaction to a white-dominated society are Eugene Genovese, *Roll Jordan Roll: The World the Slaves Made* (New York, 1974); Paul D. Escott, *Slavery Remembered* (Chapel Hill, 1979); John Blassingame, *The Slave Community: Plantation Life in the Ante-Bellum South* rev. ed. (New York, 1981); Lawrence W. Levine, *Black Culture and Black Consciousness: Afro-American Folk Thought from Slavery to Freedom* (New York, 1977); Herbert Gutman, *The Black Family in Slavery and Freedom* (New

York, 1976); Janet Sharp Herman, *The Pursuit of a Dream* (New York, 1980); and Theodore Rosengarten *All God's Dangers: The Life of Nate Shaw* (New York, 1974).

Perhaps the most crucial problem within the general problem of black adjustment to freedom was economic. A recent surge in historical debate on this problem indicates its importance. The major outlines of the debate are sketched in articles by Harold D. Woodman, "Sequel to Slavery: The New History Views the Postbellum South," *Journal of Southern History* 43 (November 1977), and Jonathan Wiener, "Class Structure and Economic Development in the American South, 1865–1955," *American Historical Review* 84 (October 1979). Some historians have challenged C. Vann Woodward's portrayal of the New South as plagued with extreme poverty and economic stagnation, which was caused by the sharecropping system. Taking a more benign view, they argue that the postbellum southern economy was a rationally organized one in which blacks made more solid economic gains than previously thought. Among these writers are Robert Higgs, *Competition and Coercion* (Cambridge, 1977) and Stephen J. De Canio, *Agriculture in the Postbellum South* (Cambridge, 1974). Countering this view are Roger Ransom and Richard Sutch in *One Kind of Freedom: The Economic Consequences of Emancipation* (Cambridge, 1977), who concede some immediate, short-term economic benefits for blacks but insist that a rapidly developing system of storekeeper monopolies, sharecropping, and tenant farming led to economic deterioration, stagnation, and dependency for all southern farmers, especially blacks. Approaching the questions from a neo-Marxist perspective, Jay Mandle's *The Roots of Black Poverty* (Durham, 1978) and Jonathan Wiener's *The Social Origins of the New South* (Baton Rouge, 1978) tend to support Ransom and Sutch's conclusions. Other books concerned with this problem are Robert Eng's *Freedom's First Generation* (Philadelphia, 1979); Donald Nieman, *To Set the Law in Motion: The Freedmens Bureau and the Legal Rights of Blacks* (Millwood, N.Y., 1979); William Gillette, *Retreat From Reconstruction* (Baton Rouge, 1979); Claude Oubre, *Forty Acres and a Mule: The Freedmens Bureau and Black Land Ownership* (Baton Rouge, 1978); Louis Gerteis, *From Contraband to Freedmen* (Westport, 1973); James L. Roark, *Masters Without Slaves: Southern Planters in the Civil War and Reconstruction* (New York, 1977); Peter Kolchin, *First Freedom: The Response of Alabama's Blacks to Emancipation and Reconstruction* (Westport, 1972); Lawrence Powell, *New Masters: Northern Planters During the Civil War and Reconstruction* (New Haven, 1980); and Daniel Novak, *The Wheel of Servitude: Black Forced Labor After Slavery* (Lexington, Mass., 1978).

Few Southern states have attracted more scholarly analysis than South Carolina. This is especially true of the antebellum period and increasingly true of the postbellum period. A survey of the black experience in South Carolina is provided in Idus A. Newby's *Black Carolinians* (Columbia, 1973). Three good treatments of the Reconstruction period are available in Francis B. Simkins and Robert H. Woody, *South Carolina During Reconstruction* (Chapel Hill, 1932); Joel Williamson, *After Slavery: The Negro in South Carolina During Reconstruction* (Chapel Hill, 1965); and Thomas Holt, *Black Over White: Negro Political Leadership in South Carolina During Reconstruction* (Urbana, 1977). More specialized analyses of that period are Martin Abbott, *The Freedmen's Bureau in South Carolina* (Chapel Hill, 1967); Willie Lee Rose, *Rehearsal for Reconstruction* (Indianapolis, 1964); Elizabeth Jacoway, *Yankee Missionaries in the South* (Baton Rouge, 1980); and George C.

Rogers, *The History of Georgetown County, South Carolina* (Columbia, 1978). On the last quarter of the nineteenth century, see George B. Tindall, *South Carolina Negroes, 1877–1900* (Columbia, 1952); William J. Cooper, Jr., *The Conservative Regime in South Carolina* (Baltimore, 1968); Francis B. Simkins, *Pitchfork Ben Tillman* (Baton Rouge, 1944); and Ernest C. Clark, *Francis Warrington Dawson* (Tuscaloosa, 1980).

For further analysis of the events in North Carolina described by Westin, see Jeffrey J. Crow and Larry E. Tise, eds., *Writing North Carolina History* (Chapel Hill, 1979); Frenise A. Logan, *The Negro in North Carolina, 1876–1894* (Chapel Hill, 1964); Helen G. Edmonds, *The Negro and Fusion Politics in North Carolina, 1874–1901* (Chapel Hill, 1951); Jeffrey J. Crow and Robert F. Durden, *Maverick Republican in the Old North State* (Baton Rouge, 1977); Dwight Billings, *Planters and the Making of a 'New South': Class Politics, and Development in North Carolina, 1865–1900* (Chapel Hill, 1979); Eric Anderson, *Race and Politics in North Carolina, 1879–1901* (Baton Rouge, 1981); and J. Morgan Kousser, "Progressivism—For Middle Class Whites Only: North Carolina Education 1880–1910," *Journal of Southern History* 46 (May 1980).

Although racial issues have generated copious amounts of historical attention, the same, unfortunately, cannot be said about art. Peter Wood's article in this volume demonstrates the contributions that a historian's scrutiny of art works can make. Those interested in pursuing this least worked area of study may wish to consult some of the biographies of Winslow Homer. See, for example, Gordon Hendricks, *The Life of Winslow Homer* (New York, 1979); Lloyd Goodrich, *Winslow Homer* (New York, 1944); William Hugh Downs, *The Life and Works of Winslow Homer* (Boston, 1911); Philip C. Beam, *Winslow Homer At Prout's Neck* (Boston, 1966); and Patti Hannaway, *Winslow Homer in the Tropics* (Richmond, 1973). Also helpful for studying Homer's work are Barbara Delman, *The Wood Engravings of Winslow Homer* (New York, 1969); Michael Quick, "Homer in Virginia," *L.A. County Museum of Art Bulletin* 24 (1978); Mary Ann Calo, "Winslow Homer's Visits to Virginia During Reconstruction," *American Arts Journal* 12 (Winter 1980); Sidney Kaplan, "The Negro in the Art of Homer and Eakins," *Massachusetts Review* 7 (Winter 1966); and Isabel Hoopes, "The Story of a Picture," *The Mentor* (August 1929). For additional aids in studying Afro-Americans in Homer's art, consult Barbara Novak, *American Painting of the Nineteenth Century* (New York, 1969); and Roger B. Stein, *Seascape and the American Imagination* (New York, 1975).

Class

For a brief survey and bibliography on classes in southern society, see Robert Shalhope, "Classes and Castes," in *The Encyclopedia of Southern History*, ed. David C. Roller and Robert W. Twyman (Baton Rouge, 1979); on the "dominant class" in the antebellum South, see Ulrich B. Phillips, *Life and Labor in the Old South* (Boston, 1929); and Wilbur J. Cash, *The Mind of the South* (New York, 1941). Eugene Genovese in *The Political Economy of Slavery: Studies in the Economy and Society of the Slave South* (New York, 1965), *The World the Slaveholders Made* (New York, 1969), and *Roll, Jordan, Roll: The World the Slaves Made* (New York, 1974), argues that the ruling class dominated the economic, political, and cultural affairs of the region; see also Michael P. Johnson, *Toward a Patriarchial Republic: The Secession of Georgia* (Baton Rouge, 1977). For the postbellum South and the debate over whether or not the hegemony of the "dominant class" persisted, see C. Vann Woodward, Origins of the New South, 1877–1913 (Baton Rouge, 1951); Sheldon Hackney, "Origins of the New South in Retrospect," *Journal of Southern History* 37 (May 1972); Carl N. Degler, *Place Over Time: The Continuity of Southern Distinctiveness* (Baton Rouge, 1977), and the sharp challenges to Woodward by Marxist social historians: Jonathan M. Wiener, *Social Origins of the New South: Alabama, 1860–1885* (Baton Rouge, 1978); Jay R. Mandle, *The Roots of Black Poverty: The Southern Plantation Economy After the Civil War* (Durham, 1979); and Dwight Billings, *Planters and the Making of a "New South": Class, Politics and Development in North Carolina, 1865–1900)* (Chapel Hill, 1979); see also James Tice Moore, "Redeemers Reconsidered: Change and Continuity in the Democratic South, 1870–1900," *Journal of Southern History* 44 (August 1978), who concludes that there is much to support "the notion of continuity between the Old and New Souths. Professor Woodward's revisionist interpretation of Redeemer origins is itself in need of revision."

A good starting point for reaching an understanding of the relationships of other classes to the "dominant class" in both the pre- and postwar South is Edward Magdol and Jon L. Wakelyn, eds., *The Southern Common People: Studies in Nineteenth Century Social History* (Westport, 1980); see also R. W. Shugg, *Origins of Class Struggle in Louisiana* (Baton Rouge, 1939); John Dollard, *Caste and Class in a Southern Town* (New Haven, 1937); Shields McIlwaine, *The Southern Poor White From Lumberland to Tobacco Road* (Norman, Okla., 1939); Frank L. Owsley, *Plain Folk of the Old South* (Baton Rouge, 1949); J. Wayne Flynt, *Dixie's Forgotten People: The South's Poor Whites* (Bloomington, 1979); and J. Wayne Flynt and Dorothy S. Flynt, *Southern Poor Whites: A Selected Annotated Bibliography of Published Sources* (New York, 1981).

Recent scholarship on the role of the church and ministers of the gospel and their relationship to the various social classes includes Donald G. Mathews, *Religion in the Old South* (Chicago, 1977); Erskine Clarke, *Wrestlin' Jacob: A Portrait of Religion in the Old South* (Atlanta, 1979); E. Brook Holifield, *The Gentlemen Theologians: American Theology in Southern Culture, 1795–1860* (Durham, 1978); and Anne C. Loveland, *Southern Evangelicals and the Social Order, 1800–1860* (Baton Rouge, 1980).

The best general work on those occasional individuals who challenged the prevailing economic, political, and cultural views of the nineteenth-century South is Carl N. Degler's *The Other South: Southern Dissenters in the Nineteenth Century* (New York, 1974); for those who challenged the prevailing views in the twentieth century, see Bruce Clayton, *The Savage Ideal: Intolerance and Intellectual Leadership in the South, 1890–1914* (Baltimore, 1972); Hugh C. Bailey, *Edgar Gardner Murphy* (Coral Gables, 1968); John M. Cooper, *Walter Hines Page: The Southerner as American* (Chapel Hill, 1979); Jacqueline Dowd Hall, *Revolt Against Chivalry: Jesse Daniel Ames and the Women's Campaign Against Lynching* (New York, 1979); Arnold Shankman, "Dorothy Tilly and the Fellowship of the Concerned" and Robert M. Randolph, "James McBride Dabbs: Spokesman for Racial Liberalism," in *From the Old South to the New: Essays on the Transitional South*, ed. Walter J. Fraser, Jr. and Winfred B. Moore, Jr. (Westport, 1981).

For the best introduction to the role of the merchants in the colonial period, see Lewis C. Gray, *History of Agriculture in the South*, 2 vols. (Gloucester, Mass., 1958), and Richard Pares, *Merchants and Planters* (London, 1960); for the antebellum period, see Lewis Atherton, *The Southern Country Store, 1800–1860* (Baton Rouge, 1949), and Harold S. Woodman, *King Cotton and His Retainers: Financing and Marketing the Cotton Crop of the South, 1800–1825* (Lexington, Mass., 1968); and for the postbellum South, see Thomas D. Clark, *Pills, Petticoats, and Plows: The Southern Country Store* (Indianapolis, 1944); Stephen J. DeCanio, *Agriculture in the Postbellum South: The Economics of Production and Supply* (Cambridge, 1974); and James L. Roark, *Masters Without Slaves: Southern Planters in the Civil War and Reconstruction* (New York, 1977).

Little has been done on the black professional. For a survey of the black experience in America, see John Hope Franklin, *From Slavery to Freedom: A History of Negro Americans* (New York, 1947).

Folk Culture and Historiography

For a recent survey and bibliography pertaining to southern folk life and culture, see Mary Washington Clarke, "Folklore," in *The Encyclopedia of Southern History*, ed. David C. Roller and Robert W. Twyman (Baton Rouge, 1979); for the larger society, see Richard M. Dorson, *American Folklore* (Chicago, 1959); collections, interpretations, and bibliographies of folk history appear frequently in such journals as the *Journal of American Folklore, Southern Folklore Quarterly, Mid South Folklore*, and *North Carolina Folklore*. Early research into southern folk ways was pioneered by Howard W. Odum in *Folk, Region, and Society* (Chapel Hill, 1966); see also the seminal essay by David Potter, "The Enigma of the South," *The Yale Review* 51 (1961), and Bertram Wyatt-Brown, "The Ideal Typology and Antebellum Southern History: A Testing of a New Approach," *Societas* 5 (1975).

Standard treatments of the southern educational experience may be found in Edgar Knight, *Public Education in the South* (Boston, 1922) and Charles W. Dabney, *Universal Education in the South*, 2 vols. (Chapel Hill, 1936). For a recent brief survey, see Wayne J. Urban, "Education," in *The Encyclopedia of Southern History*, ed. David C. Roller and Robert W. Twyman (Baton Rouge, 1979); see also F. D. Mathews, "Education in Alabama and Georgia, 1830–1860" (Ph. D. diss., Columbia University, 1965); for a view of education within and without the South, see Lawrence A. Cremin, *American Education: The National Experience, 1783–1876* (New York, 1980).

Violence and vigilantism constitute the most publicized aspects of the southern experience and accordingly have generated a proportionate amount of historical literature. Several books focus on the most notorious of the vigilante groups, the Ku Klux Klan. Among the most useful of these books are Allen W. Trelease, *White Terror: The Ku Klux Klan Conspiracy and Southern Reconstruction* (New York, 1971); David M. Chalmers, *Hooded Americanism: The First Century of the Ku Klux Klan* (New York, 1965); John W. Mecklin, *The Ku Klux Klan: A Study of the American Mind* (New York, 1924); and Stanley F. Horn, *Invisible Empire: The Story of the Ku Klux Klan, 1866–1871* (Boston, 1939). Numerous articles have also appeared on this topic. Among the articles most pertinent to Flynn's essay are Herbert

Shapiro, "The Ku Klux Klan during Reconstruction: The South Carolina Episode," *Journal of Negro History* 49 (January 1964); J. C. A. Stagg, "The Problem of Klan Violence: The South Carolina Up-Country, 1868–1871," *Journal of American Studies* 8 (December 1974); Vernon Burton, "Race and Reconstruction: Edgefield County, South Carolina," *Journal of Social History* 12 (Fall 1978); and Grady McWhiney and Francis B. Simkins, "The Ghostly Legend of the Ku Klux Klan," *Negro History Bulletin* 14 (February 1951). On the related topic of "whitecapping" violence, see the various articles of William F. Holmes, including "Whitecapping: Agrarian Violence in Mississippi, 1902–1906," *Journal of Southern History* 35 (May 1969) and "Whitecapping in Late Nineteenth Century Georgia," in *From the Old South to the New*, ed. Walter J. Fraser, Jr. and Winfred B. Moore, Jr. (Westport, 1981). The reader who may wish to test the possible connection between American vigilantism and earlier European traditions should consult Edward P. Thompson, " 'Rough Music' Le Charivari Anglais," *Annales: Economies; Societés: Civilization* 27 (Mars-Avril 1972) and Natalie Z. Davis, *Society and Culture in Early Modern France* (Stanford, 1975). To place this phenomenon within the broader context of southern and American violence, see Hugh D. Graham and Ted R. Gurr, eds., *Violence in America* (Washington, 1969); Richard M. Brown, *Strain of Violence: Historical Studies of American Violence and Vigilantism* (New York, 1975); and Allen D. Grimshaw, ed., *Racial Violence in the United States* (Chicago, 1969).

For introductions to the historiographical debate on the causes of the Civil War, see David M. Potter, *The South and the Sectional Crisis* (Baton Rouge, 1968); Thomas J. Pressly, *Americans Interpret Their Civil War* (New York, 1962); Arthur S. Link and Rembert W. Patrick, eds., *Writing Southern History* (Baton Rouge, 1965); Eric Foner, "The Causes of the American Civil War: Recent Interpretations and New Directions," *Civil War History* 20 (September 1974); and Edwin C. Rozwenc, ed., *The Causes of the American Civil War* (Boston, 1961). Many excellent volumes analyzing the general causes of the war have appeared. Among the most influential of these are Avery D. Craven, *The Coming of the Civil War* (Chicago, 1942); Allan Nevins, *Ordeal of the Union* (New York, 1947); David M. Potter, *The Impending Crisis* (New York, 1976); William J. Cooper, Jr., *The South and the Politics of Slavery, 1828–1856* (Baton Rouge, 1978); and Kenneth Stampp, *The Imperiled Union: Essays on the Background of the Civil War* (New York, 1980). More specialized books examining issues on the road to secession and war include William W. Freehling, *Prelude to Civil War* (New York, 1966); Steven A. Channing, *Crisis of Fear: Secession in South Carolina* (New York, 1970); William L. Barney, *The Secessionist Impulse* (Princeton, N.J., 1974); Eric Foner, *Free Soil, Free Labor, Free Men: The Ideology of the Republican Party Before the Civil War* (New York, 1970); Michael F. Holt, *The Political Crisis of the 1850s* (New York, 1978); Michael P. Johnson, *Toward a Patriarchal Republic: The Secession of Georgia* (Baton Rouge, 1977); J. Mills Thornton, *Politics and Power in a Slave Society: Alabama, 1800–1860* (Baton Rouge, 1978); David M. Potter, *Lincoln and his Party in the Secession Crisis* (New Haven, 1962); and Raimondo Luraghi, *The Rise and Fall of the Plantation South* (New York, 1978). On the general popularity of secession among southerners, see William J. Donnelly, "Conspiracy or Popular Movement: The Historiography of Southern Support for Secession," *North Carolina Historical Review*, January 1965.

For recent works on the Confederate period and excellent bibliographies, see

Emory Thomas' own *The Confederate Nation: 1861–1865* (New York, 1979) and *The Confederacy as a Revolutionary Experience* (Englewood Cliffs, N.J., 1971); and Frank E. Vandiver, *Their Tattered Flags* (New York, 1970); see also James I. Robertson, Jr., "Historiography of the Confederacy at War," Charles P. Roland, "Historiography of the Confederacy on the Home Front," Bell I. Wiley, "Confederate Army," Richard D. Goff, "Confederate Economy," Kenneth R. Callahan, "Confederate Guerrillas," William J. McNeill, "Confederate Morale," and Charles P. Cullop, "Confederate Propaganda" for summaries and bibliographies in *The Encyclopedia of Southern History*, ed. David C. Roller and Robert W. Twyman (Baton Rouge, 1979).

INDEX

Abolitionists, 119-25 passim
Adams, Henry, 174, 175
Adger, John B., 106, 108, 109, 110, 111, 112
African Methodist Episcopal Church, 13
Africans of the Slave Bark, "Wildfire," The, 81
Afro-Americans: adjustment to freedom, 5-21, 25-57; antebellum church ministries to slaves, 105-14; and educational reform in North Carolina, 63-73; folk life of, 163-64; images of, in American art, 75-88; as physicians prior to World War II, 143-51; rebellion against planter authority, 49-52; transition to free-labor agriculture in South Carolina, 25-57. *See also* Negroes; Slavery
Aiken, David Wyatt, 33
Aiken, William, 52
Allen, D. P., 70
All's Well, 87
Annales school of social historians, 161, 162
Aristocracy in southern thought, 97-103
Army, U.S., 49, 52, 53
Ashmore, John D., 172, 173
Atlanta Race Riot of 1906, 17, 18
Aycock, Charles B., 73

Bacchus, Josephine, 9
Baker, Kenny, 179

Baldwin, Joseph G., 176
Barrett, John M., 124, 125
Beaman, G. L., 69
Beardsley, E. H., 96, 143
Beecher, Henry Ward, 81
Beecher, James C., 52, 53
Beecher, Lyman, 81
Berger, John, 78
Birney, James G., 121, 122
Blair, Lewis Harvie, 101
Bloch, Marc, 161
Bousfield, M. O., 148, 150
Brandon, A. W., 172
Braudel, Fernand, 161
Breen, T. H., 134
Brewer, Street, 70, 71, 72
Brisbane, William Henry, 119-25
Brooks, Iveson, 26
Brown, Joseph E., 208
Buchanan, James, 209
Burke, Emily P., 180
Butler, George, 66, 67
Byrd, William II, 172

Calhoun, Andrew P., 207
Calhoun, John C., 119
Caraker, A. P., 31
Carnival, The, 82
Carter, Jimmy, 157, 218
Carter, Robert, 172
Cash, W. J., 99
Cassels, Samuel J., 107
Caucasian, 68, 69
Charivaris, 192

NOTES ON THE CONTRIBUTORS

Leon F. Litwack is Professor of History at the University of California, Berkeley. His most recent work, *Been in the Storm So Long*, won the Pulitzer Prize for history in 1979.

Lacy Ford recently received his Ph.D. in American History at the University of South Carolina.

John Scott Strickland is completing a dissertation on the interaction of African-American society, culture, and religion in South Carolina from 1680 to 1880 at the University of North Carolina, Chapel Hill.

Richard B. Westin is Professor of History at the University of Richmond. He is engaged currently in research on early twentieth-century southern education.

Peter H. Wood, Associate Professor of History at Duke University, is best known for his book, *Black Majority*.

George M. Fredrickson is Mason Professor of American History at Northwestern University. His most recent work is *White Supremacy*.

Jack P. Maddex, Jr., Professor of History at the University of Oregon, is the author of *The Virginia Conservatives, 1867–1879*.

Blake McNulty is an Associate Professor of History at the University of Wisconsin—Waukesha. He is at work on a biography of William Henry Brisbane.

Ronald L. F. Davis is a Professor of History at California State University, Northridge, and is the author of *Good and Faithful Labor: From Slavery to Sharecropping*.

E. H. Beardsley is an Associate Professor of History at the University of South Carolina and the author of *The Rise of the American Chemistry Profession*.

Charles Winston Joyner is Professor of History and Anthropology at the University of South Carolina, Coastal Carolina College, and has recently completed a book entitled *Slave Folklife*.

Grady McWhiney is Professor of History and Director and Distinguished Senior Fellow of the Center for the Study of Southern History and Culture at The University of Alabama. His most recent work is *Attack and Die: Civil War Military Tactics and the Southern Heritage.*

Charles L. Flynn, Jr., is an Assistant Professor of History at Denison University. He is the author of a forthcoming book entitled *White Land, Black Labor: Caste and Class in Late Nineteenth-Century Georgia.*

William J. Cooper, Jr., is Professor of History at Louisiana State University and is best known for his work *The South and the Politics of Slavery, 1828–1856.*

Emory M. Thomas is Professor of History at the University of Georgia. His most recent book is *The Confederate Nation, 1861–1865.*

About the Editors

Walter J. Fraser, Jr. is Professor and Head, Department of History, Georgia Southern College. He is the author of a book on Charleston during the Revolutionary era and coeditor of *From the Old South to the New: Essays on the Transitional South* (Westport, 1981).

Winfred B. Moore, Jr., is an Associate Professor of History at The Citadel. He is the coeditor of *From the Old South to the New: Essays on the Transitional South* (Westport, 1981) and is currently at work on a study of James F. Byrnes.